Philip Ostergard has given us a close reading of Lincoln's words, illuminating the connection between his public sentiments and the private stirrings of his heart. Avoiding the temptation to pigeonhole Lincoln's faith, Ostergard allows the reader to follow Lincoln on his life's journey seeking the Almighty.

Thomas F. Schwartz, PhD
Illinois State Historian
Abraham Lincoln Presidential Library and Museum

Philip Ostergard has compiled a most valuable study of Abraham Lincoln's knowledge and use of the Bible in his thoughts and writings. Such overt actions surely confirm Lincoln's belief in an all-powerful God who became his touchstone in his later life and presidency. This piece of Lincolniana will be an informative tool for all those who ponder Lincoln's religion.

Wayne C. Temple, PhD
Chief Deputy Director
Illinois State Archives
Author, *Abraham Lincoln: From Skeptic to Prophet*

Philip Ostergard provides an illuminating and accessible story of Abraham Lincoln's lifelong engagement with the Bible that came to fruition in his Second Inaugural Address. Speech by speech, letter by letter, the author guides us on Lincoln's journey in the rough and tumble world of politics. *The Inspired Wisdom of Abraham Lincoln* includes helpful charts that allow the reader to see how the Bible, for Lincoln, was a major source of political wisdom.

Ronald C. White Jr.
Author, *Lincoln's Greatest Speech: The Second Inaugural* and *The Eloquent President*
Fellow, Huntington Library
Professor emeritus of American religious history, San Francisco Theological Seminary

Lincoln is America's Jacob, a God wrestler, wounded, clinging to a national birthright and birth-responsibility. Philip Ostergard shows how early reading in the Bible eventually supplied President Lincoln with roots to nurture him during the personal and public crisis of the Civil War.

Rick Kennedy, Chair
Department of History and Political Science
Point Loma Nazarene University

ABRAHAM LINCOLN

The Inspirational Wisdom of
Abraham Lincoln

PHILIP L. OSTERGARD

JAICO PUBLISHING HOUSE

Ahmedabad Bangalore Chennai
Delhi Hyderabad Kolkata Mumbai

Published by Jaico Publishing House
A-2 Jash Chambers, 7-A Sir Phirozshah Mehta Road
Fort, Mumbai - 400 001
jaicopub@jaicobooks.com
www.jaicobooks.com

ABRAHAM LINCOLN
ISBN 978-81-8495-042-7

Jaico Print-on-Demand Edition: 2025

Printed by
Repro India Limited, Mumbai

Dedicated to my grandchildren
Jensen, Parker, Bailey, Hudson, Cooper, and Peyton,
that they might place their faith in the Divine Being,
as did Abraham Lincoln,
and attain potential greatness

CONTENTS

ACKNOWLEDGMENTS

I recall checking out a biography of Abraham Lincoln at the main library in Pasadena, California, as a boy of fourteen.

My serious study of Lincoln began once I had acquired and read the eight original volumes of *The Collected Works of Abraham Lincoln.* As I read, I made a card file of those quotations offering advice and wisdom for many situations in life.

My wife gave me a gift that helped make Lincoln a close-at-hand friend. It's a small statue, a maquette of the great sculpture by Borglum in Boston in which Lincoln is sitting on a park bench as though inviting those passing by to swap stories. As I sit at my desk writing letters and planning projects, that little work of art prods me to think, *How would Lincoln say this?*

I was also inspired by my visit to the Louis A. Warren Lincoln Library and Museum (now called The Lincoln Museum) in Fort Wayne, Indiana. While there, I was able to visit the home of Warren, a pioneer Lincoln researcher. By then retired, Warren was devoting his time to tending his garden of a thousand dahlias. As we strolled through the vast colorful expanse in full bloom, I was humbled to listen to the words of so respected a man. His love of Abraham Lincoln ignited mine.

Dr. Thomas Schwartz of the Abraham Lincoln Presidential Library in Springfield, Illinois, encouraged me in the research for this book and granted the necessary copyright permission for the numerous quotations from *The Collected Works of Abraham Lincoln.* Dr. Wayne Temple, chief deputy director of the Illinois State Archives, and Dr. Ronald Rietveld, professor of history at California State University, Fullerton, reviewed the manuscript and made a number of helpful suggestions. Dr. Ronald White, highly acclaimed Lincoln author and scholar at the Huntington Library in Pasadena, California, has been an invaluable mentor. My friend William Yee, history teacher at Alhambra High School in Alhambra, California, has been a point of focus in my mind as my study has been to help teachers of our youth. I also render my sincere thanks to a most helpful person, Kimberly Miller, my editor from Tyndale House Publishers.

While the study of Lincoln has been my lifelong avocation, my professional life has been spent in youth leadership. My greatest hope is that today's boys and girls will learn that Lincoln overcame extreme disadvantages to become a great figure in history because he built his life on biblical principles.

A CHRONOLOGY OF LINCOLN'S LIFE

February 12, 1809	Abraham Lincoln born near Hodgenville, Kentucky
Spring 1811	Family moves to 230-acre farm on Knob Creek, six miles east of Hodgenville
1812	Brother Thomas born and dies in infancy
Fall 1817	Family moves to farm in Vincennes, Indiana
October 5, 1818	Nancy Hanks Lincoln, Abraham's mother, dies of milk sickness
December 2, 1819	Thomas Lincoln, Abraham's father, marries Sarah Bush Johnston
June 1823	Father joins Pigeon Creek Baptist Church
January 20, 1828	Abraham's older sister, Sarah, dies in childbirth
March 1830	Lincoln family moves to new home near Decatur, Illinois
1831	Abraham Lincoln settles in New Salem, Illinois
Spring 1832	Lincoln is candidate for state legislature; serves as captain in Black Hawk War
August 6, 1832	Lincoln defeated in election; the only time he lost a popular vote.
August 4, 1834	Elected Illinois representative from Sangamon County
December 1834	Takes seat in 55-member Illinois House of Representatives
September 9, 1836	Lincoln is granted a law license
April 15, 1837	Moves to Springfield; becomes law partner of John T. Stuart
November 4, 1842	Marries Mary Todd
August 1, 1843	Son Robert Todd Lincoln born
March 10, 1846	Son Edward (Eddy) Baker Lincoln born
August 3, 1846	Elected to U.S. House of Representatives; serves 1847–1849

JANUARY 10, 1849	Offers amendment abolishing slavery in Washington, D.C.
FEBRUARY 1, 1850	Eddy Baker dies
DECEMBER 21, 1850	Son William Wallace Lincoln born
APRIL 4, 1853	Son Thomas (Tad) Lincoln born
1854	Aroused by signing of the Kansas-Nebraska Act, Lincoln reenters politics
NOVEMBER 7, 1854	Elected to Illinois legislature; soon resigns to become Senate candidate
FEBRUARY 8, 1855	Lincoln throws support to Trumbull for Senate
JUNE 16, 1858	Wins Republican nomination for Senate race
AUGUST 21, 1858	First Lincoln-Douglas debate held
NOVEMBER 2, 1858	Lincoln wins popular vote but Douglas, chosen by legislature, is awarded Senate seat
MAY 16, 1860	Lincoln nominated for presidency
NOVEMBER 6, 1860	Lincoln elected president
DECEMBER 20, 1860	South Carolina is first state to secede from the Union
MARCH 4, 1861	Lincoln delivers First Inaugural Address
APRIL 12, 1861	Fort Sumter is attacked
JULY 21, 1861	Union army defeated at Bull Run
FEBRUARY 1862	Grant wins first important Union victories in the West
FEBRUARY 20, 1862	Son Willie dies
JANUARY 1, 1863	Emancipation Proclamation takes effect
NOVEMBER 19, 1863	Lincoln delivers Gettysburg Address, commemorating July battle at Gettysburg, Pennsylvania, and dedication of cemetery there
NOVEMBER 26, 1863	First national observance of Thanksgiving
MARCH 12, 1864	General Ulysses S. Grant appointed commanding general of the Union army

November 8, 1864	Lincoln wins reelection
February 1, 1865	Lincoln approves resolution sending Thirteenth Amendment, which abolishes slavery, to the states
March 4, 1865	Lincoln delivers Second Inaugural Address
April 9, 1865	General Robert E. Lee surrenders at Appomattox Court House in Virginia, effectively ending the Civil War
April 14, 1865	Lincoln shot by John Wilkes Booth; dies the following morning
May 4, 1865	Lincoln interred in Oak Ridge Cemetery, Springfield, Illinois

FOREWORD

"The child is the father of the man," declared poet William Wordsworth.

So we might say that the tall, dark-haired frontier lad scratching numbers with charcoal and reading by the light of the cabin fireplace was the father of the giant figure sitting in the marble chair in the majestic Lincoln Memorial.

Abraham Lincoln drew his first gulps of water from the Sinking Spring near his family's Kentucky farm. He drank, too, of the common-sense wisdom of the wilderness, and his roots bore deeply into the moral principles and precepts of the Bible.

As a boy, Lincoln's imagination came alive as he read about our country's history. The images of seasick and storm-tossed colonists stepping ashore in the early 1600s, as well as underequipped, valiant American soldiers pressing on against the British, blossomed into feelings of patriotism that never left him.

However, when Lincoln emerged from the wilderness into the sunlight of civilization, he found that many persons dismissed the faith in which he'd been reared. As a young man newly arrived in New Salem, Illinois, Lincoln engaged in debates with humanistic and atheistic thinkers who challenged his biblically and historically based presuppositions. His philosophical mind, when confronted with these alternative views, questioned the biblical principles he'd been taught in the crude log-cabin church of his boyhood. Without question, these encounters triggered a season of doubts and skepticism. In fact, most historians agree that Lincoln wandered in doubt and uncertainty for most of two decades.

The question is, Was Lincoln's faith in a personal, loving God ever restored? Two streams of opinion originate from two differing viewpoints. Some, such as myself, believe that his faith was rekindled. Others conclude that Abraham Lincoln never recovered from his skepticism. A few insist he used Scripture in his letters and speeches merely to gain political capital.

Discerning his beliefs is somewhat difficult. First, Lincoln never made a conclusive statement about his faith, nor was he a member of any church. Furthermore, his life and death have become so legendary, such a cherished and integral part of American culture, that it is difficult to know him as a man.

Abraham Lincoln died on a Good Friday, a fact that in itself would have lent a holy aura to his life. Not long after his assassination, his kind deeds were exaggerated, his great deeds honored. People seemed ready to canonize him. Within a year of Lincoln's death, boyhood friends, neighbors, lawyers, clients in his law business, ministers, and politicians hastened to print their remembrances. A worldwide search for personal letters and scraps of paper with a few words in his handwriting was underway.

To written words, people added their stories: the yarns told by the young rail-splitter; tales of encounters with Lincoln in rooming houses, country housewarmings, riverboats, trains, late-night rallies, the legislature, and the White House. The stories of Lincoln were told from two different viewpoints. Those who knew him as a young adult recognized him as a gifted, popular, and trustworthy person. They also remembered that he did not attend church and kept his religious feelings to himself. Few of these acquaintances were aware of his midlife renewal of faith, and they raised questions about his beliefs.

Those who knew him as president—as well as the millions of Americans who followed his words—heard his public references to God and didn't know about his earlier doubts and questions. Many of these Americans not only believed that Lincoln was a devout Christian, they were sure he belonged to their denominations!

I believe that life's experiences and lessons caused the intellectually honest Lincoln to rethink his early teachings and nurtured him to a restored faith in the God of the Bible. In particular, the significant personal and public losses he endured during his presidency led him to reassess his view of God. To the nation the Civil War was an endless ordeal of sacrifice and blood; to the lonely man in the White House it was a smelting furnace, fashioning and disciplining every facet of his physical, intellectual, emotional, and spiritual being. He emerged like precious metal, refined and tensile hardened.

While the Civil War lasted "only" four years, its roots can be traced back to a great compromise forged during the Constitutional Convention, when the delegates agreed to permit slavery. In 1922, during his remarks at the dedication of the Lincoln Memorial, President Warren Harding noted that this concession in the Constitution represented "an ambiguity which only a baptism in blood could efface."[1]

For nearly one hundred years, the nation lived with the tension created by being a land established in liberty that nonetheless kept large numbers of people in chains. The Missouri Compromise, adopted in 1820, drew a line beyond which slavery would be restricted. But in 1850 powerful forces were fiercely resisting gradual extinction and aggressively expanding legal slavery in the territories created by the Louisiana Purchase. The struggle over slavery during the 1850s drew Lincoln, by then a prosperous Illinois lawyer and former state and federal legislator, back into politics.

When the man from the backwoods was elected president, he vowed to lead a people's government: "A house divided cannot stand. . . . It will become all one thing, or all the other." His position created general unease, even among some opposed to slavery. Multitudes of good men were inclined to live quietly and peacefully, even at the price of continued slavery. Lincoln's task was to rally these citizens, arouse them from their neutrality, and unite them against the tyranny of those who would control the lives of others.

In the first days of his presidency, various cabinet members, congressmen, newspaper editors, and generals thought they could manipulate him, but they soon recognized that as commander in chief he was a strong, tough personality, truly a master of men. His early no-holds-barred political fights had hardened him for the political firing line.

Lincoln foresaw the cataclysmic storm that lay in the path of the nation. Though acutely aware of his lack of qualifications for leadership, he accepted the role of president, grounding his confidence in the cumulative wisdom of the people and in the Sovereign Creator who desires men to live in peace and freedom.

The historian Albert Beveridge wrote two volumes on Lincoln, which were published in 1928. He completed the first volume by reflecting on the contradictory images of our sixteenth president: a man well liked and respected yet unconcerned with his personal appearance; a man who displayed bottomless melancholy as well as boundless humor; a man who was cautious yet unflinchingly devoted to what he thought was right. In the end, Beveridge says, these characteristics helped "*make up the man*

Lincoln, who wrought the wizardry that has mystified historians of all lands" (emphasis mine).[2]

Lincoln possessed unusual qualities and unique personality traits; however, great deficiencies stood in the way of any possible chance of success. Deprived of an education, unused to a cultural setting, and inexperienced in administrative work, what leadership traits could he muster? How could he have achieved such resounding success?

In Lincoln's own eyes, he possessed no *wizardry* and there was no *mystery*. He emphatically and repeatedly stated that solutions to the nation's trials were beyond his wisdom or power and that he was merely an instrument elected by the people to be used in the hands of the Supreme Architect. He expressed his feelings many times in words similar to the following: "Without Him, I cannot succeed; with Him, I cannot fail." (See, for example, page 120, which includes an excerpt from his farewell speech in Springfield as he headed to Washington to assume the presidency.)

Those words, I believe, are a concise summary of his faith during the last half decade of his life. His belief in an inscrutable yet trustworthy God had developed slowly, but by the end of his life was as much a part of his outlook as his belief that every American possessed a birthright of freedom and his conviction that the Declaration of Independence's statement that all men are created equal must apply to the black slave as well as the white man.

In this book, I trace the development of these three themes throughout Lincoln's writings. Part 1 of this book tells of the early life experiences of Abe Lincoln, which were an apprenticeship for the great work ahead. Here we see his faith in "government by the people" interwoven with his faith in common, ordinary people. In fact, it was more than campaign rhetoric for him to say that if the people could have their way, they would save their government. In Part 2, we see how Lincoln's growing unease over the slavery question pulled him back into politics, leading to some of the most memorable and significant political debates in American history, those with political rival Stephen Douglas.

In Part 3, Lincoln emerges as a national leader who became the instrument of the Almighty. The death of a son turned a bereaved father to a Heavenly Father. The nightmare prospect of a bloody civil war that threatened to vaporize his boyhood dream of American greatness aroused, tugged, and pulled peerless leadership qualities from the country lawyer. Yet the magnitude of the crisis also drew him back to God.

☆ ☆ ☆

Lincoln's renewed faith is evident near the climax of his Second Inaugural Address, given in the waning days of the Civil War, as he spoke to men and women who had been broken in sorrow and confused in faith by a horrifying war that pitted American against American. "The Almighty has His own purposes. . . . Shall we discern therein any departure from those divine attributes which the believers in a Living God always ascribe to Him?"[3]

Living God. Politicians may use scriptural phrases without really believing that God is actively involved in the events of the nation. Is it possible that Lincoln did the same here, or did he truly believe that God was concerned with the events of the United States, that He had allowed the war to begin, and that He had enabled the North to bring the war to conclusion?

Since we cannot settle this question from the Second Inaugural Address alone, we will study the totality of the statements in all his writings. In fact, it is the premise of my study that we should read Lincoln's words directly, as that is the only safe method of discerning his expressions of faith.

Authentically documented written statements by Abraham Lincoln are far more helpful in understanding the man than oral statements from friends and critics, recalled years after they were made. While most writers attempt to understand Lincoln's metamorphism from his backwoods culture to eminent leadership qualities using psychological methods, in this book we trace his return to faith in the Bible in his own letters and documents.

Fortunately, in 1953, the Abraham Lincoln Association, under the editorship of Roy P. Basler, gathered and published all original documents in eight volumes and an index called *The Collected Works of Abraham Lincoln.* Two small supplementary volumes were added. In limited cases, newspaper accounts of important speeches were included.

Lincoln's *Collected Works* include revealing personal letters he wrote as a young man, as well as documents and correspondence to associates, editors, ministers, generals, and the public. Through them, we can witness his reactions to life's challenges and disciplining experiences, as well as his maturing faith as chief executive in the crucible of a terrible war.

As this study uses only Lincoln documents contained in *The Collected Works*, it does not include some notable statements attributed to Lincoln by reliable secondary sources, but I make my case stronger if the reader can be certain that he or she is reading the words of Lincoln. Through nearly five thousand pages, Abraham Lincoln speaks to us without passing through the filter of those who would water down his statements or of great admirers who would magnify his image. *The Collected Works* stand as a reliable source of information. (On occasion, I do draw from other writers' insights into Lincoln and his times.)

Just a few final notes to help you navigate through the excerpts in this book. Since one of my purposes is to demonstrate how frequently Lincoln included references to God and scriptural phrases in his writings, I want you to be able to locate those easily. For that reason, such terms are in bold. Also, I give the volume and page number(s) where each Lincoln document is found in *The Collected Works of Abraham Lincoln,* which is abbreviated **CW** in this text. (Please note: The wording has been reproduced exactly as it is in *The Collected Works*, so occasional misspellings and grammatical errors appear as recorded. Bracketed letters or words indicate some sort of editorial clarification or insertion.)

As an aid to understanding and appreciating the use of Scripture throughout Lincoln's writings, three appendices are included at the end of the book. They document all Scripture verses and Bible terms; biblical characters and topics; and names and terms for deity that appear in Lincoln's writings. Unless noted otherwise, Bible verses quoted are from the King James Version of the Bible, which is the version that Abraham Lincoln used.

As you sift through the excerpts from Lincoln contained in this book, my hope is that you will gain a true picture of our sixteenth president, the man who matured from a resourceful wilderness youth into a statesman with the fortitude and faith necessary to lead and reunite a fractured nation.

PART ONE

THE APPRENTICESHIP OF AN AMERICAN LEADER

Every man is said to have his peculiar ambition. Whether it be true or not, I can say for one that I have no other so great as that of being truly esteemed of my fellow men, by rendering myself worthy of their esteem.

Abraham Lincoln
New Salem, March 9, 1832

CHAPTER 1

ABRAHAM LINCOLN'S OWN STORY

December 20, 1859

To Jesse W. Fell, Enclosing Autobiography

I was born Feb. 12, 1809, in Hardin County, Kentucky. My parents were both born in Virginia, of undistinguished families—second families, perhaps I should say. My mother, who died in my tenth year, was of a family of the name of Hanks, some of whom now reside in Adams, and others in Macon counties, Illinois.

CW III: 511

Much about life for a boy growing up two hundred years ago in the secluded Indiana wilderness is lost to us in the shadows of time long past.

Shortly before he became president, Lincoln himself filled in some of the broad details of his family and early life. By then, he had become nationally known as a result of the Lincoln-Douglas Debates, during which Lincoln had squared off against Stephen Douglas for the Illinois Senate seat. Lincoln's friend Jesse Fell, whom he'd known since his first term in the Illinois legislature twenty-five years before, had asked him to write a brief account of his life that Fell and other Lincoln supporters could use to advance his nomination for the presidency. Though Lincoln was reluctant to do so at first, eventually he wrote a brief autobiography.

My paternal grandfather, Abraham Lincoln, emigrated from Rockingham County, Virginia, to Kentucky, about 1781 or 2, where, a year or two later, he was killed by indians, not in battle, but by stealth, when [where?] he was laboring to open a farm in the forest. His ancestors, who were Quakers, went to Virginia from Berks County, Pennsylvania. An effort to identify them with the New-England family of the same name ended in nothing more definite, than a similarity of Christian names in both families, such as Enoch, Levi, Mordecai, Solomon, Abraham, and the like. My father, at the death of his father, was but six years of age; and he grew up, litterally without education. . . .

CW III: 511

This first Abraham Lincoln had been a moderately wealthy Virginia landowner who felt the urge to follow a distant relative, Daniel Boone, over the Cumberland Mountains into Kentucky. While he was clearing a parcel of land—and while his three sons watched—a bullet shot by a Native American ended his life. One warrior ran to snatch Thomas, Abraham's six-year-old son, who was sobbing over his dead father, with the intent of carrying him into the wilderness. Fortunately, another son, Josiah, quickly reacted with an accurate rifle shot, and the future president's father was unharmed.

At age twenty-eight, Thomas married Nancy Hanks Lincoln. Though Lincoln's father has sometimes been described as shiftless, records show that he was respected as an honest and honorable person, a carpenter by trade. At the time of their first son's birth, Thomas and Nancy lived on a farm on the South Fork of Nolin Creek with their daughter, Sarah. There Thomas had built the log cabin in which the future president was born. Two years later, Thomas bought and then moved the family to another farm on Knob Creek.

Incomplete surveying and unregulated legal records caused Thomas problems in Kentucky. Furthermore, he detested slavery, which was legal in that state. So Thomas moved his family again, this time across the Ohio River into Indiana. Not long after, his wife died of milk sickness, an often fatal disease contracted by drinking milk from a cow that had eaten white snakeroot. Thomas was left to raise their two children alone.

. . . He [Thomas Lincoln] removed from Kentucky to what is now Spencer County, Indiana, in my eighth year. We reached our new home about the time the State came into the Union. It was a wild region, with many bears and other wild animals still in the woods. There I grew up.

CW III: 511

Not long after the death of Nancy Hanks Lincoln, Abraham and his sister, Sarah, were left alone with their cousin Dennis Hanks for weeks as Thomas sought a new wife. He chose wisely, and Sarah Bush Johnston became Abraham's stepmother in 1819. When she arrived at the Lincoln home with her own three children, she was appalled by the conditions in which her two stepchildren were living. It is clear that she made their house a home again and that Abraham was always fond of her.

There were some schools, so called; but no qualification was ever required of a teacher, beyond "readin, writin, and cipherin," *to the Rule of Three. If a straggler supposed to understand latin, happened to so-journ in the neighborhood, he was looked upon as a wizzard. There was absolutely nothing to excite ambition for education. Of course when I came of age I did not know much. Still somehow, I could read, write, and cipher to the Rule of Three; but that was all. I have not been to school since. The little advance I now have upon this store of education, I have picked up from time to time under the pressure of necessity. . . .*

CW III: 511

All told, Lincoln probably received only a few months of formal education. Yet he was an insatiable learner. He had access to few books but devoured those he was able to borrow, including *Robinson Crusoe*, *The Pilgrim's Progress*, and *Aesop's Fables*. His great love for America was inspired, in part, by reading Weems's *Life of Washington* and Grimshaw's *History of the United States*.

☆ ☆ ☆

In 1819 the Rev. Louis A. Warren was a minister in Hodgenville, Kentucky, where Abe Lincoln was born. People wrote him asking for information about Lincoln's boyhood, inciting his interest to the extent that he pursued a lifetime of research and writing about the parentage and childhood of our sixteenth president. His books offer extensive information about wilderness life, yet specific details regarding Abe's childhood and young manhood are sparse.

Still, it is obvious that Lincoln had to overcome unimaginable disadvantages to become president. Yet what we call disadvantages might in some ways have been advantages. In our minds, we see the dirt floor and feel the cold biting wind, marveling that Abe Lincoln could ever have climbed the ladder to success. The frontier with its exposure to the elements was an efficient though harsh teacher with important lessons.

The boy Abe drew his first gulps of water from a natural spring. The young child had been rocked to sleep in the quietness of the wilderness night, with the sound of the hoot of an owl or the mating call of a lynx. Through life, many would assert that he knew no fear. As president, surrounded by arguing, unreasonable congressmen, smeared by newspaper editors, and nagged by a well-meaning wife, he would draw his clear thinking from the wisdom of the wilderness.

The hardships of the frontier disciplined its pupils into developing two great, though seemingly opposite, traits. The pioneer had to be self-reliant and, at the same time, he or she had to work with and rely upon others. We will see that these two characteristics blend beautifully. As a president presiding over a cabinet, Lincoln displayed both traits. He was unmovable in his basic decisions, and at the same time, he relied upon and elicited the best efforts of every man.

In addition to growing up in the harsh climate of the frontier, Abe endured a number of losses in his narrow family circle. A younger brother died at birth; an aunt, an uncle, and a neighbor all died of milk sickness before his mother succumbed to the same. The story is told that as a nine-year-old, Lincoln wrote a letter to a minister, asking him to stop by and pray at his mother's resting place. Not many years later, his older sister passed away in childbirth. He lost another close friend, Ann Rutledge of New Salem, who many believe was his first serious romantic interest.

Yet his wilderness upbringing also gave Abe Lincoln some advantages. Lost in the quiet of nature, undistracted by social and economic problems, the heart and mind could lift the eyes to heavenly powers. The reading of the Bible combined with the worshipful environment were nutrients in fertile soil for his faith in deity.

Abe helped to cut the timber for the building of the log cabin Baptist church of which his parents were members. His early reading of the Bible gave him a familiarity that shines forth in the many quotations of this study. Yet he never joined any church himself. Could it have been that the emotionalism of the backwoods church did not appeal to him? It is quite possible that the environment of nature contributed to his basic faith in the Bible and the Lord God, while leaving him unenthusiastic about the preaching in the wilderness church. In his mature years, he appreciated sermons preached by men who could appeal to his keen intelligence and appreciation of literature. As he struck out on his own in his early twenties, however, he might have wondered if he were leaving his faith behind for good.

CHAPTER 2

NEW SALEM

To Jesse W. Fell, Enclosing Autobiography

I was raised to farm work, which I continued till I was twenty two. At twenty one I came to Illinois, and passed the first year in . . . Macon county. Then I got to New-Salem, (at that time in Sangamon, now in Menard County, where I remained a year as a sort of Clerk in a store. . . .

CW III: 511

Abe Lincoln was twenty-one when he emerged from the wilderness. That same year, he drove an oxen-pulled wagon that carried him and his family to Illinois, where his father and stepmother settled on a farm ten miles southwest of Decatur. Striking out on his own as a hired hand, Abe made a trip on a flatboat to New Orleans and back. Three years later, Lincoln hired on again. This time the trader offered the young man a position as a store clerk in the pioneer settlement of New Salem, Illinois. Lincoln accepted the offer, later commenting that he had landed along the river shore like a "piece of floating driftwood."

Though that term aptly described his selection of New Salem as the place to disembark, it was certainly not descriptive of the man. He was anything but a floating, nonreacting object. He embodied the best traits and spirit that characterize an American. While others slept, Abe read all the books he could find; while others fiddled, he gained skill in mathematics; while others wasted time, he attended court in the County Court House, some fifteen miles distant from his home. When young men gathered together, Abe proved the wrestling king and the fastest runner. When he wielded an axe, he had no competition.

☆ ☆ ☆

New Salem was established about two years before Lincoln's arrival. The settlement, on the banks of the Sangamon River, about twenty-two miles northwest of Springfield, Illinois, quickly became a bustling village. When Abe stepped ashore, he found a boom town village of young men with the "going somewhere" spirit. Remarkably, some residents had degrees from eastern universities.

When Lincoln "drifted" ashore at New Salem, he sought help to remedy his meager bits of education. He was interested in the study of grammar and immersed himself in literature. A frontier resident introduced him to Shakespeare. He studied law books by lamplight. To support himself, he tried several jobs. Surveying work taught him some technical skills that would later give him an advantage in legal matters. He also was part owner of a store for a time.

Later Lincoln served as the town postmaster. When not working, he was a popular entertainer, debater, and storyteller in New Salem. He could mix with the best, giving and taking hard social barbs. He was always eager to spar with men of ideas.

☆ ☆ ☆

That Lincoln could establish himself so quickly in a new town, trying his hand at many trades, may not seem remarkable today, yet his rise was an American phenomenon. At the time, the idea was still relatively new that a poor man could better his lot in the world. For centuries, the great majority of common persons, living under a blanket of submission to landlords, accepted the life they were born into as their lot. Only the elite, the exclusive upper class, could try new ideas, make changes in lifestyle, and pursue dreams. When the early colonists ventured to traverse the ocean and disembarked from their ships, theirs was a new world. They could cultivate crops or starve, build shelters or freeze, succeed or fail. They owed nothing to a landlord, and they could expect help from no one.

Admittedly, early Americans like Lincoln had a strategic advantage, entering a land with virgin forests and hills of minerals; a land with ribbons of natural waterways simultaneously inviting and daunting exploration. Rocky mountains beckoned the adventurous. The future belonged to these pioneers. Fueled by the high octane of liberty, they invented machines, published papers, and leveled forests for fast-growing cities. Freedom of enterprise pumped adrenaline through their bodies to work longer hours, outproducing workers of the old country. The explosion of new ideas and vigorous labor lifted the standard of living. The virgin soil produced men and women inclined to hard work and willing to dig deeply into rich mineral veins. The powerful dynamic of free enterprise energized them.

Dr. Joyce Appleby explains the situation for the men and women who shook their allegiance to the Old World:

> As John Adams observed to Josiah Quincy, "there is no people on earth so ambitious as the people of America. The reason is," he went on to explain, "because the lowest can aspire as freely as the highest." No quality has so marked the character of American social life as individual aspiration, turning the United States into a magnet for immigrants and a wellspring of hope for the adventurous. If working for others alienates men and women from their handicraft and talents, imagining one's own future path—what came to be called careers in the early nineteenth century—grounded men and women in their own fantasies. Personal planning weakened the ties to community, but opened up the possibility of affinities based on moral and intellectual commitments. An ideology that linked economic and political freedom also fused the goals of the nation and its citizens.[1]

Lincoln recognized that his opportunities were part of his birthright as an American. Stories read in childhood, such as Weems's book on George Washington, had ignited the flame of patriotism and love of his country. He was a true believer in the rights and dignity of man, basic to all interactions with people. Born an American, he had been "conceived in liberty."

☆ ☆ ☆

March 9, 1832

Communication to the People of Sangamo County

FELLOW-CITIZENS: Having become a candidate for the honorable office of one of your representatives in the next General Assembly of this state, in accordance with an established custom, and the principles of true republicanism, it becomes my duty to make known to you—the people whom I propose to represent—my sentiments with regard to local affairs.

Abe Lincoln was only one month into his twenty-third year when, following the inner urge to be part of a government by the governed, the storytelling rail-splitter presented his candidacy to the people to be their representative of Sangamon County in the state legislative body at Vandalia. He did so by writing out this statement and submitting it to the *Sangamo Journal*. It read in part:

Upon the subject of education, not presuming to dictate any plan or system respecting it, I can only say that I view it as the most important subject which we as a people can be engaged in. That every man may receive at least, a moderate education, and thereby be enabled to read the histories of his own and other countries, by which he may duly appreciate the value of our free institutions, appears to be an object of vital importance, even on this account alone, to say nothing of the advantages and satisfaction to be derived from all being able to read the scriptures and other works, both of a religious and moral nature, for themselves. For my part, I desire to see the time when education, and by its means, morality, sobriety, enterprise and industry, shall become much more general than at present, and should be gratified to have it in my power to contribute something to the advancement of any measure which might have a tendency to accelerate the happy period.

Who more than the boy who learned to read by firelight would better understand the wonderful privilege of education? And who would better appreciate the special blessing of being able to read the Scriptures?

Fellow-Citizens, I shall conclude. Considering the great degree of modesty which should always attend youth, it is probable I have already been more presuming than becomes me. However, upon the subjects of which I have treated, I have spoken as I thought. I may be wrong in regard to any or all of them; but holding it a sound maxim, that it is better to be only sometimes right, than at all times wrong, so soon as I discover my opinions to be erroneous, I shall be ready to renounce them.

Every man is said to have his peculiar ambition. Whether it be true or not, I can say for one that I have no other so great as that of being truly esteemed of my fellow men, by rendering myself worthy of their esteem. How far I shall succeed in gratifying this ambition, is yet to be developed. I am young and unknown to many of you. I was born and have ever remained in the most humble walks of life. I have no wealthy or popular relations to recommend me. My case is thrown exclusively upon the independent voters of this county, and if elected they will have conferred a favor upon me, for which I shall be unremitting in my labors to compensate. But if the good people in their wisdom shall see fit to keep me in the background, I have been too familiar with disappointments to be very much chagrined. Your friend and fellow-citizen,

New Salem, March 9, 1832. A. LINCOLN.

CW I: 5–9 (5, 8–9)

☆ ☆ ☆

To Jesse W. Fell, Enclosing Autobiography

Then came the Black-Hawk war; and I was elected a Captain of Volunteers—a success which gave me more pleasure than any I have had since. I went the campaign, was elated, ran for the Legislature the same year (1832) and was beaten—the only time I have been beaten by the people. . . .

CW III: 512

Lincoln's campaign for a seat in the state legislature was interrupted by a call to service in the Black Hawk War.

His enlistment and service in the frontier militia was a boot camp of preparation for his service as commander in chief. To Lincoln's personal gratification, the men in his company elected him captain. Though his time of service was only eight days, Lincoln emerged more confident in his ability to command men. The only Native American his men saw was a warrior who accidently wandered into their camp. Lincoln prevented his men from killing the man.

The officer who mustered him out of the service was Robert Anderson. Interestingly, Anderson was in command of Fort Sumter when the Civil War began about thirty years later.

While Lincoln was always proud of his military service during the Black Hawk War, his participation interrupted his campaigning for the legislature, and Lincoln did not win the seat, the only election in which the common people did not elect him. On the other hand, Lincoln did win the vote in those areas where he had been able to campaign.

To Jesse W. Fell, Enclosing Autobiography

The next, and three succeeding biennial elections, I was elected to the Legislature. I was not a candidate afterwards. During this Legislative period I had studied law, and removed to Springfield to practice it. In 1846 I was once elected to the lower House of Congress. Was not a candidate for re-election. . . .

CW III: 512

Two years after the Black Hawk War, Lincoln, a member of the Whig party, was elected to the state legislature by the people of Sangamon County. After borrowing money for a new suit, he paid the fare for a carriage trip to Vandalia, which at the time was the capital of Illinois.

As the legislature was only in session a few months of the year, Lincoln continued to live in New Salem. Though he felt his education inadequate to study law, another legislator, John Stuart, encouraged him and lent him the necessary books. When he was finally able to complete the requirements for a law license, Lincoln moved to Springfield and became Stuart's law partner.

Interestingly, as the bustling village of New Salem had come into existence just before Abe arrived, it passed out of importance after he left. The village has since been restored as a popular historic site, and today when visitors walk its streets, they get some sense of the spirit of the place that helped form young Abe, storekeeper, surveyor, soldier—and the life of every gathering. If books had inspired him to pursue the American dream, in New Salem he began to live out those dreams.

CHAPTER 3

LEGISLATOR

Vandalia was a small town of nine hundred people when Abraham Lincoln arrived to take a seat in the fifty-five member Illinois House of Representatives on December 1, 1834. He roomed with John T. Stuart, the young lawyer with whom he had served in the Black Hawk War and who had encouraged Lincoln to study law. The legislature session was from November to approximately February. During his second term, he became known as part of the "Long Nine," the description given the representatives from Sangamon County, all of whom happened to be tall.

While it might seem a small part of Lincoln's political career, his service in Vandalia was important because there he learned the arts of government on the state level; made some of his first public speeches; gained the confidence to study law and be admitted to the bar; and first became acquainted with his long-time antagonist (and later his friend) Stephen Douglas.

Lincoln took his seat just sixteen years after Illinois had been granted statehood. Like many of his fellow legislators, he was a strong supporter of those internal improvements that would attract more settlers to the area and advance the interests of the common people in the state. As a result of legislation enacted during Lincoln's first term, construction on the Illinois and Michigan Canal, which would connect the Illinois River to the Great Lakes and first establish Chicago as a major transportation hub, began in 1836. While one of the largest transportation projects approved by the legislature, it was by no means the only one: In a special session that began in December 1835, 139 bills were introduced in the House; 106 in the Senate. According to Lincoln biographer Benjamin Thomas, ninety-nine of these related to roads and eighty-one to railroads. Fifteen others pertained to bridges, canals, and navigation.[1]

Lincoln's role in promoting a waterway to connect the Mississippi with the St. Lawrence is often overlooked. That his contribution was appreciated is evidenced by riverboats named the *Rail-Splitter*, the *Old Abe*, and the *A. Lincoln* that steamed up and down the waterway before he was even elected president.

☆ ☆ ☆

Once Lincoln had earned his law license in 1836, he decided to move from New Salem, which could not provide enough business to support a law practice, to Springfield. There he roomed with Joshua Speed and became Stuart's law partner. Moving from a frontier town to a larger, more refined city with an active social life initially left Abe lonely and socially uncomfortable. Yet Springfield would be his home from 1837 until the day he left for Washington, D.C.

When the Lincoln family first arrived in Illinois in 1830, Springfield was a small community of six hundred inhabitants. By the late 1830s, however, the number of residents had increased to approximately 2,500, and calls to move the seat of government from Vandalia to Springfield became stronger. In 1837, the legislators, after an intense fight, voted to move the capital to Springfield. Lincoln was a strong proponent of the move in the legislature, and Springfield's businesspeople appreciated his support.

Political comrades and opponents learned that they could never be certain of what Lincoln might do. On one occasion, the political opposition wanted to pass a motion to end a special session but lacked a quorum of members present. Wanting to witness their frustration first-hand, Lincoln and two other Whigs finally came to their seats in the temporary House chambers housed in the Methodist Episcopal Church. While Lincoln laughed, the opposition quietly rounded up absent members, who entered the meeting room, located on the first floor of the building. Lincoln suddenly realized that they had secured a quorum. The door was locked, so he could not leave. Instead he opened a window and, with his long legs, was able to step down to the ground.[2]

As a state legislator, Lincoln's skill as a public leader was first noted. Just about a year before the capital moved to Springfield, Lincoln was invited to address the Young Men's Lyceum, a leading cultural activity in

Springfield that enabled aspiring young men to test their oratorical skills. A week shy of age twenty-nine when he spoke, Abraham Lincoln had already served four years as a representative in the Illinois legislative body.

Compared to many of his later speeches, the Lyceum speech would have little lasting effect. However, it was important to Lincoln himself. In his boyhood, he had imitated the sermons of preachers. He had recently begun presenting evidence to judges and juries in courtrooms. Now, however, he was testing his wings as an orator.

Much of this early speech centers on the meaning of America. It introduces many of the themes he developed in future speeches. In fact, he would spend the rest of his life elaborating and restating the major premises of the Lyceum Address in ever more eloquent phrases.

The title of this early address, "The Perpetuation of Our Political Institutions," would not promote much interest unless one stops to think of it as did Abraham Lincoln. As a youngster, he had been moved by the stories of the founding of his country. Perhaps his young mind had even pondered how America had endured when other governments had fallen. In the Lyceum Address, Lincoln was asking a serious question, one that should arrest the attention of every American: How can this nation perpetuate its political institutions?

The principles of a people's government, predicated on the ideals of freedom and justice, make a strong nation—yet there are inherent weaknesses in the armor of democracy, so that, great as America is, without vigilant care, destruction is possible.

In their expression of thanks, the Society solicited him to furnish a copy of the eight-page address for publication. For that Americans should be thankful, since it gives us insights into Lincoln's ideals as a young legislator.

January 27, 1838

Address Before the Young Men's Lyceum of Springfield, Illinois

As a subject for the remarks of the evening, 'The perpetuation of our political institutions,' *is selected.*

In the great journal of things happening under the sun, we, the American People, find our account running, under date of the nineteenth century of the Christian era. We find ourselves in the peaceful possession, of the fairest portion of the earth, as regards extent of territory, fertility of soil, and salubrity of climate. We find ourselves under the government of a system of political institutions, conducing more essentially to the ends of civil and religious liberty, than any of which the history of former times tells us. We, when mounting the stage of existence, found ourselves the legal inheritors of these fundamental blessings. . . . a legacy bequeathed us, by a once *hardy, brave, and patriotic, but* now *lamented and departed race of ancestors. Their's was the task (and nobly they performed it) to possess themselves, and through themselves, us, of this goodly land; and to uprear upon its hills and its valleys, a political edifice of liberty and equal rights; [. . . This task of gratitude to our fathers, justice to] ourselves, duty to posterity, and love for our species in general, all imperatively require us faithfully to perform.*

How, then, shall we perform it? At what point shall we expect the approach of danger? By what means shall we fortify against it? Shall we expect some transatlantic military giant, to step the Ocean, and crush us at a blow? Never! All the armies of Europe, Asia and Africa combined, with all the treasure of the earth (our own excepted) in their military chest; with a Buonaparte for a commander, could not by force, take a drink from the Ohio, or make a track on the Blue Ridge, in a trial of a thousand years.

At what point then is the approach of danger to be expected? I answer, if it ever reach us, it must spring up amongst us. It cannot come from abroad. If destruction be our lot, we must ourselves be its ***author and finisher****. As a nation of freemen, we must live through all time, or die by suicide. . . .*

Lincoln asked the question: If a government of freedom and democracy is of great strength, what is the weakness in the armor? What can defeat a government of the people? He said Americans themselves would be "the author and finisher," a phrase that echoes words found in Hebrews 12:2.

Later in his speech, Lincoln addressed this question:

The question recurs "how shall we fortify against it?" The answer is simple. Let every American, every lover of liberty, every well wisher to his posterity, swear by the blood of the Revolution, never to violate in the least particular, the laws of the country; and never to tolerate their violation by others. . . .

Moving to the conclusion of the speech, Lincoln mentions another great danger by which America can be weakened. The scenes of the Revolutionary War, particularly the heroics of George Washington, moved people to passion. As the emotional loyalty to the country fades, Lincoln proposed, it must be replaced by reason.

Another reason which once was*; but which, to the same extent, is* now no more*, has done much in maintaining our institutions thus far. I mean the powerful influence which the interesting scenes of the revolution had upon the* passions *of the people as distinguished from their judgment. . . . The deep rooted principles of* hate, *and the powerful motive of* revenge, *instead of being turned against each other, were directed exclusively against the British nation. . . . The basest principles of our nature, were either made to lie dormant, or to become the active agents in the advancement of the noblest of causes[?]—that of establishing and maintaining civil and religious liberty.*

But this state of feeling must fade, is fading, has faded*, with the circumstances that produced it.*

I do not mean to say, that the scenes of the revolution are now *or* ever will be *entirely forgotten. . . . In history, we hope, they will be read of, and recounted, so long as the* ***bible*** *shall be read;—but even granting that they will, their influence* cannot be *what it heretofore has been. . . . At the close of that struggle, nearly every adult male had been a participator in some of its scenes. . . . In the form of a husband, a father, a son or a brother, a* living history was *to be found in every family. . . . But* those *histories are gone. They* can *be read no more forever. They* were *a fortress of strength; but, what invading foemen could* never do, *the silent artillery of time* has done*; the levelling of its walls. They are gone. . . .*

They were *the pillars of the temple of liberty; and now, that they have crumbled away, that temple must fall, unless we, their descendants, supply their places with other pillars, hewn from the solid quarry of sober reason. Passion has helped us; but can do so no more. It will in future be our enemy. Reason, cold, calculating, unimpassioned reason, must furnish all the materials for our future support and defence. Let those [materials] be moulded into* general intelligence, [sound] morality *and, in particular,* a reverence for the constitution and laws*; and, that we improved to the last; that we remained free to the last; that we revered his name to the last; [tha]t, during his long sleep, we permitted no hostile foot to pass over or desecrate [his] resting place; shall be that which to le[arn the* ***last] trump*** *shall awaken our* W*ASH[INGTON.*

Upon these] let the proud fabric of freedom r[est, as the] rock of its basis; and as truly as has been said of the only greater institution, **"the gates of hell shall not prevail against it."**

CW I: 108–115 (108–109, 112, 114–115)

The expression *last trump* appears in the apostle Paul's Resurrection chapter, in which he speaks of the awakening of all the dead (1 Corinthians 15:52). Note, too, Lincoln's mention of "the only greater institution," a clear reference to Christ's church, of which Jesus promised "the gates of hell shall not prevail against it" (Matthew 16:18). Ordinarily, it might be odd to use a phrase that seems to connect a secular nation and the church of the Lord Jesus Christ. However, it is appropriate considering Lincoln's philosophy of America and his belief that this nation is the fulfillment of the Creator's plan to give democracy to all people. The true, invisible church is ordained by God and cannot be overcome. America, as long as it is true to its birthright principles, is likewise invincible. This is a bold and far-reaching assertion from which Lincoln never retreated.

America was not better than other nations, but because of the foundations of democracy and freedom, Lincoln dared to suggest that America stands second to the greatest of all institutions, the church of the Lord Jesus Christ.

When the Lyceum Address is compared to Lincoln's later speeches, especially the Gettysburg Address and the Second Inaugural, it is evident that, instead of the oratorical flurry of this early speech, he came to rely on language that stood out for its simpler, beautiful eloquence. The dramatic reference to the church would give way in later speeches to the simple, powerful phrase "Right Makes Might."

As president, the burdens of a divided nation would kindle in him the power and wisdom to express the sublime truths of the birthright of America and our sacred obligations to all of humanity. On the first Fourth of July after his election to the presidency, President Lincoln addressed Congress in Special Session. He used the Lyceum theme, the perpetuation of political institutions (see chapter 14): "Our popular government has often been called an experiment. Two points in it, our people have already settled—the successful *establishing*, and the successful *administering* of it.

One still remains—its successful *maintenance* against a formidable [internal] attempt to overthrow it. . . ."[3]

CW IV: 439

The Gettysburg Address asks the same question: "testing whether that nation, or any nation so conceived and so dedicated, can long endure."[4] Little did the young men who listened to Lincoln deliver the Lyceum Address that night in January 1838 realize that it would take four bloody years of civil war to answer the question of the twenty-nine-year-old budding orator who stood before them.

This speech raised other issues that became mainstream in Lincoln's public statements: What were the danger points to a democracy? How might they bring decay to our democracy? Clearly Lincoln looked to the Bible as a source of wisdom as he considered these questions.

☆ ☆ ☆

While Lincoln was a passionate proponent of the ideals of American government, he was also keenly interested in the practical details that would enable America and its people to prosper. In a speech before the Illinois House of Representatives that was printed in the *Sangamo Journal,* Lincoln argued against the banking system termed the Sub-Treasury, which President Van Buren had established to replace the National Bank as a repository of government money.[5]

December 26, 1839

Speech on the Sub-Treasury

We say that public officers, selected with reference to their capacity and honesty, (which by the way, we deny is the practice in these days,) stand an equal chance, precisely, of being capable and honest, with Bank officers selected by the same rule. We further say, that with however much care selections may be made, there will be some unfaithful and dishonest in both classes. The experience of the whole world, in all by-gone times, proves this true. The Saviour of the world chose twelve disciples, and even one of that small number, selected by superhuman wisdom, turned out a traitor and a devil. And, it may not be improper here to add, that Judas carried the bag—was the Sub-Treasurer of the Saviour and his disciples. . . .

Refuting the claim that the men who ran the National Bank had all been corrupt, Lincoln said that such men are likely to show up in any institution, reminding the representatives that even Jesus had a traitor among his disciples (see John 12:6, 13:29). While Lincoln used the Lyceum Address to reflect on the perpetuation of his country, in his speech on the Sub-Treasury, Lincoln warns of the potential loss of liberty and expresses his own deep feelings of patriotism:

Many free countries have lost their liberty; and ours may *lose hers; but if she shall, be it my proudest plume, not that I was the* last *to desert, but that I* never *deserted her. I know that the great volcano at Washington . . . is belching forth the lava of political corruption. . . . Broken by it, I, too, may be; bow to it I never will. The* probability *that we may fall in the struggle* ought not *to deter us from the support of a cause we believe to be just; it* shall not *deter me. If ever I feel the soul within me elevate and expand to those dimensions not wholly unworthy of its* ***Almighty Architect****, it is when I contemplate the cause of my country, deserted by all the world beside, and I standing up boldly and alone and hurling defiance at her victorious oppressors. Here, without contemplating consequences, before High Heaven, and in the face of the world, I swear eternal fidelity to the just cause, as I deem it, of the land of my life, my liberty and my love. . . .*

CW I: 159–179 (166–167, 178–179)

Architect comes from a Greek word meaning "chief artificer, master-builder, director of works, architect, engineer." The Greek word is used in 1 Corinthians 3:10. Lincoln's usage here reflects his understanding that the human soul is designed by God, the "Almighty Architect."

☆ ☆ ☆

With fellow attorneys T. Logan and A. T. Bledsoe, Lincoln wrote an eight-page campaign circular addressed to the people of Illinois. Concerned with Whig party positions on various topics, it was a plea for party unity. While the circular is unimportant, Lincoln used an illustration from *Aesop's Fables* and a Bible verse to illustrate the principle of strength in united action. Years later, the scriptural phrase used in this political document (see Matthew 12:25 and Luke 11:17) became the linchpin of the dramatic "House Divided" Speech that propelled him to the presidency (see chapter 11).

March 4, 1843

Campaign Circular from Whig Committee

That "union is strength" is a truth that has been known, illustrated and declared, in various ways and forms in all ages of the world. That great fabulist and philosopher, Aesop, illustrated it by his fable of the bundle of sticks; and he whose wisdom surpasses that of all philosophers, has declared that **"a house divided against itself cannot stand. . . ."**

CW I: 309–318 (315)

While Lincoln was already beginning to articulate the major themes of his political life, he still was in the process of maturing. Because of his natural wit, humor, and willingness to be forthright, Lincoln was embroiled in political fights. As a young politician, he occasionally went too far in attacking an opponent. In his biography of Lincoln, Carl Sandburg tells how Lincoln once humiliated a political opponent by the name of Jesse B. Thomas after he attacked the "Long Nine" from Sangamon County. During his sarcastic tirade, Lincoln mimicked Thomas, generating cheers from the crowd. Witnesses referred to it as the "skinning of Thomas." However, afterward Lincoln apologized to the man and told friends he was not proud of his performance.[6]

The action most seriously regretted by Lincoln was his part in the writing of anonymous letters that ridiculed James Shields, the state auditor. The letters were printed in the *Sangamo Journal* in 1842. Infuriated, Shields challenged Lincoln to take part in a duel. As the one being challenged, Lincoln was able to determine the weaponry and other conditions. He made them so ridiculous that eventually Shields agreed to accept a written apology instead. Yet this incident had a profound effect on Lincoln, who did not like to discuss it and refrained from making fun of political opponents in the future.

☆ ☆ ☆

While Lincoln often came down hard on his political opponents, he showed genuine compassion to those he governed. For instance, while Abraham Lincoln did not drink, intemperance was common in the backwoods. He addressed the Springfield Washington Temperance Society a number of times, and often spoke with compassion toward those who battled drink.

In the following address, he used some interesting illustrations from the Bible to describe the struggle of those who drink to excess. He compares a man set free from drink to the man possessed by the demons named Legion, a man whom Jesus had set free from living like a wild man among the tombs (Mark 5:15 and Luke 8:35).

February 22, 1842

An Address

Delivered before The Springfield Washington Temperance Society. . . . A victim of intemperance, bursts the fetters that have bound him, and appears before his neighbors "clothed, and in his right mind." . . .

Lincoln was thirty-three years old and in the period when others insisted he was an unbeliever. By reference to the incarnation and humiliation of the Lord Jesus, Lincoln was showing respect and reverence to the most sacred doctrine in the Bible. His disarming logic contrasted the humility of the Lord Jesus condescending to become a man with the conceit of the Christian who feels superior to those who drink.

If they believe, as they profess, that ***Omnipotence condescended to take on himself the form of sinful man,*** *and, as such, to* ***die an ignominious death for their sakes****, surely they will not refuse submission to the infinitely lesser condescension, for the temporal, and perhaps eternal salvation, of a large, erring, and unfortunate class of their own fellow creatures. Nor is the condescension very great. . . .*

. . . The demon of intemperance ever seems to have delighted in sucking the blood of genius and of generosity. What one of us but can call to mind some dear relative, more promising in youth than all his fellows, who has fallen a sacrifice to his rapacity? He ever seems to have gone forth, like the ***Egyptian angel of death****, commissioned to slay if not the first, the fairest born of every family. Shall he be arrested in his desolating career? . . . He keeps our fathers, our brothers, our sons, and our friends, prostrate in the chains of moral death. To all the living every where, we cry, "come sound the moral resurrection trump, that these may rise and stand up, an* ***exceeding great army"—"Come from the four winds, O breath! and breathe upon these slain, that they may live. . . ."***

CW I: 271–279 (272, 277–278)

In writing this passage, Lincoln appears to have drawn from Philippians 2:7-8, Exodus 12:29-30, and Ezekiel 37:9-10. The prophet Ezekiel wrote a book of visions and symbolism that pictures the twelve tribes of Israel scattered to the winds, a hopeless, dead army with absolutely no possibility of awakening. In fact, they were not even skeletons but dry bones in a valley. As in the old slave spiritual, there was a great shaking, and bones began coming together. In the story in Ezekiel, they came to life and began to breathe. Lincoln uses these verses as an analogy to those hopelessly controlled by liquor.

Perhaps Lincoln's compassion for those with internal battles stemmed, in part, from his own struggles during his early adult years, which we'll explore in the next chapter.

CHAPTER 4

FRIENDS AND FAMILY

Lincoln's early life in Springfield may have revolved around politics, but it was not entirely consumed by it. During this time, he also established lifelong friendships—and met his future wife. His letters reveal some of the ups and downs of his personal life at this time. They also give us an occasional glimpse into his doubts about his faith. Unfortunately, few of his letters from his New Salem and Springfield days were saved; those that we do have, however, reveal some fascinating details.

When Abe Lincoln moved to Springfield, he was quite impressed with the grandeur of the city as compared to New Salem. He was also keenly aware of his social inferiority and, at first, felt quite lonely. During this time, he was corresponding with Mary Owens, a young lady of polished manners who had met Lincoln while she was visiting New Salem. (She should not be confused with Mary Todd, who later married Lincoln.) The following letter was written about a year after his move to Springfield.

May 7, 1837

To Mary S. Owens

This thing of living in Springfield is rather a dull business after all, at least it is so to me. I am quite as lonesome here as [I] ever was anywhere in my life. I have been spoken to by but one woman since I've been here, and should not have been by her, if she could have avoided it. I've never been to church yet, nor probably shall not be soon. I stay away because I am conscious I should not know how to behave myself. . . .

CW I: 78–79 (78)

Despite his openness to Mary about his loneliness, their courtship seemed to flounder after Lincoln moved to Springfield. Each became bothered by what they perceived as the weaknesses of the other—Abe was bothered by Mary's weight; Mary by his lack of social graces. Eventually Lincoln wrote Mary a letter in which he left the future of their relationship to her, saying he wanted to do right by her but in which he revealed no great passion for her. Mary never responded to the letter, effectively ending their relationship.

☆ ☆ ☆

Just as Lincoln met Mary Owens when she came to visit her sister in New Salem, so he met Mary Todd when she came to stay with a sister in Springfield. Mary was one of seven children of Robert and Eliza Parker Todd. Mary's father was a prominent banker, merchant, and lawyer in Lexington, Kentucky. Though a slaveholder, Robert Todd opposed bringing slaves into Kentucky. Mary's mother died when she was six years old. Her father remarried and had nine more children with his second wife. Mary did not get along with her stepmother and was sent to a boarding school. As was customary for girls of society, she attended a finishing school.

At age twenty-one, Mary went to Springfield to live with her sister Elizabeth, who was married to Ninian W. Edwards, the son of the territorial governor of Illinois. As a member of a prominent family, Mary was under pressure to be socially acceptable. She was courted by both Stephen Douglas and Lincoln, who felt out of her class. Yet Abraham and Mary became engaged.

Ninian Edwards knew Lincoln, for the two were in the "Long Nine" of the Illinois legislature. He discouraged his wife's sister from seeing Lincoln. It is uncertain how much his disapproval had to do with it, but the twenty-three-year-old Mary Todd and thirty-three-year-old Abraham Lincoln broke their engagement in January 1841. (A common story is that the breakup occurred during the final wedding preparations—even after the tables had been set. That is completely false.)

Lincoln entered a period of extreme melancholy. Secondary sources tell us that Lincoln's friends were watchful during this period, concerned that he might take his own life. Psychiatrists today confirm that Lincoln suffered recurring bouts of depression. To unload the crushing depression,

Lincoln turned to John Stuart, who had encouraged and tutored him in the study of the law. At the time Lincoln wrote this letter, they were law partners.

January 23, 1841

To John T. Stuart

I am now the most miserable man living. If what I feel were equally distributed to the whole human family, there would not be one cheerful face on the earth. Whether I shall ever be better I can not tell; I awfully forebode I shall not. To remain as I am is impossible; I must die or be better, it appears to me. The matter you speak of on my account, you may attend to as you say, unless you shall hear of my condition forbidding it. I say this, because I fear I shall be unable to attend to any business here, and a change of scene might help me. If I could be myself, I would rather remain at home with Judge Logan. I can write no more. Your friend, as ever—

A. Lincoln

CW I: 229–230

Lincoln possessed an unusual appreciation of literature, memorizing long passages from Shakespeare. He was familiar with the whole Bible, often quoting from the Gospels and the literary works of Job, the Psalms, and Ecclesiastes. Not surprisingly then, Lincoln explained his melancholy in terms similar to a famous passage of Scripture. Job complained in chapter after chapter that God had allowed everything to go wrong and should just let him die.

In his hyperbole regarding his misery, Lincoln sounds a bit like Job in the Bible, who, after suffering numerous losses, lamented, "Oh that my grief were throughly weighed, and my calamity laid in the balances together! For now it would be heavier than the sand of the sea" (Job 6:2-3).

☆ ☆ ☆

The Speed family lived near Louisville, Kentucky, and several members become close to Lincoln. Joshua Speed was a partner in a Springfield general store. When Abe Lincoln moved to the city, Joshua offered him living quarters above the store. They became close friends.

Joshua Speed moved back to Kentucky about the time of Lincoln's broken engagement. While still in the midst of his depression, Abe made a three-week trip to visit Joshua and his sister Mary. While there, Joshua's mother, Lucy Speed, gave Lincoln a Bible. He expressed his appreciation in a letter to Mary Speed:

September 27, 1841

To Mary Speed

. . . I intend to read it regularly when I return home. I doubt not that it is really, as she says, the best cure for the "Blues" could one but take it according to the truth. . . .

Your sincere friend

A. LINCOLN

CW I: 259–261

Lincoln never forgot the gift from Joshua's mother, Lucy Speed, as is clear from the way he signed a photo for her when he was president.

October 3, 1861

Inscription on Photograph Given to Mrs. Lucy G. Speed

For Mrs. Lucy G. Speed, from whose pious hand I accepted the present of an Oxford Bible twenty years ago.

A. LINCOLN

CW IV: 546

Like Lincoln, Joshua Speed was uncertain about entering into marriage. The two corresponded and encouraged each other regarding their respective courtships. In early 1842, Miss Fanny Henning, soon to be married to Speed, became seriously ill. Lincoln reminded his friend that his deep concern was evidence of his true love and that his love should settle all questions as to the wisdom of the marriage.

February 3, 1842

To Joshua F. Speed

I hope and believe, that your present anxiety and distress about her *health and* her *life, must and will forever banish those horrid doubts, which I know you sometimes felt, as to the truth of your affection for her. If they can be once and forever removed, (and I almost feel a presentiment that the* ***Almighty*** *has sent your present affliction expressly for that object) surely, nothing can come in their stead, to fill their immeasurable measure of misery. . . . Should she, as you fear, be destined to an early grave, it is indeed, a great consolation to know that she is so well prepared to meet it. Her religion, which you once disliked so much, I will venture you now prize most highly.*

CW I: 267–268

Lincoln wrote the following letter to his friend, anticipating that it would arrive shortly after Fanny Henning and Joshua Speed were married on February 15:

February 13, 1842

To Joshua F. Speed

When this shall reach you, you will have been Fanny's husband several days. You know my desire to befriend you is everlasting. . . .

I am now fully convinced, that you love her as ardently as you are capable of loving. Your ever being happy in her presence, and your intense anxiety about her health, if there were nothing else, would place this beyond all dispute in my mind. . . .

I hope with tolerable confidence, that this letter is a plaster for a place that is no longer sore.* ***God*** *grant it may be so. . . .*

CW I: 269–270

Just a few months later, Lincoln sent this letter to his friend.

July 4, 1842

To Joshua F. Speed

I always was superstitious; and as part of my superstition, I believe God made me one of the ***instruments*** *of bringing your Fanny and you together, which union, I have no doubt He had fore-ordained. Whatever he designs, he will do for* me *yet.* ***"Stand still and see the salvation of the Lord"*** *is my text just now. . . .*

CW I: 288–290 (289)

Lincoln often used the term *instrument* to express his belief that God had a plan for his life (see the introduction to part 3). This early

*A medicated or protective dressing; something applied to heal and soothe.

usage as a figure of speech helps us understand his meaning when he speaks of his own relationship to God in the service of his country. In this letter to Speed, he also uses the words Moses used to encourage the panicked Israelites as they spotted the Egyptian warriors pursuing them (Exodus 14:13).

Lincoln's boyhood imagination had captured the great dramatic action of major Bible stories. When he read the account of Moses leading his people out of Egypt, Lincoln's vivid mind saw the Egyptian chariots about to overtake the fleeing Israelites. Moses, preparing to part the Red Sea, stood upon a high rock and shouted, "Stand still, and see the salvation of the LORD" (Exodus 14:13).

☆ ☆ ☆

Just as Lincoln had encouraged Speed to marry Fanny, so now Joshua, along with some of Lincoln's other friends, encouraged him to commit to Mary Todd. Abraham Lincoln and Mary Todd were married on November 4, 1842, by the Rev. Charles Dresser in the Ninian Edwards home. Though it was a little below what the aspiring southern belle would have desired, they made their first home in a rented room in the Globe Tavern, for which they paid four dollars each week for room and board.

☆ ☆ ☆

Even after his marriage, Lincoln did not forget his family of origin. After his father's death, Lincoln helped provide for his stepmother. He had to be especially cautious that his stepbrother not get access to that money. We get a sense of his concern in the letter written to that stepbrother, John D. Johnston. He was a shiftless person who always needed money but lacked the ambition to work. In a classic example of how to help such a person, Lincoln wrote:

December 24, 1848

To John D. Johnston[1]

Dear Johnston:

Your request for eighty dollars, I do not think it best, to comply with now. At various times when I have helped you a little, you have said to me, "We can get along very well now" but in a very short time, I find you in the same difficulty again. . . .

What I propose is that you shall go to work, "tooth and nails" for some body who will give you money [for] it. . . . I now promise you, that for every dollar you will, between this and the first of next May, get for your own labor, either in money, or in your own indebtedness, I will then give you one other dollar. By this, if you hire yourself at ten dollars a month, from me you will get ten more, making twenty dollar[s] a month for your work. . . . Now if you will do this, you will soon be out of debt, and what is better, you will have a habit that will keep you from getting in debt again.

Affectionately Your brother A. LINCOLN

CW II: 15–16

CHAPTER 5

A QUESTIONING FAITH

During Abe Lincoln's youth, the very few available books awakened his mind to the world of imagination and literature. He read the Bible, fiction such as *Robinson Crusoe*, and nonfiction works such as the *Revised Laws of Indiana*. Abe's appetite for the printed page lured him to consider new ideas.

In New Salem, he associated with those of intellectual interests, some of whom had attended college before moving to the frontier village. A debating society welcomed Lincoln, and he was introduced to the writings of François Voltaire, C. F. Volney's *The Ruins of Empires*, and Thomas Paine's *Age of Reason*.

Many of Lincoln's new friends dismissed the Bible as archaic and of the backwoods. Emerging as he had from the wilderness, Lincoln naturally regretted his lack of formal education and questioned the simple faith of his parents. For the sake of illustration, imagine a college student, raised in a staunch political home. When confronted in college with strong opposing ideas, he or she turns from the parents' ideologies, but later, entering into adult responsibilities and having sifted various political views, the young adult may turn back to the views of early upbringing. Yet no matter which school of thought this young person finally follows, the conclusions are more sound and convictions more grounded because the person made the beliefs his or her own.

When elected to the legislature, Lincoln made a marked decision to shake off the disadvantages of his limited surroundings, though he would forever remain a man of the people. He bought a new suit of clothes and dropped the name "Abe," choosing from then on to sign his name "A. Lincoln." Lincoln also left behind the religious experiences in the wilderness church of his parents, where emotions were freely expressed. While we don't know exactly what he thought of the religion on the frontier, it's easy to imagine him poking fun at the excesses of the "fire and brimstone" preachers of his day.

Lincoln was a doubter at this time, and some of his friends from his early days called him a skeptic. Nonetheless, he often included references to the Bible and the Christian faith in his writings and speeches, without a hint of skepticism. In his letters to his most intimate friends, he spoke of God and the Bible quite freely. In the setting of the Lyceum Address, speaking to young men who like himself were reading and exploring ideas, reference to God was not necessarily expected, yet he spoke with acceptance of biblical truths.

☆ ☆ ☆

Along with several others, Lincoln aspired for an open seat in the United States House of Representatives in 1843. Yet when seeking the Whigs' nomination, Lincoln had a problem: He was not a member of a church. His opponents labeled him a skeptic, not a good label for a political candidate in that time. He addressed their questions in a letter to Martin Morris, an old friend from Petersburg, not far from New Salem where Abe had lived. Morris was a member of the Whig committee that would select the party's candidate for the seat.

March 26, 1843

To Martin S. Morris

My wife has some relatives in the Presbyterian and some in the Episcopal Churches, and therefore, whereever it would tell, I was set down as either the one or the other, whilst it was every where contended that no ch[r]istian ought to go for me, because I belonged to no church, was suspected of being a deist, and had talked about fighting a duel. . . .

CW I: 319–321 (320)

Despite this defense, Lincoln did not get the nomination for the Whig party that year. Though most of the state voted Democratic, Sangamon County and the rest of that congressional district was solidly Whig, so the nomination would have assured his election. However, Lincoln was not the only Whig interested in that seat. Lincoln and a friend, Edward Baker, for whom he named his second son, both desired to run, as did another qualified Whig candidate, John Hardin. To preserve party unity, it appears that they made a loose agreement to take turns. Hardin served first, then Edward Baker, and in 1846, Lincoln was elected by a solid majority.

☆ ☆ ☆

While some raised questions about Lincoln's Christianity based on his admission of doubts and decision not to join a church, others questioned his piety based on questions surrounding his character as a young politician. Many of these came to light after Lincoln's death, when his longtime law partner, William Herndon, began collecting recollections from those who knew Lincoln as a young man. Some early acquaintances said they remembered him as "vacillating, less principled" and a "political hack."[1] He was known for publishing anonymous letters in local newspapers that ridiculed and mocked his opponents (a pretty common tactic in that day, by the way).

Without question, Lincoln was an unusually gifted humorist, the life of any gathering. Lincoln relished the frequently no-holds-barred political debate in Vandalia and Springfield. Often it made for hilarious entertainment. Even his political opponents appreciated his biting wit and humorous storytelling. In 1842, for instance, these friends from across the aisle were entertaining President Martin Van Buren. To ensure that their distinguished guest would have an enjoyable evening, they invited Lincoln to come along.

If money is a test of a man's character, Lincoln passed with flying colors early in life. While in New Salem, Lincoln was part owner of a store for a time. His partner, who had a drinking problem, eventually died, leaving Lincoln with a debt of over $500. Lincoln not only took responsibility for his debt, he also assumed responsibility for the debts of the partner, making what he called a national debt of $1,100, a staggering sum at that time. As a result, Lincoln first earned the nickname "Honest Abe."[2]

Ralph Waldo Emerson, the nineteenth-century orator and writer, summed up Lincoln's sterling reputation in the essay "Greatness" in his 1876 book *Letters and Social Aims*: "Abraham Lincoln is perhaps the most remarkable example of this class that we have seen,—a man who was at home and welcome with the humblest, and with a spirit and a practical vein in the times of terror that commanded the admiration of the wisest. His heart was as great as the world, but there was no room in it to hold the memory of a wrong."[3]

☆ ☆ ☆

While questions about his character never amounted to much, many constituents remained concerned about his faith. Though Lincoln did receive the nomination for this congressional seat in 1846, once again he had to address charges that he was a skeptic. In fact, because his opponent was a well-known Methodist circuit rider named Peter Cartwright, the issue of church membership was even more important. (Note that the word *infidelity* had a broader meaning as used in the following document than the word generally has today.)

July 31, 1846

Handbill Replying to Charges of Infidelity

To the Voters of the Seventh Congressional District.

FELLOW CITIZENS:

A charge having got into circulation in some of the neighborhoods of this District, in substance that I am an open scoffer at Christianity, I have by the advice of some friends concluded to notice the subject in this form. That I am not a member of any Christian Church, is true; but I have never denied the truth of the Scriptures; and I have never spoken with intentional disrespect of religion in general, or of any denomination of Christians in particular. It is true that in early life I was inclined to believe in what I understand is called the "Doctrine of Necessity"—that is, that the human mind is impelled to action, or held in rest by some power, over which the mind itself has no control; and I have sometimes (with one, two or three, but never publicly) tried to maintain this opinion in argument. The habit of arguing thus however, I have, entirely left off for more than five years. And I add here, I have always understood this same opinion to be held by several of the Christian denominations. . . .

I do not think I could myself, be brought to support a man for office, whom I knew to be an open enemy of, and scoffer at, religion. Leaving the higher matter of eternal consequences, between him and his **Maker**, I still do not think any man has the right thus to insult the feelings, and injure the morals, of the community in which he may live. If, then, I was guilty of such conduct, I should blame no man who should condemn me for it; but I do blame those, whoever they may be, who falsely put such a charge in circulation against me. A LINCOLN

CW I: 382

Lincoln was thirty-seven when he wrote the above handbill, emerging from a period of his life in which his thinking had been affected by writers opposed to the Bible and the faith of his childhood. A less thoughtful man would have taken the simple step of joining the church with his wife as a means to end the controversy. That wasn't Lincoln's way, however. In his letter to Allen Ford, editor of the *Gazette* in Lacon, Illinois, Lincoln states his own rigid test of truth as I've emphasized below.

August 11, 1846

To Allen N. Ford

. . . *One lesson in morals which he might, not without profit, learn of even me—and that is, never to add the weight of his character to a charge against his fellow man, without* knowing *it to be true. I believe it is an established maxim in morals that he* who makes an assertion without knowing whether it is true or false, is guilty of falsehood; and the accidental truth of the assertion, does not justify or excuse him.

CW I: 383–384

☆ ☆ ☆

Lincoln continued to partner with John Stuart, even after Stuart became a congressman in 1839. In 1841, they parted ways and Lincoln formed a new partnership with Steven Logan. Their association ended in 1844 when Lincoln opened his own law office, hiring the younger William Herndon. In a letter to his junior law partner, Lincoln passes on a bit of wisdom.

July 10, 1848

To William H. Herndon

The way for a young man to rise, is to improve himself every way he can, never suspecting that any body wishes to hinder him. Allow me to assure you, that suspicion and jealousy never did help any man in any situation. There may sometimes be ungenerous attempts to keep a young man down; and they will succeed too, if he allows his mind to be diverted from its true channel to brood over the attempted injury. Cast about, and see if this feeling has not injured every person you have ever known to fall into it. . . .

CW I: 497–498 (497)

☆ ☆ ☆

The young man with a prophet's vision of America, the eloquent herald of Lyceum, was clearly different from most of his political cronies in Springfield. His boyhood dream, a childhood faith, and granite character set him apart. Though he relished the muddy political brawl, he was in an apprenticeship for the arena in which he would carry the standard for democracy.

Though he had a remarkable knowledge and appreciation of the Bible, questions plagued him regarding God and His purposes for His creatures. Before 1850 he did not accompany his wife to church services. He was wandering in a wilderness of doubts and questions.

Acknowledgement of God was one thing, but was God a personal God? Did the God of creation actually see mortal creatures as individuals in their making of right or wrong decisions? Surely a God so great as to control the oceans, the lightning storms, and the stars in their orbits would not be involved in the little details of a single person's life. Would God choose and benefit one nation over another? Why would He allow wicked men to butcher weaker men?

Lincoln was still mulling over these questions when he was elected to the U.S. House of Representatives in 1846. What he never doubted, however, was the superiority of the American system to any other. At last he had the opportunity to advance his country's interests at a national level.

CHAPTER 6

UNITED STATES CONGRESSMAN

The first session of the Thirtieth Congress of the United States opened in December 1847, more than a year after the election. Congressman Abraham Lincoln was sworn into the House of Representatives on December 6. Prior to that date, however, he had been working on comments on tariffs that would be debated at the start of the session. In his remarks, he quoted from Genesis 3:19 to support his contention that tariffs were a necessary protection for the common laborer.

December 1, 1847

Fragments of a Tariff Discussion

In the early days of the world, the Almighty said to the first of our race ***"In the sweat of thy face shalt thou eat bread"****; and since then, if we except the* light *and the* air *of heaven, no good thing has been, or can be enjoyed by us, without having first cost labour. And, inasmuch [as] most good things are produced by labour, it follows that [all] such things of right belong to those whose labour has produced them. But it has so happened in all ages of the world that* some *have laboured, and* others *have, without labour, enjoyed a large proportion of the fruits. This is wrong, and should not continue. To [secure] to each labourer the whole product of his labour, or as nearly as possible, is a most worthy object of any good government. . . .*

CW I: 407–415 (411–412)

Throughout his political career, Lincoln would extol the virtues of honest labor—his convictions no doubt influenced by the many forms of labor he undertook as a young man. He believed that the slave was entitled to the fruit of his labor just as much as any other man. At this point in his career, however, he thought it best to allow slavery to continue in the South, where he hoped it would eventually die out. Slavery should not be allowed in new states and territories. Stephen Oates summarizes Lincoln's position:

> I hold it to be a paramount duty of us in the free states, due to the Union of the states, and perhaps to liberty itself (paradox though it may seem) to let the slavery of the other states alone; while, on the other hand, I hold it to be equally clear, that we should never knowingly lend ourselves directly or indirectly, to prevent that slavery from dying a natural death.[1]

☆ ☆ ☆

Lincoln's position on slavery helps explain his opposition to the Mexican War, the great issue before the House of Representatives when Lincoln took office. In 1845, the United States had annexed Texas, which about ten years before had gained independence from Mexico. President James Polk, a Democrat, then ordered General Zachary Taylor to advance to the Rio Grande. Mexico had never recognized the annexation of its former territory, and skirmishes between the two country's forces soon broke out.

Lincoln, like most in the Whig party, feared that new territory in the South would mean the extension of slavery. (Part of the reason Texas had seceded from Mexico was that country's opposition to slavery, which many Texans felt was critical to their economy.) As the opposition party, the Whigs argued that President Polk had deliberately sent American soldiers into disputed territory in order to aggravate Mexico into starting a war. On December 22, 1847, Lincoln laid a series of resolutions on the table of the U.S. House of Representatives, demanding that Polk reveal the actual "spot" on which the war with Mexico had begun.

On January 12, Lincoln gave a ten-page speech to the House in which he, like an attorney in a courtroom, pursued the question of whether the aggression had started in U.S. or Mexican territory. Arguing that Texas's boundary stopped at the Nueces River, north of the Rio Grande, he concluded that United States forces had improperly entered Mexican territory and were responsible for starting the war.[2] That explains his mention of the blood of Abel, found in Genesis 4:10.

Lincoln's charges actually only echoed allegations the Whigs had been making for months. Yet because his views were unpopular back home, Lincoln knew speaking out might cost him reelection. And, in the end, the president made no response to Lincoln's queries.

January 12, 1848

Speech in United States House of Representatives: The War with Mexico

Any people anywhere, being inclined and having the power, have the right *to rise up, and shake off the existing government, and form a new one that suits them better. This is a most valuable,—a most sacred right—a right, which we hope and believe, is to liberate the world. . . . As to the country now in question, we bought it of France in 1803, and sold it to Spain in 1819, according to the President's statements. After this, all Mexico, including Texas, revolutionized against Spain; and still later, Texas revolutionized against Mexico. In my view, just so far as she carried her revolution, by obtaining the* actual, *willing or unwilling, submission of the people,* so far, *the country was hers, and no farther. Now sir, for the purpose of obtaining the very best evidence, as to whether Texas had actually carried her revolution, to the place where the hostilities of the present war commenced, let the President answer the interrogatories, I proposed, as before mentioned, or some other similar ones. Let him answer, fully, fairly, and candidly. Let him answer with* facts, *and not with arguments. . . . As a nation* should *not, and the Almighty* will *not, be evaded, so let him attempt no envasion—no equivocation. And if, so answering, he can show that the soil was ours, where the first blood of the war was shed—that it was not within an inhabited country, or, if within such, that the inhabitants had submitted themselves to the civil authority of Texas, or of the United States . . . I, shall be most happy to reverse the vote I gave the other day. I have a selfish motive for desiring that the President may do this. I expect to give some votes, in connection with the war, which, without his so doing, will be of doubtful propriety in my own judgment, but which will be free from the doubt if he does so. But if he* can *not, or* will *not do this . . . , then I shall be fully convinced, of what I more than suspect already, that he is deeply conscious of being in the wrong—that he feels the blood of this war, like the* ***blood of Abel****, is crying to Heaven against him. . . . He now finds himself, he knows not where. . . .*

CW I: 431–442 (438–440)

☆ ☆ ☆

In a very frank letter, Lincoln asked John Peck, a friend who was a Baptist minister and agent of the American Bible Society, how he could defend the United States in its policy regarding the Mexican War. After reiterating the facts, Lincoln asks his friend to consider Jesus' charge to treat others as we wish to be treated (see Matthew 7:12 and Luke 6:31).

May 21, 1848

To John M. Peck

If you deny that they are facts, I think I can furnish proof which shall convince you that you are mistaken.

If you admit that they are facts, then I shall be obliged for a reference to any law of language, law of states, law of nations, law of morals, law of religion,—any law human or divine, in which an authority can be found for saying those facts constitute "no aggression".

Possibly you consider those acts too small for notice. Would you venture to so consider them, had they been committed by any nation on earth, against the humblest of our people? I know you would not. Then I ask, is the precept ***"Whatsoever ye would that men should do to you, do ye even so to them" . . . ?***

CW I: 472–473 (473)

Lincoln's Congressional voting record makes clear he opposed slavery in principle. The following paragraph, taken from a House resolution written by Lincoln, was only a beginning, the first tottering baby step toward emancipation. In the full three-page document, he proposed that residents of the District of Columbia be able to vote on a referendum to abolish slavery there.

January 10, 1849

Representatives
Concerning Abolition of Slavery in the District of Columbia

Section I Be it enacted by the Senate and House of Representatives of the United States of America, in Congress assembled: That no person not now within the District of Columbia, nor now owned by any person or persons now resident within it, nor hereafter born within it, shall ever be held in slavery within said District.

CW II: 20–22 (20)

Though the bill had broad restrictions that would only keep slaves from being brought into the District of Columbia, Lincoln could not rally support and withdrew the bill without a vote. Though this first tiny step was unsuccessful, a decade later, his challenge would be to win emancipation by personal persuasion, wisdom, and exceptional leadership.

☆ ☆ ☆

Though it was unusual for a congressman's family to accompany him to Washington in those days, Lincoln's wife and two sons moved with him to Washington. They boarded at Mrs. Sprigg's boarding house, a popular residence for many Whigs in Congress. Yet Mary was apparently unhappy there. According to Benjamin Thomas, she was lonesome among so few women and didn't get along with those whom she did meet.[3] After only three months, she, Robert, and Eddy Lincoln moved to Lexington to be among her relatives.

The following letter gives us a peek into Abe and Mary's relationship during this time and allows us to see a little of the private lives of husband and wife while he was a congressman in Washington, D.C.

April 16, 1848

To Mary Todd Lincoln

Dear Mary:

In this troublesome world, we are never quite satisfied. When you were here, I thought you hindered me some in attending to business; but now, having nothing but business—no variety—it has grown exceedingly tasteless to me. I hate to sit down and direct documents, and I hate to stay in this old room by myself. You know I told you in last sunday's letter, I was going to make a little speech during the week; but the week has passed away without my getting a chance to do so; and now my interest in the subject has passed away too. Your second and third letters have been received since I wrote before. Dear Eddy thinks father is "gone tapila" [probably meaning "capitol"] Has any further discovery been made as to the breaking into your grand-mother's house? If I were she, I would not remain there alone. You mention that your uncle John Parker is likely to be at Lexington. Dont forget to present him my very kindest regards.

I went yesterday to hunt the little plaid stockings, as you wished; but found that McKnight has quit business, and Allen had not a single pair of the description you give, and only one plaid pair of any sort that I thought would fit "Eddy's dear little feet." I have a notion to make another trial to-morrow morning. If I could get them, I have an excellent chance of sending them. Mr. Warrick Tunstall, of St. Louis is here. He is to leave early this week, and to go by Lexington. He says he knows you, and will call to see you; and he voluntarily asked, if I had not some package to send to you.

I wish you to enjoy yourself in every possible way. . .

. . . All the house—or rather, all with whom you were on decided good terms—send their love to you. The others say nothing.

Very soon after you went away, I got what I think a very pretty set of shirt-bosom studs—modest little ones, jet, set in gold, only costing 50 cents a piece, or 1.50 for the whole.

Suppose you do not prefix the "Hon" to the address on your letters to me any more. I like the letters very much, but I would rather they should not have that upon them. It is not necessary, as I suppose you have thought, to have them to come free.

And you are entirely free from head-ache? That is good—good—considering it is the first spring you have been free from it since we were acquainted. I am afraid you will get so well, and fat, and young, as to be wanting to marry again. Tell Louisa I want her to watch you a little for me. Get weighed, and write me how much you weigh.

I did not get rid of the impression of that foolish dream about dear Bobby till I got your letter written the same day. What did he and Eddy think of the little letters father sent them? Dont let the blessed fellows forget father. . . .

Most affectionately
A. Lincoln

CW I: 465–466

Though much is made of his difficulty in living with Mary, we should remember that on the last day of his life, they had a private lunch, and in the afternoon he took her for a carriage ride on which they spoke of returning to Illinois and living quietly. They spent their last evening together at Ford's Theater. While president, he wrote many short notes to Mary. No doubt they were appreciated, even though most were but a half dozen words.

April 28, 1864

To Mary Todd Lincoln

Mrs. A. Lincoln
Metropolitan Hotel
New-York

The draft will go to you. Tell Tad the goats and father are very well—especially the goats.

A. Lincoln

CW VII: 320

☆ ☆ ☆

At some period of time, the Lincolns were able to visit Niagara Falls. Lincoln paused for meditation, considering the awe-inspiring wonder through the eyes of various beholders, as a scientist, a philosopher, and as a naturalist. As the following letter shows, he was inspired by the infinite timelessness the falls represent.

September 25, 1848

Fragment: Niagara Falls

Niagara-Falls! By what mysterious power is it that millions and millions, are drawn from all parts of the world, to gaze upon Niagara Falls? There is no mystery about the thing itself. Every effect is just such as any inteligent man knowing the causes, would anticipate, without [seeing] it. If the water moving onward in a great river, reaches a point where there is a perpendicular jog, of a hundred feet in descent, in the bottom of the river,—it is plain the water will have a violent and continuous plunge at that point. It is also plain the water, thus plunging, will foam, and roar, and send up a mist, continuously, in which last, during sunshine, there will be perpetual rain-bows. . . . Yet this is really a very small part of that world's wonder. It's power to excite reflection, and emotion, is it's great charm. The geologist will demonstrate that the plunge, or fall, was once at Lake Ontario, and has worn it's way back to it's present position; he will ascertain how fast *it is wearing now, and so get a basis for determining how* long *it has been wearing back from Lake Ontario, and finally demonstrate by it that this world is at least fourteen thousand years old. A philosopher . . . will say Niagara Falls is only the lip of the basin out of which pours all the surplus water which rains down on two or three hundred thousand square miles of the earth's surface. He will estim[ate with] approximate accuracy, that five hundred thousand [to]ns of water, falls with it's full weight, a distance of a hundred feet each minute—thus exerting a force equal to the lifting of the same weight, through the same space, in the same time. . . . This vast amount of water, constantly pouring* down, *is supplied by an equal amount constantly* lifted up, *by the sun; . . . and he is overwhelmed in the contemplation of the vast power the sun is constantly exerting in quiet, noiseless opperation of lifting water* up *to be rained* down *again.*

But still there is more. It calls up the indefinite past. When Columbus first sought this continent—when Christ suffered on the cross—when Moses led Israel through the Red-Sea—nay, even, when Adam first came from the hand of his Maker—then as now, Niagara was roaring here. . . . Co[n]temporary with the whole race of men, and older than the first man, Niagara is strong, and fresh to-day as ten thousand years ago. The Mammoth and Mastadon—now so long dead, that fragments of their monstrous bones, alone testify, that they ever lived, have gazed on Niagara. In that long—long time, never still for a single moment. Never dried, never froze, never slept, never rested,

CW II: 10–11

☆ ☆ ☆

Lincoln had long been fascinated with the power of America's waterways. In his youth, he made a flatboat trip down the Mississippi to New Orleans. After moving with his parents to Illinois, he constructed a crude river craft, intending to navigate the Sangamon River and make a second trip down the Mississippi. When the craft could not make it over a shallow place at New Salem, Lincoln's ingenuity and engineering attracted the attention of onlooking strangers. When he returned, they welcomed the tall, ungainly stranger.

Legislator Abraham Lincoln supported internal improvements, especially those having to do with the waterways and river transportation. After his eight years in the state legislature, he was chosen by Sangamon County as a delegate to a River and Harbor Convention in Chicago in 1847, and later was appointed one of three commissioners for the Illinois and Michigan Canal.[4]

During his single term in the U.S. House of Representatives, Lincoln made an important speech on federal involvement in internal improvements. In it he countered the arguments of those who believed that each state should make its own improvements.

June 20, 1848

Speech in United States House of Representatives on Internal Improvements

. . . There is something of local advantage in the most general objects. But the converse is also true. Nothing is so local *as to not be of some* general *benefit. Take, for instance, the Illinois and Michigan canal. . . . Considered apart from it's effects, it is perfectly local. Every inch of it is within the state of Illinois. . . . in a very few days we were all gratified to learn, among other things, that sugar had been carried from New-Orleans through this canal to Buffalo in New York. . . .*

CW I: 480–490 (483)

After a session of Congress, Lincoln returned by riverboat to Springfield. He was intrigued as he watched empty barrels and boxes being used to float a vessel that had run aground. Challenged by the problem of giving buoyancy to a vessel in shallow water, he partnered with a local mechanic and constructed a model of a boat that used expandable air chambers to lift boats over sandbars. Lincoln took the model with him to Washington, D.C., for the second year of his congressional term. Though he applied for a patent in 1849, he never realized monetary gain from this invention.[5]

☆ ☆ ☆

At the time he applied for his patent, Lincoln knew he would not be returning to the House. His opposition to the Mexican War had stirred up a hornet's nest in his own state, and it appeared that his career in politics had ended. The Illinois Whigs had nominated Stephen Logan, so like his friend Edward Baker, he would serve only one term.

Lincoln had worked feverishly for the crumbling and disintegrating Whig party and climbed the political ladder, only to reluctantly step downward. Pondering the closing door, he considered applying for some government position that would afford good security for his family. Without enthusiasm, he decided to apply for the General Land Office.

June 1, 1849

To Moses Hampton

At last I concluded to take the General Land-Office if I can get it. I have come to this conclusion, more to prevent what would be generally bad for the party here, and particularly bad for me, than a positive desire for the office. Will you please write old Zach (not Mr. Ewing, but Old Zach) as pretty a letter for me as you think the truth will permit? Time is important. ***What you do, do quickly.***

Your friend, as ever.

A. Lincoln

CW (Second Supplement): 1

In this letter, Lincoln uses a phrase similar to the one Jesus used in sending Judas from the Upper Room where He celebrated the Last Supper with His disciples (John 13:27).

☆ ☆ ☆

In the end, Lincoln was not chosen for the position. Lincoln decided to return to his Springfield law practice and travel with the Eighth Illinois Circuit Court. He was moving along in life, having lived forty of his eventual fifty-six years. In his biography of Lincoln, David Herbert Donald wrote: "With that his public career was apparently over. As he settled back in Springfield, he must have remembered a note he gave a few months earlier to an autograph collector who requested his 'signature with a sentiment'; 'I am not a very sentimental man; and the best sentiment I can think of is that if you collect the signatures of all persons who are no less distinguished than I, you will have a very undistinguishing mass of names.'"[6]

☆ ☆ ☆

Lincoln's childhood dreams and the New Salem aspirations were wilting. He was disappointed, frustrated, and puzzled as he pondered the future. Yet had Abraham Lincoln been appointed to the General Land Office, he would have faded into obscurity. Had the political winds suddenly changed and he been reelected, he would not have experienced the awakenings of faith described in the next chapter. Life-changing experiences are more likely after traumatic experiences. Had Lincoln advanced to leadership in the House of Representatives and to the ultimate of his ambitions, giving orations as a senator, he would have missed the Douglas debates and thus would never have been lifted in public recognition. The "House Divided" would in time have ceased to be "divided"—*not with freedom of the slaves*—but with the black race in continued legal bondage.

Yet Lincoln's single term in the House of Representatives had been a most important apprenticeship for the unique, overwhelming, and as yet unthought of challenge ahead. He had met many of the lawmakers, generals, politicians, and newsmen who would appear on the stage of the great drama in which he would play the lead part. An example was Alexander Stephens, the friend who eventually would accept the vice presidency of the Confederacy.

Disappointing as his single term had been, it had enabled this country lawyer to learn the workings of Congress.

CHAPTER 7

FAITH REKINDLED

To Jesse Fell, Enclosing Autobiography

From 1849 to 1854, both inclusive, practiced law more assiduously than ever before. Always a whig in politics, and generally on the whig electoral tickets, making active canvasses. . . .

CW III: 511–512 (512)

A much wiser and politically astute Lincoln went back to trying cases in the Sangamon Circuit Court of rural Illinois. Twice each year he spent three months traveling from county seat to county seat with a judge and fellow lawyers to settle cases, which meant long separations from his family. While he was on the road, he enlivened the atmosphere of the hotels where he stayed with his humor. He also met many of the common people who would provide the backbone of his support in the great struggle for democracy.

Given his disappointment over the failure (in his mind at least) of his political career, the early 1850s were a difficult time for Lincoln. Yet his personal interactions with his former constituents reminded him of one thing: America was a land of opportunity for all. G. S. Boritt, author and director of the Civil War Institute at Gettysburg College, has said he admired Lincoln even as a young boy growing up in Hungary. In his book *Lincoln and the Economics of the American Dream*, he discusses Lincoln's vision that the American dream would be available to all inhabitants. He writes:

> Most important, his underlying moral assumption, his devotion to the idea that America stood for fair reward for man's labor, for

> equal, constantly expanding opportunity for all, was strengthened until it became a nation-pervading force. Thus in the end—and in the final analysis—Lincoln accepted the Civil War to save, above all, his Dream—the Union, however precious, being merely its carrying vessel.[1]

☆ ☆ ☆

The year 1850 was particularly difficult for Abraham and Mary Lincoln. In February, their second son died after being ill for nearly two months. Not quite four years old, Edward Baker Lincoln had been named after the man whom Lincoln replaced in the House of Representatives.

The child's tombstone read:

Edward B.
Son of
A. & M. LINCOLN
DIED
Feb. 1, 1850
Aged
3 years 10 months
18 days
Of such is the kingdom of Heaven

Though Lincoln had not resolved the questions of his early biblical teachings, he and his wife adorned their son's memorial with the beautiful Scripture from the story of the Master calling for little children to be brought to Him (see Matthew 19:14; Mark 10:14; Luke 18:16).

Mary Lincoln arranged for Dr. James Smith of the First Presbyterian Church in Springfield to hold a memorial service for her young son. Dr. Smith was renowned as a debater against prominent atheists. In his 676-page book *The Christian's Defense*, Reverend Smith explained that he had been a skeptic but had found answers to his questions in the Bible.[2] Just the fall before, Lincoln had come across Smith's book in the Todd library when he had returned to Lexington with Mary to settle her father's estate. The book made a deep impression on Lincoln, who asked a friend to introduce him to the minister when he and Mary returned home. Before long, Lincoln rented a church pew, which was a common practice in those days, and occasionally attended services with Mary, who joined the church.[3]

Documents show that Lincoln's relationship with Dr. James Smith continued into his presidency when he appointed Dr. Smith as a diplomat to the clergyman's native land, Scotland.[4]

☆ ☆ ☆

Abraham Lincoln lost another close family member less than a year after his son's death. Just five days before his father, Thomas, died, Lincoln sent the following letter to his stepbrother. The reminder of God's care for His creatures is a clear reference to Matthew 10:29-30 and Luke 12:6-7.

January 12, 1851

To John D. Johnston

*I sincerely hope Father may yet recover his health; but at all events tell him to remember to call upon, and confide in, our great, and good, and merciful Maker; who will not turn away from him in any extremity. He notes **the fall of a sparrow**, and **numbers the hairs of our heads**; and He will not forget the dying man, who puts his trust in Him. Say to him that if we could meet now, it is doubtful whether it would not be more painful than pleasant; but that if it be his lot to go now, he will soon have a joyous [meeting] with many loved ones gone before; and where [the rest] of us, through the help of God, hope ere-long [to join] them. . . .*

CW II: 96–97

☆ ☆ ☆

Disillusioned in politics, devastated by the loss of a son, with his youthful dreams and ideals fading, Lincoln might have settled for the prosperous lifestyle of a country attorney. Because of his ambition, keen intellect, and sharp wit, Lincoln had stood out from his peers for many years. He was well liked by his fellow lawyers, who appreciated his effervescence, wit, and humor, which enlivened the courtrooms and hotel lobbies.

Yet he'd first been motivated to declare his political candidacy as a young man because of his love for and belief in America's ideals. So even as he traveled the court circuit again, the smoldering coals of Lincoln's unrealized dreams could not lie dormant. The flickering, but nonetheless live, embers of a vision for the future of America would not quite allow him to settle permanently into his law career.

Passing through the valley of sorrow following Eddy's death was the real climax of Lincoln's apprenticeship. In the depths of grief, Abraham Lincoln refused to succumb to bitterness and rested in the acceptance of God's will. Lincoln's study of *The Christian's Defense* and his sporadic church attendance were infant steps on the pathway of faith, which would blossom into great pronouncements addressed to liberty-loving people of all nations. It was during these years that a disciplined man emerged and began walking the path to lead his country through what he would call the "fiery trial."

The presidency would be a crucible of conflict and overwhelming sorrow for Lincoln. He would be caricatured by cartoonists as the cause of endless casualty lists. Opponents would remain unaware of the grieving man at the telegraph office, waiting for a sign of optimism from the front lines.

Of course, in the 1850s, Lincoln, like all who knew him, assumed he had retired from public life. He and Mary welcomed two sons into their home in 1850 and 1853, William and Thomas. Yet already the undercurrents of the slavery issue, which the United States never seemed able to quell for long, were beginning to stir again. This time, Lincoln would allow himself to be pulled into the resulting fray.

PART TWO

A HOUSE DIVIDED

A house divided against itself cannot stand. I believe this government cannot endure, permanently half slave *and half* free. *I do not expect the Union to be* dissolved—*I do not expect the house to* fall—*but I* do *expect it will cease to be divided. It will become* all *one thing or* all *the other.*

Lincoln's "A House-Divided" Speech
Springfield, Illinois, June 16, 1858

CHAPTER 8

INCITED, IGNITED

To Jesse Fell, Enclosing Autobiography

I was losing interest in politics, when the repeal of the Missouri Compromise aroused me again. What I have done since then is pretty well known. . . .

CW III: 511–512 (512)

Through the centuries, *Might* had decided what was *Right*. Yet the Declaration of Independence challenged that assumption. The trampled-upon common man, subjected to tyranny for thousands of years, heard the Liberty Bell. And while the bell was still pealing, the Founding Fathers ratified the Constitution of the United States, the historical document that did more than any other to protect human rights.

Yet to assure passage of the Constitution, the young nation had agreed to permit slavery. Many of the Founding Fathers spoke of their hope of its eventual extinction, and the United States took a few steps in the early nineteenth century that seemed destined to help fulfill that expectation. In 1808, for instance, Congress banned further importation of slaves. In 1820, Lincoln's hero Henry Clay helped forge the Missouri Compromise, a series of laws designed to keep the balance between slave and free states as a number of new states were being formed from the western territories. As a result of this legislation, slavery was prohibited in any of the territory acquired through the Louisiana Purchase north of the southern boundary of Missouri—except within Missouri itself, which was set to join the nation. (Since Missouri's settlers were largely from the South, slavery was already an established practice there.)

The Compromise of 1850 was another attempt to maintain the

balance following the Mexican War, which had raised the question of slave expansion once again. As a result of this legislation, the United States welcomed Texas, along with states like California, into the nation. Again, Henry Clay played a large role in creation of this legislation, although it was guided to passage by Senator Daniel Webster of Massachusetts and Senator Stephen Douglas of Illinois.

In 1854, the news that the Missouri Compromise had been nullified by a new law, the Kansas-Nebraska Act, exploded across the prairies. Lincoln, the circuit-riding attorney, avidly read every newspaper he could to find out more.

The Kansas-Nebraska Act opened new lands for settlement. More significantly, it threatened to overturn the careful balance between slave and free states. Rather than determining which territories would be slave and which would be free, Congress this time mandated that settlers themselves would determine whether slavery would be allowed in the new territories. The author of this legislation was Stephen Douglas, who had become an advocate of "popular sovereignty."

While giving settlers the right to decide whether or not to allow slavery sounds democratic, it led to great turmoil in the Kansas territory, with many people on both sides of the slavery issue flooding into the state just for the opportunity to vote one way or the other. Bloodshed between the two sides was common. John Brown, who favored insurrection as a means to abolish slavery, first gained national notoriety there for his role in killing five proslavery farmers. The conflict in "Bleeding Kansas" also led to the formation of the Republican Party, which Lincoln would join within a few years.

Later, when President Lincoln would call Congress into special session, he would use a phrase, packed with meaning, to describe America: the "last best hope of earth." We do not know when he first used that phrase, but it could easily have begun percolating in his mind at this time, when his vision of a peaceful, free America was fading fast.

Thus, while the outwardly carefree and jovial Abraham Lincoln continued to impress and entertain spectators in the courtrooms of Illinois in the early 1850s, inwardly, a heavy-hearted circuit lawyer's boyhood vision and hopes for America were becoming a bad dream. For the first time he sensed that his nation, destined for greatness, could end in a premature death.

☆ ☆ ☆

As news of ominous votes in Congress reached the quiet towns of central Illinois, Lincoln's companions on the circuit noted that he kept more and more to himself. His thoughts seemed far away. Stephen Oates wrote of the lonely, dejected Lincoln: "Friends who saw him sitting alone in rural courthouses thought him more withdrawn than ever. Once when they went to bed in a rude hostelry, they left him sitting in front of the fireplace staring intently at the flames. The next morning he was still there, studying the ashes and charred logs."[1] Henry Whitney, a fellow attorney who traveled the eighth circuit with Lincoln, also remembered the future president sitting through the night by a cold fire.[2]

Lincoln biographer Benjamin Thomas picks up the story:

> Three months later [after the passage of the Kansas-Nebraska Act] we shall find [Lincoln] back in politics. But he will emerge as a different Lincoln from the ambitious politician whose hopes were seemingly blighted in 1849. His ambition, reawakened, will become as compelling as before, but it will be restrained now by devotion to a cause. When he speaks again, it will be with a new seriousness, a new explicitness, a new authority. From his young manhood a lucid thinker and a clever man before a crowd, he will stand forth hereafter as a political analyst and debater of surpassing power.
>
> The impact of a moral challenge, purging Lincoln of narrow partisanship and unsure purpose, is about to transform an honest, capable, but essentially self-centered small-town politician of self-developed but largely unsuspected talents into a statesman who will grow to world dimensions.[3]

☆ ☆ ☆

A decade before, on March 4, 1843, Lincoln had used a biblical phrase, "house divided" for the political purpose of rallying his party (see chapter 3). The illustration had fomented in his brain so that in 1858 it would become the rapier that would pierce the complacency of Illinois voters in the Lincoln-Douglas Debates. Of absolute importance was the uniting of the divided house, the forging together of a people's government that would rid the country of the sickening cancer of slavery. Were the people's government to fail, all would be lost, and the bonds would tighten upon the slave; if the people's government held, justice and democracy would be victorious and all chains would be broken.

Though from a free state, Stephen Douglas seems to have had no personal objection to slavery. The compromises he agreed to in crafting the Kansas-Nebraska Act possibly were motivated in part by his desire to gain Southern support for his plan to run the transcontinental railroad through Chicago.

From his entrance into the Illinois legislature in 1836, Stephen Douglas was the archrival of Lincoln, who was beginning his second term. Only five foot four inches tall, Douglas was a gifted orator, a meteor of light to the Democratic Party. Known as the "Little Giant," Douglas was admired for his tenacity and eagerness to see the nation's continued westward expansion. Unlike Lincoln's, Douglas's political career advanced steadily.

Though Douglas was widely admired, Lincoln was not easily fooled by anyone and never shied away from criticizing Douglas's policies. In a long address in which he responded to a speech by Douglas, Lincoln displayed his natural gift as an entertainer, humorously upbraiding Douglas for twisting words around to mean whatever Douglas wanted them to mean.

August 14, 1852

Speech to the Springfield Scott Club

When the builders of the ***tower of Babel*** *got into difficulty about language, if they had just called on Judge Douglas, he would, at once, have construed away the difficulty, and enabled them to finish the structure, upon the truly democratic platform on which they were building. . . .*

The biblical story of the tower of Babel is found in Genesis 11:1-9. Lincoln continued chiding Douglas for using words with meanings other than the ones intended.

As an example, take a sentence from an old and well known book, not much suspected for duplicity, or equivocal language; which sentence is as follows:

"And Enoch walked **with** ***God; and he was not, for God took him. . . ."***

CW II:135–157 (141)

Lincoln gave illustrations of various ways the word *with* might be used, each altering the meaning of the statements. Lincoln continued to rib Douglas, making reference to Enoch, who is profiled in Genesis 5:24.

Because Douglas was viewed as an exceptionally able senator, many people were surprised at his willingness to shake the uneasy peace over the expansion of slavery that the country had reached through the Missouri Compromise and the Compromise of 1850. By repealing the slavery restriction guidelines established by the Missouri Compromise, Douglas did just that. He himself predicted that the bill would be met with fierce opposition when it was introduced to the Senate.

Not surprisingly, then, once Congress adjourned, Douglas hurried home to begin defending this legislation—and his own record. Everywhere he went, he faced derision and jeering from angry crowds. Yet this seemed only to mobilize him, and slowly he began to win his constituents back.

In October 1854, however, Lincoln responded to Douglas's defenses with a reasoned but impassioned address of his own. He spent twelve days working meticulously on this speech, which became a pattern of many to follow. It is a demonstration of his knowledge of the Bible that he could select and use the six scriptural quotations without the use of Bible tools that are available today.

Known as the Peoria Address, in it Lincoln explained his view that the Founding Fathers had intended that slavery would eventually be ended. While not criticizing the Southerners, he also discussed why he was so personally opposed to slavery, both because of its injustice and because it contradicted the American ideal of liberty for all. While affirming the principle of self-government, he explained why popular sovereignty, which really meant that the expansion of slavery would be determined by the small number of settlers in a few new states, was not a reasonable approach.

October 16, 1854

Speech at Peoria, Illinois

This declared *indifference, but as I must think, covert real zeal for the spread of slavery, I can not but hate. I hate it because of the monstrous injustice of slavery itself. I hate it because it deprives our republican example of its just influence in the world—enables the enemies of free institutions, with plausibility, to taunt us as hypocrites—causes the real friends of freedom to doubt our sincerity, and especially because it forces so many really good men amongst ourselves into an open war with the very fundamental principles of civil liberty—criticising the Declaration of Independence, and insisting that there is no right principle of action but* self-interest.

Unlike the abolitionists, Lincoln was not demanding that slavery be prohibited where it already existed. His disagreement with Douglas was that the senator would allow it to extend to new territories. Note his reference to Jesus' words in Matthew 6:34.

. . . What did we mean, when we, in 1852, endorsed the compromises of '50? . . . I meant not to resist the admission of Utah and New Mexico, even should they ask to come in as slave States. I meant nothing about additional territories, because, as I understood, we then had no territory whose character as to slavery was not already settled. As to Nebraska, I regarded its character as being fixed, by the Missouri compromise, for thirty years—as unalterably fixed as that of my own home in Illinois. As to new acquisitions I said ***"sufficient unto the day is the evil thereof. . . ."***

Lincoln bemoaned the idea that slavery was a "sacred right," a position being expressed more often by Southern leaders like John Calhoun.

Little by little, but steadily as man's march to the grave, we have been giving up the old *for the* new *faith. Near eighty years ago we began by declaring that all men are created equal; but now from that beginning we have run down to the other declaration, that for* some *men to enslave* others *is a "sacred right of self-government." These principles can not stand together. They are as opposite as* ***God and mammon****; and whoever holds to the one, must despise the other. . . .*

Let north and south—let all Americans—let all lovers of liberty everywhere—join in the great and good work. If we do this, we shall not only have saved the Union; but we shall have so saved it, that the succeeding millions of free happy people, the world over, shall rise up, and ***call us blessed****, to the latest generations.*

In Matthew 6:24 and Luke 16:13, Jesus warns his followers that they cannot serve both God and money. Lincoln argues that, in the same way, self-government cannot coexist with slavery. Lincoln's words in the next paragraph bring to mind Proverbs 31:28, "Her children arise up, and call her blessed." A similar phrase is found in Luke 1:48, part of the Magnificat, in which Mary, who has just been told she'll be mother to the Messiah, expresses her exuberance: "All generations shall call me blessed."

Douglas had argued that God made man and placed good and evil before him, allowing him to choose for himself and making him responsible for the choice he would make (see Genesis 2:16-17; 3:1-6). Lincoln answered with an interesting twist on this biblical story.

God did not place good and evil before man, telling him to make his choice. On the contrary, he did tell him there was one tree, of the fruit of which, he should not eat, upon pain of certain death. I should scarcely wish so strong a prohibition against slavery in Nebraska.

Douglas had said that the revered statesmen Henry Clay and Daniel Webster, both members of the Whig party, would support his repeal of the Missouri Compromise. Quoting words from John 1:11 and Acts 13:46, but without suggesting any conveyance of spiritual thought, Lincoln answered:

The truth is that some support from whigs is now a necessity with the Judge, and for thus it is, that the names of Clay and Webster are now invoked. His old friends have deserted him in such numbers as to leave too few to live by. ***He came to his own, and his own received him not****, and* ***Lo! He turns unto the Gentiles****. . . .*

CW II: 247–283 (255, 260, 276, 278, 282)

Though Lincoln had been out of the state legislature since 1842, he remained a leading political figure in Illinois and decided that he would run for a seat in that body again. A month after making his Peoria speech, Lincoln was elected, but he quickly resigned his seat when he realized he had a good chance of securing a much bigger prize. In February 1855, the legislature would choose a United States senator. Obtaining this seat had been a lifetime dream for Lincoln. Since the Whigs controlled the legislature, he had a good possibility of winning the position. However, he faced two opponents who also had strong support: Democrats James Shields and Lyman Trumbull. Joel A. Matteson was actually the official Democratic candidate but in a political maneuver, the Democrats backed the incumbent, James Shields.

The first ballot put Lincoln ahead. He received 44 votes; Shields, 41;

Trumbull, 5. Trumbull would not yield his votes, and the balloting continued. On the seventh ballot before a crowded house, the Shields votes swung to Matteson. Lincoln, seeing that he was out of the running and that Matteson must be stopped, gave his votes to Trumbull. In an instant, the Senate seat, which had almost been within his grasp, slipped away.

As disappointing as this loss was, Lincoln continued speaking out. In the fall of 1856, he gave a rousing speech at a Republican rally. The *Peoria Weekly Republican* reported on Lincoln's speech.

October 9, 1856

Speech at Peoria, Illinois

On this occasion he went over the whole battle field of the two great contending armies, one *for* and the other *against* slavery and slave labor, and showed, most triumphantly, that our young, gallant and world-renowned commander was the man for the day—the man to right the ship of State, and, like the stripling of Israel, to slay the boasting Goliaths of slaveocracy that have beset the national capitol and defiled the sanctums of liberty, erected and consecrated by the old prophets and fathers of this republic.

CW II: 379

During this time, Lincoln continued practicing law—but his political ambitions, fueled by a desire to preserve American ideals, had been fully restored.

CHAPTER 9

INTO THE ARENA

Nearly 150 years after the Civil War ended, it is sometimes hard to believe that slavery was ever allowed in a free nation—or to understand why great men like Abraham Lincoln did not simply settle it by a direct order of emancipation. Without question, Lincoln agonized over these issues himself during the 1850s, but it was protected by the Constitution.

Even in Lincoln's day, slavery was recognized by many people as an open sore and shame to democracy. So why did the Founding Fathers allow slavery in the Constitution? Quite simply, the Southern states would not have become part of a union that prohibited slavery. The convention had two choices: (1) include slave states but add provisions that would lead to a gradual extinction of slavery, or (2) prohibit slavery, knowing the Southern states would form their own nation with a constitution allowing slavery. The Founding Fathers adopted the first course, and as a result, the Constitution required each slave to be counted as three-fifths of a white person when a state's population was determined (Article I, Section 2); permitted the importation of slaves until 1808 (Article I, Section 9); and required fugitive slaves to be returned to their owners (Article IV, Section 2).

Yet, after careful research, Lincoln determined that these concessions to the Southern states did not signify the Founders' approval of slavery. In the Cooper Union Address, an 1860 speech that helped cement his national reputation, Lincoln impressed the political leaders in the East with an exceptionally well-prepared analysis of the voting records of the thirty-nine Founding Fathers of the Constitution, thirty-six of whom believed that Congress should control slavery in the territories and prevent its expansion. (This speech is covered in detail in chapter 12.)

In Henry Clay, a founder of the Whig party and a senator from Kentucky, Lincoln found a model statesman who he felt took a reasonable approach to the vexing problem of slavery for that time. Though a slave owner, Clay felt the practice was a blight on the American system and favored its gradual elimination. He treated his slaves well and freed most of them before his death. He was known as "the Great Compromiser" for his leadership in the creation of the Missouri Compromise and the Compromise of 1850.

Abolitionists, however, did not look favorably on Clay. In the following letter, written to a man with strong antislavery views, Lincoln points out the danger of looking too narrowly at an issue.

October 3, 1845

To Williamson Durley

Durley

. . . *If by your votes you could have prevented the* extension, *&c. of slavery, would it not have been* good *and not* evil *so to have used your votes, even though it involved the casting of them for a slaveholder?* ***By the* fruit *the tree is to be known. An* evil *tree can not bring forth* good *fruit.*** *If the fruit of electing Mr. Clay would have been to prevent the extension of slavery, could the act of electing have been* evil?

CW I: 347–348 (347)

Lincoln includes one of the most practical and thought-provoking teachings of Jesus in his letter. A man should not be known by what he professes or his outward habits, but by the consequences or the fruits of his actions (see Matthew 7:16; 12:33; and Luke 6:43-44).

When Clay died, Lincoln delivered a heartfelt eulogy in the Hall of Representatives in Springfield's statehouse.

July 6, 1852

Eulogy on Henry Clay

On the fourth day of July, 1776, the people of a few feeble and oppressed colonies of Great Britain, inhabiting a portion of the Atlantic coast of North America, publicly declared their national independence, and made their appeal to the justice of their cause, and to the God of battles, for the maintenance of that declaration. That people were few in numbers, and without resources, save only their own wise heads and stout hearts.

Lincoln wrote twelve pages honoring Clay's efforts for gradual emancipation and returning the slaves to Liberia. He refers to the disasters that ultimately fell on Egypt for refusing to free the enslaved children of Israel (see Exodus 7–14).

This suggestion of the possible ultimate redemption of the African race and African continent, was made twenty-five years ago. Every succeeding year has added strength to the hope of its realization. May it indeed be realized! Pharaoh's country was cursed with plagues, and his hosts were drowned in the Red Sea for striving to retain a captive people who had already served them more than four hundred years. May like disasters never befall us! If as the friends of colonization hope, the present and coming generations of our countrymen shall by any means, succeed in freeing our land from the dangerous presence of slavery; and, at the same time, in restoring a captive people to their long-lost father-land, with bright prospects for the future; and this too, so gradually, that neither races nor individuals shall have suffered by the change, it will indeed be a glorious consummation.

CW II: 121–132 (121, 132)

☆ ☆ ☆

Lincoln's hopes that America could yet avoid a bitter struggle over slavery through the efforts of "moderate" men like Clay were shaken with the Kansas-Nebraska Act. He watched in growing dismay as Kansas became the center of the national firestorm that lasted until the state was finally admitted to the Union as a free state in 1861.

When he wrote this letter to his old friend Joshua Speed, a slave owner, that outcome was not so sure. He made the case against slavery in Kansas by comparing men who plan death for others to Haman, who plotted against Mordecai and the Jews and only prepared trouble for himself. In one of the most interesting plots in all literature, Haman had constructed a scaffold for hanging Mordecai only to be the one to be hanged on it (Esther 7:10).

August 24, 1855

To Joshua F. Speed

That Kansas will form a Slave constitution, and, with it, will ask to be admitted into the Union, I take to be an already settled question; and so settled by the very means you so pointedly condemn. By every principle of law, ever held by any court, North or South, every negro taken to Kansas is free; yet in utter disregard of this—in the spirit of violence merely—that beautiful Legislature gravely passes a law to hang men who shall venture to inform a negro of his legal rights. This is the substance, and real object of the law. If, like ***Haman****, they should hang upon the gallows of their own building, I shall not be among the mourners for their fate.*

CW II: 320–323 (321)

☆ ☆ ☆

Lincoln continued to criticize Stephen Douglas during this time.

December 1856

Fragment on Stephen A. Douglas

Twenty-two years ago Judge Douglas and I first became acquainted. We were both young then; he a trifle younger than I. Even then, we were both ambitious; I, perhaps, quite as much so as he. With me, *the race of ambition has been a failure—a flat failure; with* him *it has been one of splendid success. His name fills the nation; and is not unknown, even, in foreign lands. I affect no contempt for the high eminence he (Douglas) has reached. So reached, that the oppressed of my species, might have shared with me in the elevation, I would rather stand on that eminence, than wear the richest crown that ever pressed a monarch's brow.*

CW II: 382–383

☆ ☆ ☆

The Republican Party, which counts Abraham Lincoln as one of its most distinguished members, was formed in 1854 by antislavery radicals furious over the Kansas-Nebraska Act. Given the party's extreme views, Lincoln did not immediately align himself closely with it. However, in the spring of 1856 Lincoln helped moderate the views of the Republican platform and gave an impassioned speech designed to meld the radical and more moderate elements of the party.

Later that year, he expressed his hope that, with God's help, the Union would survive this crisis over slavery. Lincoln's words may have reminded many listeners that God calls Himself Immanuel, or "God with us." (Isaiah 7:14; 8:10).

December 10, 1856

Speech at Republican Banquet, Chicago, Illinois

As Webster said, "Not Union without liberty, nor liberty without Union; but Union and liberty, now and forever, one and inseparable.

We can *do it. The human heart* is *with us*—***God is with us***. *We shall again be able not to declare, that "all States as States, are equal," nor yet that "all citizens as citizens are equal," but to renew the broader, better declaration, including both these and much more, that "all* men *are created equal."*

CW II: 383–385 (383, 385)

☆ ☆ ☆

As one possible solution to the slavery issue, Lincoln advocated the colonization of blacks to Africa. Some rather ridiculously objected that the numbers would be too great a task. In reply, he used a scriptural story, which is detailed in Exodus 12:37, Numbers 1:46, and Numbers 11:21.

June 26, 1857

Speech at Springfield, Illinois

The ***children of Israel****, to such numbers as to include four hundred thousand fighting men, went out of Egyptian bondage in a body.*

Lincoln then identified the real reason colonization of the slaves would never be seriously considered.

The plainest print cannot be read through a gold eagle; and it will be ever hard to find many men who will send a slave to Liberia, and pay his passage while they can send him to a new country, Kansas for instance, and sell him for fifteen hundred dollars . . .

CW II: 398–410 (409–410)

☆ ☆ ☆

Below is a preliminary draft of the great speech in which Lincoln launched a missile that would streak across the prairie skies. His words were a thunderbolt: "A house divided cannot stand." This phrase is borrowed from Jesus, who first used the analogy when the Pharisees accused him of performing miracles under the power of Satan (see Matthew 12:25,

Mark 3:25, and Luke 11:17). As He pointed out, any kingdom at war with itself cannot survive. Lincoln had first used the metaphor on March 4, 1843, (see chapter 3) in rallying support of his party, declaring that "union is strength." After mulling over the concept for fifteen years, he readied the phrase as he honed his logic in preparation for the great debates with Douglas.

May 18, 1858

Fragment of a Speech

I believe the government cannot endure permanently half slave and half free. I expressed this belief a year ago; and subsequent developments have but confirmed me. I do not expect the Union to be dissolved. I do not expect the house to fall; but I do expect it will cease to be divided. It will become all one thing or all the other.

Welcome, or unwelcome, agreeable, or disagreeable, whether this shall be an entire slave nation, is *the issue before us. Every incident—every little shifting of scenes or of actors—only clears away the intervening trash, compacts and consolidates the opposing hosts, and brings them more and more distinctly face to face. The conflict will be a severe one; and it will be fought through by those who* do *care for the result, and not by those who do not care—by those who are* for, *and those who are against a legalized national slavery. . . .*

To give the victory to the right, not bloody bullets, *but* peaceful ballots *only, are necessary. Thanks to our good old constitution, and organization under it, these alone are necessary. It only needs that every right thinking man, shall go to the polls, and without fear or prejudice,* vote *as he* thinks.

CW II: 448–454 (452–454)

By this time, Lincoln was determined to pursue the Republican nomination for the U.S. Senate seat in Illinois. He made his intentions clear in a letter to his good friend and fellow attorney Ward Lamon.

June 11, 1858

To Ward H. Lamon

As to the inclination of some Republicans to favor Douglas, that is one of the chances I have to run, and which I intend to ***run with patience****.*

CW II: 458–459 (459)

His promise to persevere in his campaign seems to echo Hebrews 12:1, where Paul admonishes believers to run the race of life with endurance. The campaign would indeed require Lincoln's patience and persistence—in fact, it was one of the most memorable Senate campaigns in U.S. history. The Lincoln-Douglas Debates (covered in chapter 11) were the product of the fight between the two great Illinois legislators.

CHAPTER 10

A LECTURE ON DISCOVERIES AND INVENTIONS

Though Lincoln became more and more preoccupied with the slavery question in the mid-1850s, he remained interested in learning more about the natural world. His sharp legal mind grasped the intricacies of the federal Constitution, but he also had an engineering bent with a natural ability to solve mechanical problems. In fact, this ability enabled him to serve as an advocate and contributor to the development of weapons technology at the start of the Civil War.

This written lecture (the first of two parts) demonstrates that Lincoln had spent time with a Bible in hand writing out his remarks.[1] Giving credence to the supernatural stories is evidence that he had shed most of his former questions and was laying a foundation of solid faith. He accepted the biblical account of the fall of man and the counting of generations from Adam; he remarked that the task of building Noah's ark was so great a task that it must have been miraculous.

April 6, 1858

First Lecture on Discoveries and Inventions

All creation is a mine, and every man, a miner.

The whole earth, and all within *it,* upon *it, and* round about *it, including* himself, *in his physical, moral, and intellectual nature, and his susceptabilities, are the infinitely various "leads" from which, man, from the first, was to dig out his destiny.*

In the beginning, the mine was unopened, and the miner stood naked, *and* knowledgeless, *upon it.*

Because of Abraham Lincoln's appreciation of the wisdom literature of the Bible, it is possible that at least part of the inspiration for the first paragraph of this lecture came from Job 28, in which the author compares mining rich veins of ore for gold to searching for the gold of true wisdom.

Fishes, birds, beasts, and creeping things, are not miners, but feeders *and* lodgers, *merely. Beavers build houses; but they build them in nowise differently, or better now, than they did, five thousand years ago. Ants, and honey-bees, provide food for winter; but just in the* same way *they did, when Solomon refered the sluggard to them as patterns of prudence.*

Man is not the only animal who labors; but he is the only one who improves *his workmanship. This improvement, he effects by* Discoveries, *and* Inventions.

After this lecture introduction, Lincoln offers many biblical illustrations, adding the unusual feature for him of providing chapter and verse.

His first important discovery was the fact that he was naked; and his first invention was the fig-leaf-apron. . . . At the first interview of the Almighty with Adam and Eve, after the fall, He made "coats of skins, and clothed them" Gen: 3-21.

The Bible makes no other alusion to clothing, before *the flood. Soon* after *the deluge Noah's two sons covered him with a* garment*; but of what* material *the garment was made is not mentioned. Gen. 9-23*

Abraham mentions **"thread"** *. . . to indicate that spinning and weaving were in use in his day—Gen. 14.23. . .* "Linen breeches,["] *are mentioned,—Exod. 28.42—*

In his own preparation for this part of the lecture, Abraham Lincoln read the instructions in Exodus 35 for the making of the Tabernacle.

This passage illustrates how the Lord God gives special abilities to individuals:

. . . "All the women that were wise hearted, [given special wisdom—ed.] did spin *with their hands" (35-25) and, "all the women whose hearts stirred them up in wisdom,* spun *goat's hair" (35-26).*

Lincoln continued with his listing of discoveries and inventions.

The work of the "weaver" *is mentioned— (35-35). In the book of Job, a very old book, date not exactly known, the* **"weavers shuttle"** *is mentioned. . . .*

How could the **"gopher wood"** *for the Ark, have been gotten out without an axe? . . .*

Tubal-cain was ***"an instructor of every artificer in*** **brass** ***and*** **iron** *["]—Gen: 4-22. Tubal-cain was the seventh in decent from Adam; . . .*

After *the flood, frequent mention is made of* iron, *and* instruments *made of iron. Thus* ***"instrument of iron,"*** *at Num: 35-16;* ***"bed-stead of iron"*** *at Deut. 3-11—;* ***"the iron furnace["]*** *at 4-20— and* ***"iron tool"*** *at 27-5. At 19-5 —very distinct mention of "the ax to cut down the tree" is made; and also at 8-9, the promised land is described as* ***"a land whose stones are iron, and out of whose hills thou mayest dig brass."*** *. . .*

The oldest recorded allusion to the wheel and axle is the mention of a ***"chariot"*** *Gen: 41-43. This was in Egypt, upon the occasion of Joseph being made Governor by Pharaoh. It was about twentyfive hundred years after the creation of Adam. . . . the mention of chariot-wheels, at Exod. 14-25, and the mention of chariots in connection with* horses, *in the same chapter, verses 9 & 23. . . .*

If we pass by the Ark, which may be regarded as belonging rather to the miracalous, *than to* human *invention, the first notice we have of water-craft, is the mention of* ***"ships"*** *by Jacob—Gen: 49-13. It is not till we reach the book of Isaiah that we meet with the mention of* ***"oars"*** *and* ***"sails."***

As mans food *. . . man was put into the garden of Eden* ***"to dress it, and to keep it."*** *And when afterwards, in consequence of the first transgression,* labor *was imposed on the race, as a* penalty*—a* curse*— we find the first born man—the first heir of the curse—was* ***"a tiller of the ground."*** *. . .*

Climbing upon the back of an animal, and making it carry us, might not, occur very readily. . . .

The earliest instance of it mentioned, is when ***"Abraham rose up early in the morning, and saddled his ass,*** *["] Gen. 22-3 preparatory to sacraficing Isaac as a burnt-offering; . . .*

". . . when the servant of Abraham went in search of a wife for Isaac, he took ten camels *with him; and, on his return trip,* ***"Rebekah arose, and her damsels, and they rode upon the camels, and followed the man."*** *Gen 24-6[.] . . .*

. . . Moses and the children of Israel sang to the Lord ***"the*** **horse,** ***and his*** **rider** ***hath he thrown into the sea."*** *Exo. 15-1. . . .*

. . . Joseph's bretheren, on their first visit to Egypt, ***"laded their asses with the corn, and departed thence"*** *Gen. 42-26.*

. . . plows and chariots came into use early enough to be often mentioned in the books of Moses—Deut. 22-10. Gen. 41-43. Gen. 46-29. Exo. 14-25[.] . . .

. . . As yet, the wind is an untamed, *and* unharnessed *force; . . . power was applied to sail-vessels, at least as early as the time of the prophet Isaiah.*

In speaking of running streams, *as a motive power . . . application to mills and other machinery . . . The language of the Saviour* ***"Two women shall be grinding at the mill &c"*** *indicates that, even in the populous city of Jerusalem, at that day, mills were operated by hand—having, as yet had no other than human power applied to them. . . .*

CW II: 437–442

☆ ☆ ☆

About four months after delivering the first lecture, Abraham Lincoln and Stephen Douglas began crisscrossing Illinois as they engaged in their spirited debates. (Their exchanges are covered in the next chapter.) Lincoln thrived on debate and loved the crowds. From childhood, he had been enthralled by the story of the march of humanity toward democracy. In the second part of his lecture, he envisioned the struggles and progress for the economic betterment of the human race.

Lincoln began the second part of his only public lecture with a tantalizing comparison of "Old Fogy" with "Young America." Old Fogy, or Adam, "stood, a very perfect physical man, as poets and painters inform us; but he must have been very ignorant, and simple in his habits. He had had no sufficient time to learn much by observation; and he had no near neighbors to teach him anything." By contrast, young America has many resources:

February 11, 1859

Second Lecture on Discoveries and Inventions

We have all heard of Young America. He is the most current *youth of the age. Some think him conceited, and arrogant; but has he not reason to entertain a rather extensive opinion of himself? Is he not the inventor and owner of the* present, *and sole hope of the* future? *Men, and things, everywhere, are ministering unto him. Look at his apparel, and you shall see cotten fabrics from Manchester and Lowell; flax-linen from Ireland; wool-cloth from [Spain;] silk from France; furs from the Arctic regions, with a buffalo-robe from the Rocky Mountains, as a general out-sider. At his table, besides plain bread and meat made at home, are sugar from Louisiana; coffee and fruits from the tropics; salt from Turk's Island; fish from New-foundland; tea from China, and spices from the Indies. The whale of the Pacific furnishes his candle-light; he has a diamond-ring from Brazil; a gold-watch from California, and a spanish cigar from Havanna. He not only has a present supply of all these, and much more; but thousands of hands are engaged in producing fresh supplies, and other thousands, in bringing them to him. The iron horse is panting, and impatient, to carry him everywhere, in no time; and the lightening stands ready harnessed to take and bring his tidings in a trifle less than no time. . . .*

The great difference between Young America and Old Fogy, is the result of Discoveries, Inventions, *and* Improvements. *These, in turn, are the result of* observation, reflection *and* experiment. *For instance, it is quite certain that ever since water has been boiled in covered vessels, men have seen the lids of the vessels rise and fall a little, with a sort of fluttering motion, by force of the steam; but so long as this was not specially observed, and reflected and experimented upon, it came to nothing. At length however, after many thousand years, some man observes this long-known effect of hot water lifting a pot-lid, and begins a train of reflection upon it. He says "Why, to be sure, the force that lifts the pot-lid, will lift any thing else, which is no heavier than the pot-lid." "And, as man has much hard lifting to do, can not this hot-water power be made to help him?" He has become a little excited on the subject, and he fancies he hears a voice answering "Try me" He does try it; and the* observation, reflection, *and* trial *gives to the world the control of that tremendous, and now well known agent, called steam-power.*

There are more mines above the Earth's surface than below it. All nature—the whole world, material, moral, and intellectual,—is a mine; and, in Adam's day, it was a wholly unexplored mine. . . .

I have already intimated my opinion that in the world's history, certain inventions and discoveries occurred, of peculiar value, on account of their great efficiency in facilitating all other inventions and discoveries. Of these were the arts of writing and of printing—the discovery of America, and the introduction of Patent-laws. The date of the first, as already stated, is unknown; but it certainly was as much as fifteen hundred years before the Christian era; the second—printing—came in 1436, or nearly three thousand years after the first. The others followed more rapidly—the discovery of America in 1492, and the first patent laws in 1624. . . .

At length printing came. It gave ten thousand copies of any written matter, quite as cheaply as ten were given before; and consequently a thousand minds were brought into the field where there was but one before. This was a great gain*; and history shows a great* change *corresponding to it, in point of time. I will venture to consider* it, *the true termination of that period called "the dark ages." Discoveries, inventions, and improvements followed rapidly, and have been increasing their rapidity ever since. The effects could not come, all at once. It required time to bring them out; and they are still coming. . . . It is very probable—almost certain—that the great mass of men, at that time, were utterly unconscious, that their* conditions, *or their* minds *were capable of improvement. They not only looked upon the educated few as superior beings; but they supposed themselves to be naturally incapable of rising to equality. To immancipate the mind from this false and under estimate of itself, is the great task which printing came into the world to perform. It is difficult for us,* now *and* here, *to conceive how strong this slavery of the mind was; and how long it did, of necessity, take, to break it's shackles, and to get a habit of freedom of thought, established. It is, in this connection, a curious fact that a new country is most favorable—almost necessary—to the immancipation of thought, and the consequent advancement of civilization and the arts. . . .*

Next came the Patent laws. These began in England in 1624; and, in this country, with the adoption of our constitution. Before then [these], any man might instantly use what another had invented; so that the inventor had no special advantage from his own invention. The patent system changed this; secured to the inventor, for a limited time, the exclusive use of his invention; and thereby added the fuel of interest *to the* fire *of genius, in the discovery and production of new and useful things.*

CW III: 356–363 (356–358, 361–363)

With his likeable nature and boundless humor, Lincoln delivered his lecture several times in different locations, quite well. However, attendance was often spotty, which disappointed him. Given his campaign against Douglas, he quickly turned his thoughts back to the political arena.

CHAPTER 11

THE LINCOLN-DOUGLAS DEBATES

About two months after Lincoln delivered his first lecture on discoveries and inventions, the Republican state convention met in Springfield on June 16, 1858. The new party nominated Lincoln as its candidate for the U.S. Senate. He had prepared his acceptance speech well, debating in his mind whether or not to use the emotionally arousing phrase "house divided" (see Matthew 12:25; Mark 3:25; Luke 11:17). The night before, he had asked about twenty fellow Republicans whether they thought he should use that phrase. In general, they opposed the idea. Prompted by his own intuitive wisdom, Lincoln went ahead and used it anyway.

June 16, 1858

"A House Divided:" Speech at Springfield, Illinois

If we could first know where *we are, and* whither *we are tending, we could then better judge* what *to do, and* how *to do it.*

We are now far into the fifth *year, since a policy was initiated, with the* avowed *object, and* confident *promise, of putting an end to slavery agitation.*

Under the operation of that policy, that agitation has not only, not ceased, *but has* constantly augmented.

In my *opinion, it* will *not cease, until a* crisis *shall have been reached, and passed.*

"A house divided against itself cannot stand."

I believe this government cannot endure, permanently half slave *and half* free.

I do not expect the Union to be dissolved—*I do not expect the house to* fall—*but I* do *expect it will cease to be divided.*

It will become all *one thing, or* all *the other.*

Either the opponents *of slavery, will arrest the further spread of it, and place it where the public mind shall rest in the belief that it is in course of ultimate extinction; or its* advocates *will push it forward, till it shall become alike lawful in* all *the States,* old *as well as* new—North *as well as* South. . . .

The new year of 1854 found slavery excluded from more than half the States by State Constitutions, and from most of the national territory by Congressional prohibition.

Four days later, commenced the struggle, which ended in repealing that Congressional prohibition.

This opened all the national territory to slavery; and was the first point gained.

This necessity had not been overlooked; but had been provided for, as well as might be, in the notable argument of "squatter sovereignty," *otherwise called* "sacred right of self government," *which latter phrase, though expressive of the only rightful basis of any government, was so perverted in this attempted use of it as to amount to just this: That if any* one *man, choose to enslave* another, *no* third *man shall be allowed to object.*

Lincoln then addressed fears that Douglas was too powerful an adversary. (The comparison of a living dog to a dead lion is also made in Ecclesiastes 9:4.)

They remind us that he *is a very* great man, *and that the largest of* us *are very small ones. Let this be granted. But* ***"a* living dog *is better than a dead lion."*** *Judge Douglas, if not a* dead *lion for this work, is at least a* caged *and* toothless *one. . . .*

The result is not doubtful. We shall not fail—if we stand firm, we shall not fail.

Wise councils *may* accelerate *or* mistakes delay *it, but, sooner or later the victory is* sure *to come.*

CW II: 461-68 (461–462, 467, 468–469)

Tumultuous enthusiastic cheers shook the great hall of the Illinois statehouse.

William Herndon declared that the speech would win the White

House. When Stephen Douglas heard that Lincoln would be his opponent in the campaign, he told a newspaperman, Lincoln "is as honest as he is shrewd; and if I beat him, my victory will be hardly won."[1]

☆ ☆ ☆

As expected, the words of Lincoln's speech echoed throughout the state where Douglas, drawing great crowds, began responding to the emotional phrase "house divided." In Chicago, he answered Lincoln's speech by declaring that the right to popular sovereignty, which enabled the people of the states and territories to choose their own institutions, including slavery, was "dearer to every true American than any other." He warned that any limitation on it would destroy the principle of self-government.[2]

On the next night on the same platform in that Chicago hotel, Lincoln answered Douglas, explaining his own viewpoint on American government.

July 10, 1858

Speech at Chicago, Illinois

I know that it has endured eighty-two years, half slave and half free. I believe*—and that is what I meant to allude to there—I* believe *it has endured because, during all that time, until the introduction of the Nebraska Bill, the public mind did rest, all the time, in the belief that slavery was in the course of ultimate extinction. . . .*

I have always hated slavery, I think as much as any Abolitionist. . . . I have always been quiet about it until this new era of the introduction of the Nebraska Bill began. . . .

. . . Such was the belief of the framers of the Constitution itself. Why did those old men, about the time of the adoption of the Constitution, decree that Slavery should not go into the new Territory, where it had not already gone? Why declare that within twenty years the African Slave Trade, by which slaves are supplied, might be cut off by Congress?

We had slavery among us, we could not get our constitution unless we permitted them to remain in slavery, we could not secure the good we did secure if we grasped for more, and having by necessity submitted to that much, it does not destroy the principle that is the charter of our liberties. Let that charter stand as our standard. . . .

In the next paragraph, Lincoln offers an interesting discourse on a verse whose meaning perplexes many: Matthew 5:48:

. . . ***"As your Father in Heaven is perfect, be ye also perfect."*** *The Savior, I suppose, did not expect that any human creature could be perfect as the Father in Heaven; but He said, "As your Father in Heaven is perfect, be ye also perfect." He set that up as a standard, and he who did most towards reaching that standard, attained the highest degree of moral perfection. So I say in relation to the principle that all men are created equal, let it be as nearly reached as we can. If we cannot give freedom to every creature, let us do nothing that will impose slavery upon any other creature. [Applause.] Let us then turn this government back into the channel in which the framers of the Constitution originally placed it. Let us stand firmly by each other. If we do not do so we are turning in the contrary direction, that our friend Judge Douglas proposes—not intentionally—as working in the traces tend to make this one universal slave nation.[A voice—"that is so."] He is one that runs in that direction, and as such I resist him.*

CW II: 484–502 (492, 501)

We should not miss Lincoln's argument here. The Savior called human beings to a standard that they obviously could never fully attain. But though mankind would never reach the high standard, we should keep that standard as the perfect goal to which we should ever strive. In America's case, that means continually working to ensure liberty is available to all.

☆ ☆ ☆

Led by a proslavery faction, Kansas's constitutional convention had met in 1857 and then sent to the U.S. Congress the Lecompton Constitution, asking for admission to the United States as a slave state. President Buchanan, weary of the ongoing battle in Congress, urged the legislators to get behind him in supporting it.

Douglas, at odds with the president for various reasons, joined the Republicans in opposing the measure. Due to some irregularities in the voting process, the senator claimed it was not a fair vote. It was a strange situation for Douglas, who had pushed the compromise that called for Kansas's citizens to decide for themselves whether to permit slavery in their state. Due in large part to his efforts, the Lecompton Constitution was not accepted, which prevented Kansas from becoming a slave state.

Lincoln became alarmed, suspecting trouble in the end. In fact, he was right to be concerned. Some prominent Republicans, such as Horace Greeley of New York, were so impressed with how firmly Douglas had stood up against the president to oppose the acceptance of the Lecompton Constitution that they had encouraged the Illinois Republicans to get behind Douglas's reelection bid. Fortunately for Lincoln, they refused to do so, supporting Lincoln instead.

Lincoln chided Douglas, poking fun at Douglas as he claimed credit for helping to defeat the Lecompton Act. The following excerpt ends with a reference to the parable found in Luke 15:7.

July 17, 1858

Speech at Springfield, Illinois

Does he place his superior claim to credit, on the ground that he performed a good act which was never expected of him? He says I have a proneness for quoting scripture. If I should do so now, it occurs that perhaps he places himself somewhat upon the ground of the parable of the lost sheep which went astray upon the mountains, and when the owner of the hundred sheep found the one that was lost, and threw it upon his shoulders, and came home rejoicing, it was said that there was more rejoicing over the one sheep that was lost and had been found, than over the ninety and nine in the fold. [Great cheering, renewed cheering.] The application is made by the Saviour in this parable, thus, ***"Verily, I say unto you, there is more rejoicing in heaven over one sinner that repenteth, than over ninety and nine just persons that need no repentance."***

CW II:504-21 (510, 511)

☆ ☆ ☆

After the exchange between Douglas and Lincoln at the Chicago hotel, Douglas and his wife traveled around the state in a private railroad car with banners that read: Stephen A. Douglas, Champion of Popular Sovereignty. Lincoln followed along in a public coach, speaking after Douglas in each city. Six thousand people in Lewiston heard him speak on the Declaration of Independence and the Founders' belief that all men were created in God's image (Genesis 1:26-27).

August 17, 1858

Speech at Lewiston, Illinois

. . . "We hold these truths to be self evident; that all men are created equal; that they are endowed by their Creator with certain unalienable rights; that among these are life, liberty and the pursuit of happiness." This was their majestic interpretation of the economy of the Universe. This was their lofty, and wise, and noble understanding of the justice of the Creator to His creatures. [Applause.] Yes, gentlemen, to all *His creatures, to the whole great family of man. In their enlightened belief, nothing stamped with the* ***Divine image and likeness*** *was sent into the world to be trodden on, and degraded, and imbruted by its fellows. They grasped not only the whole race of man then living, but they reached forward and seized upon the farthest posterity. They erected a beacon to guide their children and their children's children, and the countless myriads who should inhabit the earth in other ages. Wise statesmen as they were, they knew the tendency of prosperity to breed tyrants, and so they established these great self-evident truths, . . . so that truth, and justice, and mercy, and all the humane and Christian virtues might not be extinguished from the land; . . .*

Abraham Lincoln concluded with a lofty profession. Many persons make similar claims, for words come easily to political office seekers, but when we consider the words of all his addresses, it's difficult to discount his spirit of dedication.

You may do anything with me you choose, if you will but heed these sacred principles. You may not only defeat me for the Senate, but you may take me and put me to death. While pretending no indifference to earthly honors, I do claim *to be actuated in this contest by something higher than an anxiety for office. I charge you to drop every paltry and insignificant thought for any man's success. It is nothing; I am nothing; Judge Douglas is nothing.* But do not destroy that immortal emblem of Humanity—the Declaration of American Independence.

CW II: 544–547 (546, 547)

☆ ☆ ☆

Abraham Lincoln was the candidate of the Republican party in Illinois in 1858. Douglas, the Democratic incumbent, was drawing crowds all over Illinois; Lincoln was following him, speaking to the same crowds, sometimes on the same day. Rather than working out times and places as they traveled, Lincoln thought it would be an advantage for both men to schedule a series of debates.

For Lincoln it was a bold idea, as Douglas was respected as the premier debater of the country—powerful, experienced, and always well prepared. They agreed upon seven places and times; they alternated as to who would get to speak first. The opening speaker would have one hour; the other would have one and a half hours; and the first speaker would have the final half hour. In our day, we cannot conceive of listening to a three-hour debate, yet people traveled great distances to listen.

Harold Holzer wrote in *The Lincoln-Douglas Debates*:

> But even in Illinois, the impassioned response to the longtime arch-rivals broke new ground. Theirs were not mere political discussions but gala pageants; public spectacles fueled by picnic tables groaning with local fare; emblazoned with gaudy banners and astringently worded broadsides; and echoing with artillery salutes and martial music. . . . Hotels overflowed with guests, and those who could not book rooms slept on sofas in lobbies.[3]

The first debate with Douglas was held in Ottawa on August 21, 1858. Attendance was more than double the permanent population of the city. People came by train, by canal-boat, by wagon, buggy, and on horseback. Lincoln arrived on a special train bulging with excited supporters. Douglas led a mile-long procession in a beautifully appointed head carriage, as crowds cheered him from the sidewalks, from windows, piazzas, housetops, and every available standing point.

Enthusiastic crowds listened to the arguments. Lincoln presented ideas similar to those he'd expressed in his Peoria and House Divided speeches. He used his keynote phrase, "A house divided against itself cannot stand," and chided Douglas for accepting the Dred Scott verdict as though it were from absolute authority: "Thus saith the Lord." (In 1857, the Supreme Court had handed down the famous Dred Scott decision, which declared that no slave or ex-slave could be a U.S. citizen and, therefore, had no right to appeal to a federal court. Furthermore, it ruled that Congress could not prohibit slavery in the federal territories.)

August 21, 1858

First Debate with Stephen A. Douglas at Ottawa, Illinois

This man sticks to a decision which forbids the people of a Territory from excluding slavery, and he does so not because he says it is right in itself—he does not give any opinion on that—but because it has been decided by the court, *and being decided by the court he is, and you are bound to take it in your political action as* law—*not that he judges at all of its merits, but because a decision of the court is to him a* "Thus saith the Lord." *[Applause.] He places it on that ground alone, and you will bear in mind that thus committing himself unreservedly to this decision,* commits him to the next one *just as firmly as to this. He did not commit himself on account of the merit or demerit of the decision, but it is a* Thus saith the Lord. *The next decision, as much as this, will be a* thus saith the Lord. *There is nothing that can divert or turn him away from this decision.*

CW III: 1–37; Lincoln's reply, 13–30 (27–28)

☆ ☆ ☆

The second debate was held August 27, 1858, in Freeport.[4] This was the only debate in which Lincoln did not speak of the "house divided." However, Senator Douglas brought up that phrase, arguing that the Founding Fathers had founded the nation half slave and half free, and that Lincoln, by refusing to be in favor of admittance of a slave state into the Union, would be closing the door to the addition of more states.

☆ ☆ ☆

About two weeks later, Lincoln gave a memorable address that was not part of the debate series. He included an illustration from Matthew 7:6, verifying that actions cause regrettable consequences, and he gave a serious warning to our nation of a danger by which we can lose liberty. This passage strikes some of the same themes as the Lyceum Address (described in chapter 3).

September 11, 1858

Speech at Edwardsville, Illinois

Now, when by all these means you have succeeded in dehumanizing the negro; when you have put him down, and made it forever impossible for him to be but as the beasts of the field; when you have extinguished his soul, and placed him where the ray of hope is blown out in darkness like that which broods over the spirits of the damned; are you quite sure the demon which you have roused **will not turn and rend you?** *What constitutes the bulwark of our own liberty and independence? . . . Our reliance is in the* love of liberty *which God has planted in our bosoms. Our defense is in the preservation of the spirit which prizes liberty as the heritage of all men, in all lands, every where. Destroy this spirit, and you have planted the seeds of despotism around your own doors. Familiarize yourselves with the chains of bondage, and you are preparing your own limbs to wear them. Accustomed to trample on the rights of those around you, you have lost the genius of your own independence, and become the fit subjects of the first cunning tyrant who rises. And let me tell you, all these things are prepared for you with the logic of history, if the elections shall promise that the next Dred Scott decision and all future decisions will be quietly acquiesced in by the people. [Loud applause.]*

CW III: 91–96 (95–96)

The last sentence contains a serious warning to those who would retreat to their own cozy mentalities. When people acquiesce while laws are passed and decisions handed down that are harmful to the interests of a minority group, they are "planting seeds" of despotism for themselves. This was the foundation stone of all of Lincoln's thinking.

Just four days later, on September 15, Lincoln engaged in his third debate with Douglas in Jonesboro, Illinois. Seven times, Lincoln used the phrase "house divided."[5]

☆ ☆ ☆

As he considered the issue of slavery, Lincoln often thought of it as it related to the labor of America's citizens. During his entire public life, Lincoln extolled the benefits of labor yet saw slavery as a perversion of what God had intended for man's good.

September 17, 1859

Fragment on Free Labor

There is no permanent class of hired laborers amongst us. Twentyfive years ago, I was a hired laborer. The hired laborer of yesterday, labors on his own account to-day; and will hire others to labor for him to-morrow. Advancement—improvement in condition—is the order of things in a society of equals. As Labor is the common burthen *of our race, so the effort of* some *to shift their share of the burthen on to the shoulders of* others, *is the great, durable, curse of the race. Originally a curse for transgression upon the whole race, when, as by slavery, it is concentrated on a part only, it becomes the double-refined curse of God upon his creatures.*

Lincoln refers to the curse upon man as mentioned in Genesis 3:19. Slavery takes the great curse off the backs of some to be doubly heavy upon others. In contrast is the great system of free labor:

Free labor has the inspiration of hope; pure slavery has no hope. The power of hope upon human exertion, and happiness, is wonderful. The slave-master himself has a conception of it; and hence the system of tasks *among slaves. The slave whom you can not drive with the lash to break seventy-five pounds of hemp in a day, if you will task him to break a hundred, and promise him pay for all he does over, he will break you a hundred and fifty. You have substituted* hope, *for the* rod. *And yet perhaps it does not occur to you, that to the extent of your gain in the case, you have given up the slave system, and adopted the free system of labor.*

CW III: 462–463

☆ ☆ ☆

The fourth debate with Douglas was held in Charleston, which made it a sort of homecoming for Lincoln. Holzer writes: "His aged stepmother still lived in a primitive cabin not many miles from town. . . . Supporters unfurled above the street between the courthouse and the capitol building a huge, flag-festooned, eighty-foot-long banner that featured a portrait of the young Lincoln driving his oxteam [sic] into the area back in 1828. It was, again, a forerunner of 'railsplitter' image making to come."[6]

☆ ☆ ☆

Lincoln had a way of exposing the hypocrisy of the pro-slavery groups:

October 1, 1858

A Fragment on Pro-slavery Theology

The sum of pro-slavery theology seems to be this: "Slavery is not universally right, *nor yet universally* wrong; *it is better for* some *people to be slaves; and, in such cases, it is the Will of God that they be such."*

Certainly there is no contending against the Will of God; but still there is some difficulty in ascertaining, and applying it, to particular cases. . . .

Lincoln then gives his audience an example illustrating how slavery is one of those instances. He asks them to imagine a prosperous slave owner being challenged to do what is right and free his slave. That man would likely say that the Bible doesn't specifically forbid slavery, a point which Lincoln concedes—while reminding his listeners that Scripture doesn't give unqualified support to the practice either.

The Almighty gives no audible answer to the question, and his revelation—the Bible—gives none—or, at most, none but such as admits of a squabble, as to it's meaning. . . .

The slave owner might even point out how he provides his slave the basic necessities for life, which the slave might not otherwise have. (Of course, he completely ignores his selfish desire to profit from the slave's backbreaking labor.)

But, slavery is good for some people!!! As a good *thing, slavery is strikingly perculiar, in this, that it is the only good thing which no man ever seeks the good of,? for himself.*

Nonsense! Wolves devouring lambs, not because it is good for their own greedy maws, but because it [is] good for the lambs!!!

CW III: 204–205

☆ ☆ ☆

October 7, 1858

Fifth Debate with Stephen A. Douglas at Galesburg, Illinois

And I will remind Judge Douglas and this audience, that while Mr. Jefferson was the owner of slaves, as undoubtedly he was, in speaking upon this very subject, he used the strong language that "he trembled for his country when he remembered that God was just;" and I will offer the highest premium in my power to Judge Douglas if he will show that he, in all his life, ever uttered a sentiment at all akin to that of Jefferson.

CW III: 207–245, Lincoln, 219–237 (220)

☆ ☆ ☆

October 13, 1858

Sixth Debate with Stephen A. Douglas at Quincy, Illinois

Judge Douglas asks you "why cannot the institution of slavery, or rather, why cannot the nation, part slave and part free, continue as our fathers made it forever?*" In the first place, I insist that our fathers* did not *make this nation half slave and half free, or part slave and part free. [Applause, and "That's so."] I insist that they found the institution of slavery existing here. They did not make it so, but they left it so because they knew of no way to get rid of it at that time. ["Good," "Good," "That's true."] When Judge Douglas undertakes to say that as a matter of choice the fathers of the government made this nation part slave and part free,* he assumes what is historically a falsehood.

CW III: 245–283 (276)

☆ ☆ ☆

In the rivals' final debate, Lincoln articulated what he believed to be the Founding Fathers' view of slavery as expressed in the Declaration of Independence.

October 15, 1858

Seventh and Last Debate with Stephen A. Douglas at Alton, Illinois

I think the authors of that notable instrument intended to include all *men, but they did not mean to declare all men equal* in all respects. *They did not mean to say all men were equal in color, size, intellect, moral development or social capacity. They defined with tolerable distinctness in what they did consider all men created equal—equal in certain inalienable rights, among which are life, liberty and the pursuit of happiness. This they said, and this they meant. They did not mean to assert the obvious untruth, that all were then actually enjoying that equality, nor yet, that they were about to confer it immediately upon them. In fact they had no power to confer such a boon. They meant simply to declare the* right *so that the* enforcement *of it might follow as fast as circumstances should permit.*

They meant to set up a standard maxim for free society which should be familiar to all: constantly looked to, constantly labored for, and even though never perfectly attained, constantly approximated and thereby constantly spreading and deepening its influence and augmenting the happiness and value of life to all people, of all colors, everywhere. . . .

We are now far into the fifth year since a policy was initiated with the avowed object and confident promise of putting an end to the slavery agitation. Under the operation of this policy, that agitation has not only not ceased but has constantly augmented. In my opinion it will not cease until a crisis shall have been reached and passed. ***"A house divided against itself cannot stand."*** *I believe this government cannot endure permanently half Slave and half Free. I do not expect the house to fall—but I do expect it will cease to be divided. It will become all one thing, or all the other. Either the opponents of Slavery will arrest the further spread of it, and place it where the public mind shall rest in the belief that it is in the course of ultimate extinction, or its advocates will push it forward till it shall become alike lawful in all the States—old as well as new, North as well as South.*

In speaking of Stephen Douglas facing up to the true facts regarding slavery—

That extract and the sentiments expressed in it, have been extremely offensive to Judge Douglas. He has warred upon them as Satan does upon the Bible. . . . His perversions upon it are endless. Here now are my views upon it in brief. . . .

The Bible says somewhere that we are desperately selfish. I think we would have discovered that fact without the Bible. I do not claim that I am any less so than the average of men, but I do claim that I am not more selfish than Judge Douglas. . . .

Lincoln could not recall where the word *selfish* was found in the Bible but was correct in noting that the Bible calls man a "lover of self."[7]

That is the real issue. That is the issue that will continue in this country when these poor tongues of Judge Douglas and myself shall be silent. It is the eternal struggle between these two principles—right and wrong—throughout the world. They are the two principles that have stood face to face from the beginning of time; and will ever continue to struggle. The one is the common right of humanity and the other the divine right of kings.

Though Douglas often insinuated that Lincoln's views mirrored the "radical" beliefs of the abolitionists, Lincoln repeatedly told the audience of his conviction that the Constitution—which made some provisions for slavery—was to be upheld above all else. Otherwise, the American system would collapse. This explains his remarks about upholding the fugitive slave laws, which required Northerners to return runaway slaves.

Why then do I yield support to a fugitive slave law? Because I do not understand that the Constitution, which guarantees that right, can be supported without it. And if I believed that the right to hold a slave in a Territory was equally fixed in the Constitution with the right to reclaim fugitives, I should be bound to give it the legislation necessary to support it.

CW III: 283–325; Lincoln's reply 297–318 (301, 305, 310, 315, 317)

☆ ☆ ☆

Lincoln had accepted the nomination for the Senate with his dramatic "A House Divided" Speech." Three and a half months later, with the campaign over, he addressed his supporters in the place where it all began.

October 30, 1858

Fragment: Last Speech of the Campaign at Springfield, Illinois

My friends, to-day closes the discussions of this canvass. The planting and the culture are over; and there remains but the preparation, and the harvest. . . .

I have borne a laborious, and, in some respects to myself, a painful part in the contest. Through all, I have neither assailed, nor wrestled with any part of the constitution. The legal right of the Southern people to reclaim their fugitives I have constantly admitted. The legal right of Congress to interfere with their institution in the states, I have constantly denied. In resisting the spread of slavery to new teritory, and with that, what appears to me to be a tendency to subvert the first principle of free government itself my whole effort has consisted. To the best of my judgment I have labored for, *and not* against *the Union. As I have not felt, so I have not expressed any harsh sentiment toward our Southern bretheren. I have constantly declared, as I really believed, the only difference between them and us, is the difference of circumstances.*

I have meant to assail the motives of no party, or individual; and if I have, in any instance (of which I am not conscious) departed from my purpose, I regret it. . . .

As he wrapped up his final speech, Lincoln made the surprising statement that his candidacy did not spring from personal ambition; in fact, he had prayed that his campaign would have been unnecessary. Lincoln expressed a willingness to let his opponent have the honor of election to the Senate, provided that the cause for which Lincoln had fought should be successful. This statement was either a claim so lofty that it must be considered a false profession of character or a genuine statement from a man more concerned with the fortunes of his nation than his own ambition. Such statesmanship is above both personal and party interest and is an uncommonly rare quality.

Ambition has been ascribed to me. God knows how sincerely I prayed from the first that this field of ambition might not be opened. I claim no insensibility to political honors; but today could the Missouri restriction be restored, and the whole slavery question replaced on the old ground of "toleration" by necessity *where it exists, with unyielding hostility to the spread of it, on principle, I would, in consideration, gladly agree, that Judge Douglas should never be* out, *and I never* in, *an office, so long as we both or either, live.*

CW III: 334–335

The *Illinois State Journal* reported on this final campaign address:

Annotation

"We have neither time nor room to give even a sketch of his remarks to-day. Suffice it to say, the speech was one of his very best efforts, distinguished for its clearness and force, and for the satisfactory manner in which he exposed the roorbacks and misrepresentations of the enemy. The conclusion of this speech was one of the most eloquent appeals ever addressed to the American people. It was received with spontaneous bursts of enthusiasm unequalled by any thing ever before enacted in this city." From this account it may be inferred that the fragment is the conclusion of the speech, perhaps the only portion which Lincoln committed to paper.[8]

☆ ☆ ☆

The long-running campaign against the "Little Giant" was over. In 1858, senators were chosen by the state legislative bodies and Douglas was selected by a vote of 54 to 46. Members of the House of Representatives, however, were elected by popular vote. In his book *The Lincoln-Douglas Debates*, Harold Holzer includes a chart showing the Illinois election results, giving the numbers for the seven counties in which debates were held. (Because the U.S. senators were chosen by the state legislators, not the people, these totals do not include votes for Lincoln; however, the Republican candidates for the House were clearly helped by his presence on the ticket.) Republicans garnered 16,127 votes; Democrats, 14,609. Statewide, Republicans received 125,668 votes; Democrats, 122,181.[9] Clearly, Lincoln had helped the Republican ticket.

Lincoln did not retreat from the public after his defeat. He was clearly glad to have been in the campaign though he appears to have expected to drop out of the public eye once again.

November 19, 1858

To Anson G. Henry

I am glad I made the late race. It gave me a hearing on the great and durable question of the age, which I cold have had no other way; and though I now sink out of view, and shall be forgotten, I believe I have made some marks which will tell for the cause of civil liberty long after I am gone.

CW III: 339–340 (339)

☆ ☆ ☆

Following is a letter to Henry L. Pierce in which Lincoln declines an invitation to a celebration honoring the birthday of Thomas Jefferson.

April 6, 1859

To Henry L. Pierce and Others

This is a world of compensations; and he who would be *no slave, must consent to* have *no slave. Those who deny freedom to others, deserve it not for themselves; and, under a* ***just God****, can not long retain it.*

CW III: 374–376 (376)

☆ ☆ ☆

As he had in the fifth debate, Lincoln quoted Thomas Jefferson to show the Founding Fathers' ambivalence to slavery, even though Jefferson was a slave owner himself.

September 16, 1859

Speech at Columbus, Ohio

. . . "I tremble for my country when I remember that God is just!" We know how he looked upon it when he thus expressed himself. There was danger to this country—danger of the avenging justice of God in that little unimportant popular sovereignty question of Judge Douglas. He supposed there was a question of God's eternal justice wrapped up in the enslaving of any race of men, or any man, and that those who did so braved the ***arm of Jehovah****—that when a nation thus dared the Almighty every friend of that nation had cause to dread His wrath. Choose ye between Jefferson and Douglas as to what is the true view of this element among us.*

CW III: 400–424 (410)

In the Old Testament, "God's arm" is synonymous with His power. The most beautiful and well-known usage is in Isaiah 53:1: "Who hath believed our report? and to whom is the arm of the Lord revealed?" In all likelihood, Lincoln used the name *Jehovah* rather than *God* to match the literary tone of the Old Testament.

☆ ☆ ☆

Lincoln counters the arguments of Douglas that the Bible established the rightfulness of slavery.

September 17, 1859

Speech at Cincinnati, Ohio

THE BIBLE THEORY

In Kentucky, perhaps, in many of the Slave States certainly, you are trying to establish the rightfulness of Slavery by reference to the Bible. You are trying to show that slavery existed in the Bible times by Divine ordinance. Now Douglas is wiser than you, for your own benefit, upon that subject. Douglas knows that whenever you establish that Slavery was right by the

Bible, it will occur that that Slavery was the Slavery of the white *man—of men without reference to color. . . .*

At the time of the feeding of the five thousand, the Lord Jesus knew that many of the people were there for the "loaves and fishes"—the free meal rather than the hearing of His words (John 6:26). Lincoln adapted the illustration.

If we shall adopt a platform that fails to recognize or express our purpose, or elect a man that declares himself inimical to our purpose, we not only take nothing by our success, but we tacitly admit that we act upon no [other] principle than a desire to have ***"the loaves and fishes,"*** *by which, in the end our apparent success is really an injury to us. . . .*

The good old maxims of the ***Bible*** *are applicable, and truly applicable to human affairs, and in this as in other things, we may say here that* ***he who is not for us is against us; he who gathereth not with us scattereth.***

CW III: 438–462 (445, 461, 462)

At the end of the excerpt above, Lincoln drew on Jesus' words in Matthew 12:30 and Luke 11:23. In doing so, he was declaring the impossibility of taking a neutral stand on this issue.

Lincoln sounded a hopeful tone in a speech given in Clinton, Illinois. *The Collected Works* contains this excerpt from *The Weekly Central Transcript*, the town's newspaper.

October 14, 1859

Speech at Clinton, Illinois

"Our position," says Mr. L., "is right—our principles are good and just, but I would desire to impress on every Republican present to have patience and steadiness under all circumstances—whether defeated or successful. But I do hope that as there is a **just and righteous God in Heaven**, our principles will and shall prevail sooner or later."

He closed his eloquent and masterly exposition of the true intent of our cherished and time-honored principles and the sophistries and delusions of our enemies, amid the loud, prolonged and stentorian cheering of the vast audience, that made the rafters of the court-house ring again.

CW III: 487–488 (488)

☆ ☆ ☆

Once again, when it seemed that Lincoln's desire for political success was within reach, his dream of being a senator slipped from his grasp. Not as a man seeking political office, but as a true patriot, he had given more than his best. Disappointed, exhausted mentally, physically, emotionally, he would drop out of political sight and attend the Eighth Judicial Circuit again.

One day, wearily walking the last steps toward home and rest, he slipped in the muddy path. Catching his balance, he muttered, "It's a slip and not a fall."[10] In his quest for political office, once again he had slipped; significantly, he had not fallen.

An appointment to the Senate by the legislature would have given him his desire, and he certainly would have dedicated his gifts as a statesman to the interests of his nation. But would he have been able to make more than a noble effort to help the slave? Would he have been on the springboard to the presidency in time to guide the country through the fiery trial of the Civil War?

Abraham Lincoln was not fully aware of the unbounded enthusiastic reactions of his countrymen to the substance of his debate speeches. Little did Lincoln realize the impact of his debate addresses upon Illinois; and infinitely little did he realize the impact upon the newspaper readers over the country who had followed the debates. Yet many of his political friends did notice, and it is at this time that Lincoln wrote his brief autobiography for Jesse Fell. After filling in the broad details of his life, Lincoln concluded:

To Jesse W. Fell, Enclosing Autobiography

If any personal description of me is thought desirable, it may be said, I am, in height, six feet, four inches, nearly; lean in flesh, weighing, on an average, one hundred and eighty pounds; dark complexion, with coarse black hair, and grey eyes—no other marks or brands recollected. Yours very truly A. Lincoln.

CW III: 511

When Fell received the autobiography, he sent it to a journalist friend in Pennsylvania, who wrote an article on Lincoln. That article was then picked up by many other papers. Before long, leading Republican party members were eager to hear from the storytelling country lawyer.

Soon a letter arrived. It would trigger the events that would change Lincoln's life—and America—forever.

CHAPTER 12

NATIONAL PROMINENCE

The envelope arrived unexpectedly at Lincoln's home on Jackson Street. It was postmarked New York City; the return address was that of a good friend. To Lincoln's surprise, it was an invitation to speak at the Plymouth Church, which was led by the elite minister of the land, the Reverend Doctor Henry Ward Beecher. To the devastated Abraham Lincoln, the prestige of the minister and church made this a stunning invitation.

The invitation affirmed that Lincoln had held his own with one of the nation's premier debaters, Stephen Douglas. The political leaders had read the papers, and they wanted to see this gangling prairie stump speaker firsthand. At the beginning of the Senate campaign, Stephen Douglas had said of Lincoln: "I shall have my hands full. He is the strong man of the party—full of wit, facts, dates—and the best stump speaker, with his droll ways and dry jokes, in the West."[1]

Unquestionably, the debates with Stephen Douglas lifted the prairie attorney to notoriety. But to most Easterners, Abe Lincoln remained what the *New York Times* called him: "a lawyer of some local Illinois reputation."[2] The invitation would give the Illinois firebrand a national platform.

Historian Allan Nevins notes that, not long before the lecture, its location was changed from Plymouth Church to the Cooper Union Institute. He writes: "Fifteen hundred people tramped through the massive doors and downstairs to the great, round, subterranean hall with its many pillars, long, square stage, and flaring gas lamps."[3] It was the largest gathering of the city's elite since the days of Clay and Webster. To give the occasion even more cachet, the well-known poet and journalist William Cullen Bryant presided.

"As he warmed to his theme," Nevins writes, "as the glow of his earnestness lighted up his craggy face, as men caught the force of his ideas and language, he carried his audience with him. . . . The crowd, which had grown steadily more enthusiastic, gave Lincoln an ovation, shouting, clapping, and waving hats and handkerchiefs."[4]

Horace Greeley and the other newspaper editors provided national coverage of the speech, boosting the status of Lincoln from prairie lawyer to a respected national figure.

Recognizing that this lecture was the opportunity of a lifetime, Lincoln had diligently prepared. Against Stephen Douglas, he had furiously defended the concept that the Founding Fathers had meant to include the black man in the phrase "all men are created equal." They had allowed slavery in the Union only because the alternative would have been two separate nations, one with and one without slavery. Lincoln had also argued that the Founding Fathers had designed to put slavery on the path to extinction.

In his comprehensive book *Lincoln at Cooper Union*, Harold Holzer shows that Lincoln carefully researched the facts. In the address, he gave the names of the thirty-nine Founding Fathers of the Constitution and explained how each had voted on various bills. According to Lincoln, the final count was "thirty-six to three in favor of restricting slavery, an overwhelming endorsement by 'our fathers' of the very anti-slavery expansion sentiments shared by the Republicans of 1860."[5]

Lincoln argued that though the Founders allowed slavery in the Constitution out of necessity, at the same time they disallowed slavery in the Ordinance of 1787 for the Northwest Territories, which included states north of the Ohio River. Lincoln concluded by saying that twenty-three of the thirty-nine signers believed the federal government had the power to regulate slavery.[6] His arguments were solid and convincing, supported by incontestable facts.

From the time the boy Lincoln was learning to read by firelight and was writing with charcoal upon whatever he could find for a tablet, he was absorbed with the idea that his progenitors had stepped ashore along the Atlantic seaboard, establishing a new, untried system of government, a government to be planned and executed by the governed. The seasick and storm-driven colonists were free men when they stepped ashore and would build a government where people would rule themselves. From early in life, ideas percolated in his mind as Lincoln came to a solid faith that God had allowed America to rise up to break the yoke of tyranny. It would be the nation's privileged destiny not only for its citizens to be free themselves, but to unlock the shackles for all mankind.

In his youthful effort in the Lyceum speech, Lincoln had pictured the power of a nation of free persons. Fueled by the high octane of liberty, energized, empowered men would meet every emergency and conquer every foe. Freedom causes men to work hard, be more dedicated, waste less time in squabbles, and cooperate in the building of their country.

In his Lyceum speech, Lincoln had used the dramatic comparison of America to the greatest institution, the Church of the Lord Jesus Christ, and dramatically proclaimed that the "gates of hell would not prevail." In the Cooper Union speech, that phrase gave way to a less passionate, very simple, but more powerful phrase: "Right Makes Might."

"Right Makes Might." Lincoln's phrase had inward power. History's long story of one bloody conqueror after another reflected the fact that *might* and *glory* had extinguished one dream after another. The might of the conqueror was cold and self-defeating. The word *right* subscribes to an eternal principle. *Might* is physical; *right* is spiritual.

America was not great because the people were many, or the smartest, but because they had a government of the people. Following is the close of his address:

February 27, 1860

Address at Cooper Institute, New York City

Wrong as we think slavery is, we can yet afford to let it alone where it is, because that much is due to the necessity arising from its actual presence in the nation; but can we, while our votes will prevent it, allow it to spread into the National Territories, and to overrun us here in these Free States? If our sense of duty forbids this, then let us stand by our duty, fearlessly and effectively. Let us be diverted by none of those sophistical contrivances wherewith we are so industriously plied and belabored—contrivances such as groping for some middle ground between the right and the wrong, vain as the search for a man who should be neither a living man nor a dead man—such as a policy of "don't care" on a question about which all true men do care—such as Union appeals beseeching true Union men to yield to Disunionists, reversing the ***divine rule****, and* ***calling, not the sinners, but the righteous to repentance****. . . .*

Neither let us be slandered from our duty by false accusations against us, nor frightened from it by menaces of destruction to the Government nor of dungeons to ourselves. LET US HAVE FAITH THAT RIGHT MAKES MIGHT, AND IN THAT FAITH, LET US, TO THE END, DARE TO DO OUR DUTY AS WE UNDERSTAND IT.

CW III: 522-550 (550)

Was Lincoln's climax only an oratorical ending? Or was he confidently resting upon a *divine power* who tips the balance in favor of Right? That question will be answered in the long years of his presidency. We will see his mental anguish as that question taunts and tortures him in his "Meditation on the Divine Will" (see chapter 15). The question of the divine will would also be a primary focus in his Second Inaugural.

☆ ☆ ☆

Lincoln had gone east to make one all-important speech, but while there he was pressed to make additional addresses in Rhode Island, New Hampshire, and Connecticut. In early March, the *Dover Inquirer* reported on one of these speeches. In addition to briefly summarizing the speech, the article reported his concluding words, another instance in which Lincoln paraphrased Matthew 9:13 (see also Mark 2:17 and Luke 5:32).

March 2, 1860

Speech at Dover, New Hampshire

Mr. Lincoln spoke nearly two hours and we believe he would have held his audience had he spoken all night. . . .

'Neither should we be diverted by trick or stratagem, by a senseless clamor about "popular sovereignty," by any contrivances for groping for some middle ground between the right and the wrong—the "don't care" policy of Douglas—or Union appeals to true Union men to yield to the threats of Disunionists, which was reversing the divine rule, and calling, **not the sinners but the righteous to repentance**—none of these things should move or intimidate us; but having faith that right makes might, let us to the end, dare to do our duty.'

CW III: 552–554 (552, 554)

☆ ☆ ☆

Lincoln visited his son Robert at Phillips Exeter Academy while in the East. He addressed his son's school, located in Exeter, New Hampshire, and while there wrote a letter to his wife. While that letter has never been located, Robert's recollection of one passage from the letter is included in *The Collected Works.*

March 4, 1860

Letter to Mary Todd Lincoln

I have been unable to escape this toil. If I had foreseen it, I think I would not have come east at all. The speech at New York, being within my calculation before I started, went off passably well and gave me no trouble whatever. The difficulty was to make nine others, before reading audiences who had already seen all my ideas in print.

CW III: 555

☆ ☆ ☆

On March 5, Lincoln gave a lengthy speech in Hartford, Connecticut. A reporter found the following notes Lincoln had written and used to deliver his speech.[7]

SIGNS OF DECAY—BUSHWHACKING—
IRREPRESSIBLE CONFLICT—
JOHN BROWN
SHOE-TRADE—
True, or not true.
If true, what?
Mason
Plasters.
If not true, what?
[Illegible] is the question.
We must deal with it.
Magnitude of question.
What prevents just now?
Right—wrong—indifference
Indifference unphilosophical
Because nobody is indifferent
Must be converted to
Can be, or can not be done.
I suppose can not.

But if can, what result?
Indifference, then, must be rejected.
And what supported?
Sectionalism
Conservatism
John Brown
Conclusion

CW IV: 1

The notes resulted in an eloquent speech. The newspaper the *Daily Courant*, published his words, including the excerpts below.

March 5, 1860

Speech at Hartford, Connecticut

And I am glad to know that there is a system of labor where the laborer can strike if he wants to! I would to God that such a system prevailed all over the world. . . .

They may be justified in this, believing, as they do, that slavery is right, and a social blessing. We cannot act otherwise than we do, believing that slavery is wrong. If it is right, we may not contract its limits. If it is wrong, they cannot ask us to extend it. Upon these different views, hinges the whole controversy. Thinking it right, they are justified in asking its protection; thinking it wrong, we cannot consent to vote for it, or to let it extend itself. If our sense of duty forbids this extension, let us do that duty. This contrivance of a middle ground is such that he who occupies it is neither a dead or a living man. Their "Union" contrivances are not for us, for they reverse the scriptural order and ***call the righteous, not sinners to repentance****. They ask men who never had an aspiration except for the Union, to swear fealty to the Union. Let us not be slandered from our duties, or intimidated from preserving our dignity and our rights by any menace; but let us have* ***faith that Right, Eternal Right makes might****, and as we understand our duty, so do it!*

CW IV: 2-13 (7-8)

Though the content of this speech was largely a repeat of the Cooper Union address, Lincoln added one important word: *eternal*—Eternal Right makes Might.

☆ ☆ ☆

The fourth and last of the New England speeches for which we have a transcript was delivered in New Haven, Connecticut. Lincoln's remarks were quite like those in the major address at Cooper Union Institute.

March 6, 1860

Speech at New Haven, Connecticut

If our sense of duty forbids this, then let us stand by our duty, fearlessly and effectively. Let us be diverted by none of those sophistical contrivances wherewith we are so industriously plied and belabored—contrivances such as groping for some middle ground between the right and the wrong, vain as the search for a man who should be neither a living man nor a dead man—such as a policy of "don't care" on a question about which all true men do care—such as Union appeals beseeching true Union men to yield to Disunionists, reversing the divine rule, and ***calling, not the sinners, but the righteous to repentance****. . . .*

Neither let us be slandered from our duty by false accusations against us, nor frightened from it by menaces of destruction to the Government, nor of dungeons to ourselves. Let us have faith that ***right makes might****; and in that faith, let us, to the end, dare to do our duty, so we understand it.*

CW IV: 13–30 (29–30)

☆ ☆ ☆

On May 18, 1860, Abraham Lincoln was nominated for the presidency by the Republican National Convention in Chicago.

Joshua Giddings, a good friend of Lincoln's, wrote to the nominee immediately after his acceptance, saying Lincoln had been nominated because of his honesty and freedom from corrupt men and that he should place himself under obligation to no one. Lincoln sent this response.

May 21, 1860

To Joshua R. Giddings

Hon: J. R. Giddings:
Springfield, Ills.

My good friend: Your very kind and acceptable letter of the 19th. was duly handed me by Mr. Tuck. It is indeed, most grateful to my feelings, that the responsible position assigned me, comes without conditions, save only such honorable ones as are fairly implied. I am not wanting in the purpose, though I may fail in the strength, to maintain my freedom from bad influences. Your letter comes to my aid in this point, most opportunely. May the ***Almighty*** *grant that the cause of truth, justice, and humanity, shall in no wise suffer at my hands.*

CW IV: 51–52 (51)

☆ ☆ ☆

Lincoln's official acceptance of the Republican nomination for president appears below.

May 23, 1860

To George Ashmun

To George Ashmun
Hon: George Ashmun: Springfield, Ills. May 23. 1860
President of the Republican National Convention.

Sir: I accept the nomination tendered me by the Convention over which you presided, and of which I am formally apprized in the letter of yourself and others, acting as a committee of the convention, for that purpose.

The declaration of principles and sentiments, which accompanies your letter, meets my approval; and it shall be my care not to violate, or disregard it, in any part.

Imploring the assistance of ***Divine Providence****, and with due regard to the views and feelings of all who were represented in the convention; to the rights of all the states, and territories, and people of the nation; to the inviolability of the constitution, and the perpetual union, harmony, and prosperity of all, I am most happy to co-operate for the practical success of the principles declared by the convention. Your obliged friend, and fellow citizen*

A. Lincoln

CW IV: 52

☆ ☆ ☆

Some people urged Lincoln to outline his policies and commitments, particularly on what should be done about the vexing issue of slavery. He felt that he had adequately done so and would amplify at the proper time. Lincoln wrote to his friend Senator Lyman Trumbull, noting the story of Peter's denial (see Matthew 26:69-75; Mark 14:66-72; Luke 22:55-62; John 18:15-27).

June 5, 1860

To Lyman Trumbull

Remembering that Peter denied his Lord with an oath, after most solemnly protesting that he never would, I will not swear I will make no committals; but I do think I will not.

CW IV: 71

☆ ☆ ☆

Abraham Lincoln did not make speeches during the election campaign. He rested upon what he had already spoken and written. Between the election to the presidency and the inauguration, he was often asked to restate his policies. In his letter to a Tennessee newspaper editor, Lincoln declined to repeat what he had already stated. The following sentence is an allusion to Luke 16:31.

October 23, 1860

To William S. Speer

"If they hear not Moses and the prophets, neither will they be persuaded though one rose from the dead."

CW IV: 130

PART THREE

INSTRUMENT OF THE ALMIGHTY

And I shall be most happy indeed if I shall be an humble instrument in the hands of the Almighty, and of this, His almost chosen people, for perpetuating the object of that great struggle.

President Abraham Lincoln
to the New Jersey Senate, February 21, 1861

I have often wished that I was a more devout man than I am. Nevertheless, amid the greatest difficulties of my Administration, when I could not see any other resort, I would place my whole reliance in God, knowing that all would go well, and He would decide for the right.

Remarks to Baltimore Presbyterian Synod,
October 24, 1863

CHAPTER 13

THE INAUGURAL JOURNEY

With the nation near the crisis point, the presidential campaign of 1860 was unlike any before or since. Lincoln and Douglas were the front-runners, but there were two additional candidates: John Breckenridge of Kentucky, who represented the Democrats from the South, and John Bell, a third-party candidate who appealed to many former Whigs who still hoped the problem of slavery would just go away.

Stephen Douglas represented himself as the national candidate who could best advance the American spirit of government by the people through his push for popular sovereignty. Lincoln answered that popular sovereignty was an empty phrase that would simply allow men by their vote to gain control of the lives of other men.

Douglas touted his experience in both the House of Representatives and Senate and contrasted it with Lincoln's one term in Congress. Douglas claimed success in legislation that had held the nation together while Lincoln was preaching that the nation was a "divided house" that could not stand.

Though Douglas had been recognized as the premier political orator on the national scene, Lincoln's great asset was his passion. People appreciated his warm, down-to-earth convictions. Though people did not know what to do about existing slavery, the words of Lincoln rang true: All men are created equal. Though he had reassured the Southerners that he had no intention of abolishing slavery in their states, Americans knew he was firmly opposed to the practice.

Lincoln was elected president on November 6, 1860, with 39 percent of the popular vote. He carried all the Northern states except New Jersey and Missouri. He carried none of the Southern states. Of the electoral college votes, Lincoln received 180 votes; Breckenridge received 72, Bell, 39, and Douglas, 12.

Since it would be nearly four months before Lincoln would assume the presidency, he was urged by some to issue statements that might hold off the threatened secession of Southern states. He chose to weigh every option, think soberly, and unhurriedly prepare his plan of action.

Editors who were opposed to Lincoln were ready to quote his words out of context and misuse his statements. As Lincoln knew that whatever he said would be used against him, he said little, even though he was carefully thinking through his strategy.

Henry J. Raymond was the editor of the *New York Times* and a supporter of Lincoln's. In this letter to Raymond, Lincoln deplores that men in responsible positions can be grossly unfair. In his letter, he paraphrases Jesus' words in Matthew 12:39, Mark 8:12, and Luke 11:29.

November 28, 1860

To Henry J. Raymond

This is just as I expected, and just what would happen with any declaration I could make. These political fiends are not half sick enough yet. "Party malice" and not "public good" possesses them entirely. ***They seek a sign, and no sign shall be given them.*** *At least such is my present feeling and purpose. [Yours very truly*

A. Lincoln]

CW IV: 145–146 (146)

In the meantime, Southerners panicked as they considered the ramifications of Lincoln's election. Slaveholders, of course, wondered about the impact on their livelihoods if their slaves were suddenly freed. Some Southerners who did not own slaves worried that, should slaves be freed, they would suddenly face enormous competition for available jobs. And, as horrible as it is to consider today, many strongly opposed the idea of blacks attending their schools and churches—and being treated as their social equals.

☆ ☆ ☆

Even as the nation's editors criticized him for doing nothing, Lincoln was quietly contacting an old friend he hoped could help him convince the

Southern states not to secede. Alexander Stephens, a lawyer from Georgia, had been friends with Abraham Lincoln since the two had served together in the House of Representatives in 1848. Rather symptomatic of the division of the country was the separation of the two as the gulf widened between North and South. In this eroding relationship we see Lincoln at his best, using his gift of personal charisma to hold an impossible friendship together.

Lincoln wrote his old friend two days after South Carolina announced its decision to leave the Union. Not until late January did Georgia, the home state of Stephens, secede. In the intervening weeks, there was this exchange:

December 22, 1860

To Alexander H. Stephens

For your own eye only.
Hon. A. H. Stephens
Springfield, Ills.

My dear Sir

Your obliging answer to my short note is just received, and for which please accept my thanks. I fully appreciate the present peril the country is in, and the weight of responsibility on me.

Do the people of the South really entertain fears that a Republican administration would, directly, *or* indirectly, *interfere with their slaves, or with them, about their slaves? If they do, I wish to assure you, as once a friend, and still, I hope, not an enemy, that there is no cause for such fears.*

The South would be in no more danger in this respect, than it was in the days of Washington. I suppose, however, this does not meet the case. You think slavery is right *and ought to be extended; while we think it is* wrong *and ought to be restricted. That I suppose is the rub. It certainly is the only substantial difference between us. Yours very truly*

A. Lincoln

CW IV: 160–161

A portion of the reply of Alexander Stephens on December 30, 1860, is recorded in a footnote in *The Collected Works.*[1]

> Personally, I am not your enemy—far from it; and however widely we may differ politically, yet I trust we both have an earnest desire

> to preserve and maintain the Union. . . . When men come under the influence of fanaticism, there is no telling where their impulses or passions may drive them. This is what creates our discontent and apprehensions, not unreasonable when we see . . . such reckless exhibitions of madness as the John Brown raid into Virginia, which has received so much sympathy from many, and no open condemnation from any of the leading members of the dominant party. . . . In addressing you thus, I would have you understand me as being not a personal enemy, but as one who would have you do what you can to save our common country. A word fitly spoken by you now would be like "apples of gold in pictures of silver."

The phrase "A word fitly spoken is like apples of gold in pictures of silver" comes from Proverbs 25:11. Another analogy of this image helps describe Lincoln's approach to the mammoth problems the country faced. He understood that all humanity hungers for liberty, the apple of gold. But unless the apple is within the frame of silver, a solid respected government of law, there can be no enjoyment of the fruit of democracy. The exquisitely beautiful figure of speech expresses a cornerstone of Lincoln's philosophy. "Liberty" is the golden apple desired by all mankind, valueless except in the background of silver, that is, unless it is supported by constitutional law.

Radicals like John Brown seemingly were willing to disregard the Constitution to correct a gross injustice. Stephens was correct, however, in observing that radicals like Brown whipped up the flames of passion, driving a wedge between North and South. Because Lincoln refused to give in to the strong feelings of the abolitionists, many felt he was soft on slavery. To the contrary, he opposed the radical movements because they raised passions and stirred angry feelings, thereby creating only further violence and strife.

When Georgia took up the question of secession, Alexander Stephens told his fellow delegates: "My judgment is against secession for existing causes. I have not lost hope of securing our rights in the Union and under the Constitution. . . . I have been, and am still opposed to secession as a remedy against anticipated aggression."[2]

Despite his firm words, the State of Georgia voted to secede at the end of January, and Alexander Stephens became vice president of the Confederacy.

Not long after this correspondence, the president-elect used the golden apple image in this fragment on the Constitution. This statement, though short, is the backbone of his political philosophy.

January 1861

Fragment on the Constitution and the Union

All this is not the result of accident. It has a philosophical cause. Without the Constitution *and the* Union, *we could not have attained the result; but even these, are not the primary cause of our great prosperity. There is something back of these, entwining itself more closely about the human heart. That something, is the principle of "Liberty to all"—the principle that clears the* path *for all—gives* hope *to all—and, by consequence,* enterprize, *and* industry *to all.*

The expression *of that principle, in our Declaration of Independence, was most happy, and fortunate.* Without *this, as well as* with *it, we could have declared our independence of Great Britain; but* without *it, we could not, I think, have secured our free government, and consequent prosperity. No oppressed, people will* fight, *and* endure, *as our fathers did, without the promise of something better, than a mere change of masters.*

The assertion of that principle, *at* that time, *was* the *word,* "fitly spoken" *which has proved an "apple of gold" to us. The* Union, *and the* Constitution, *are the 'picture of silver,' subsequently framed around it. The picture was made, not to* conceal, *or* destroy *the apple; but to* adorn, *and* preserve *it. The* picture *was made* for *the apple*—not *the apple for the picture.*

So let us act, that neither picture, *or* apple *shall ever be blurred, or bruised or broken.*

That we may so act, we must study, and understand the points of danger.

CW IV: 168–169

So now the man from the backwoods—one who had been shaped and stirred by the ideals of his country—stood at the crossroads. Abraham Lincoln had debated the champion of proslavery forces; he had poured out his soul, passionately voicing the emotions of an enslaved race. Though a most unlikely candidate, Lincoln, the man of the people, had prevailed.

The great debates and the rousing rallies were over. He must face the stark reality. He had experienced visions of a bloodbath—unless both sides would cease the rocking of the boat. The burden, the responsibility of the control of the pilot's wheel, was now his.

Yet any hopes that the slavery question could be settled peacefully quickly faded on December 20, 1860, when South Carolina seceded from the Union. Less than two weeks later, on January 9, 1861, South Carolina troops fired upon the *Star of the West*, a merchant ship delivering supplies to Fort Sumter. By February 1, Mississippi, Florida, Alabama, Georgia, Louisiana, and Texas had also seceded. Inauguration Day was over a month away.

How should Lincoln handle a crisis that had emerged even before he took office? A mere politician might have accepted the secession, concluding that the two countries could exist side by side. A military man with dictatorial aspirations might have seized the opportunity and restored order by force.

The country waited anxiously to see what Lincoln's response would be. When he and his son Robert boarded the train in Springfield that would take them to Washington, a great crowd was waiting at the station. In the absence of photographs, all we have is an artist's rendering of Lincoln as he appeared on the rear platform. Rain was falling when he spoke:

February 11, 1861

Farewell Address at Springfield, Illinois

My friends—No one, not in my situation, can appreciate my feeling of sadness at this parting. To this place, and the kindness of these people, I owe every thing. Here I have lived a quarter of a century, and have passed from a young to an old man. Here my children have been born, and one is buried. I now leave, not knowing when, or whether ever, I may return, with a task before me greater than that which rested upon Washington. ***Without the assistance of that Divine Being, who ever attended him, I cannot succeed. With that assistance I cannot fail.*** *Trusting in Him, who can go with me, and remain with you and be every where for good, let us confidently hope that all will yet be well. To His care commending you, as I hope in your prayers you will commend me, I bid you an affectionate farewell.*

CW IV: 190

His marching into the storm could have been construed as a foolish act of unwise confidence in his own abilities, but Lincoln did not trust in his own leadership; rather, he stated emphatically that he relied upon the assistance of Almighty God. Over and over on the two-week whistle-stop tour to Washington, Lincoln said, "Without Him I cannot succeed; with Him and with the people of America, I cannot fail."

Quite possibly Lincoln had in mind the beautiful metaphor of the vine and the words of Jesus in John 15:5, "Without me ye can do nothing." Jesus reasoned with His disciples that they were like branches. Obviously, a branch cannot bear fruit apart from the vine, but rooted and drawing life from the vine, it will be successful and bear fruit.

After the train's departure, the crowd at the railroad station lingered; the tall, ungainly man who had walked their streets and told stories to their children was gone. Eyes followed the chugging, departing train down the tracks, until swallowed up in the horizon, it remained only a trace of smoke in the cloudy sky.

☆ ☆ ☆

Fifty or more times, crowds waited for Lincoln for hours at preannounced places, greeted by the one-time prairie lawyer as old friends. His neighborly talk and friendly humor inspired people to unite with him in the great task.

Not all his words during the whistle-stops were recorded in writing. Fortunately, some accounts have been reconstructed from newspaper printings; his warm, magnetic personality comes through clearly.

The first whistle-stops included appearances in

Tolono, Illinois
Danville, Illinois
Indiana State Line
Lafayette, Indiana
Thorntown and Lebanon, Indiana

Lincoln's train finally reached Indianapolis, where Governor Oliver Morton gave a welcoming speech. In his response, Lincoln picked up a phrase used in the early speech to the Lyceum of Springfield, on January 27, 1838, showing the great power in unity. He compared a free people, unified in their love of liberty, to the church of the Lord Jesus Christ.

United in freedom and justice, a nation is powerful and will overcome all enemies. Abraham Lincoln urged his great nation to stand for democracy in confidence that, united in a love of liberty, they would be invincible, much like Christ's description of His church in Matthew 16:18.

February 11, 1861

Reply to Oliver P. Morton at Indianapolis, Indiana

Gov. Morton and Fellow Citizens of the State of Indiana:

Most heartily do I thank you for this magnificent reception, and while I cannot take to myself any share of the compliment thus paid, more than that which pertains to a mere instrument, an accidental instrument, perhaps I should say, of a great cause, I yet must look upon it as a most magnificent reception, and as such, most heartily do I thank you for it. . . .

While I do not expect, upon this occasion, or on any occasion, till after I get to Washington, to attempt any lengthy speech, I will only say that to the salvation of this Union there needs but one single thing—the hearts of a people like yours. [Applause.] When the people rise in masses in behalf of the Union and the liberties of their country, truly may it be said, ***"The gates of hell shall not prevail against them."*** *[Renewed applause.]*

In all the trying positions in which I shall be placed, and doubtless I shall be placed in many trying ones, my reliance will be placed upon you and the people of the United States—and I wish you to remember now and forever, that it is your business, and not mine; that if the union of these States, and the liberties of this people, shall be lost, it is but little to any one man of fifty-two years of age, but a great deal to the thirty millions of people who inhabit these United States, and to their posterity in all coming time. It is your business to rise up and preserve the Union and liberty, for yourselves, and not for me. I desire they shall be constitutionally preserved.

I, as already intimated, am but an ***accidental instrument****, temporary, and to serve but for a limited time, but I appeal to you again to constantly bear in mind that with you, and not with politicians, not with Presidents, not with office-seekers, but with you, is the question, "Shall the Union and shall the liberties of this country be preserved to the latest generation?" [Loud and prolonged applause.]*

CW IV: 193–194

☆ ☆ ☆

In another address, given on the day he set off for Washington, Lincoln drew from Ecclesiastes 3:7.

February 11, 1861

Speech from the Balcony of the Bates House at Indianapolis, Indiana

I appear before you now to thank you for this very magnificent welcome which you have given me, and still more for the very generous support which your State recently gave to the political cause of the whole country, and the whole world. [Applause.] Solomon has said, that ***there is a time to keep silence****.*

CW IV: 194–196 (194–195)

☆ ☆ ☆

February 12, 1861 (Lincoln's birthday)

Remarks in Lawrenceburg, Indiana

If the politicians and leaders of parties were as true as the PEOPLE, *there would be little fear that the peace of the country would be disturbed. I have been selected to fill an important office for a brief period, and am now, in your eyes, invested with an influence which will soon pass away; but should my administration prove to be a very wicked one, or what is more probable, a very foolish one, if you, the* PEOPLE, *are but true to yourselves and to the Constitution, there is but little harm I can do,* thank God*!*

CW IV: 197

☆ ☆ ☆

February 12, 1861

Speech at Cincinnati, Ohio

Allow me to say that I think what has occurred here to-day could not have occurred in any other country on the face of the globe, without the influence of the free institutions which we have unceasingly enjoyed for three-quarters of a century. . . . [Applause.]

Fellow citizens of Kentucky—friends—bretheren, may I call you . . . I take your response as the most reliable evidence that it may be so, along

with other evidence, trusting that the good sense of the American people, on all sides of all rivers in America, under the ***Providence of God, who has never deserted us****, that we shall again be brethren, forgetting all parties—ignoring all parties. My friends I now bid you farewell.*
CW IV: 197–199 (198–199)

☆ ☆ ☆

Whistle-stops:
Germans in Cincinnati, Ohio
London, Ohio

☆ ☆ ☆

February 13, 1861

Address to the Ohio Legislature, Columbus, Ohio

. . . I cannot but turn and look for the support without which it will be impossible for me to perform that great task. I turn, then, and look to the American people and to that God who has never forsaken them. . . .

A few sentences later, Lincoln repeated the statement.

This is a most consoling circumstance, and from it we may conclude that all we want is time, patience and ***a reliance on that God who has never forsaken this people****.*
CW IV: 204–205 (204)

☆ ☆ ☆

Whistle-stops:
Newark, Ohio
Cadiz Junction, Ohio

☆ ☆ ☆

February 14, 1861

Speech at Steubenville, Ohio

Though the people have made me by electing me, the instrument to carry out the wishes expressed in the address, I greatly fear that I shall not be the repository of the ability to do so. Indeed I know I shall not, more than in purpose, unless sustained by the great body of the people, and by the Divine Power, without whose aid we can do nothing. . . . If anything goes wrong, however, and you find you have made a mistake, elect a better man next time. There are plenty of them. . . .

CW IV: 206–207 (207)

☆ ☆ ☆

Whistle-stops:

Wellsville, Ohio
Rochester, Pennsylvania
Monongahela House, Pittsburgh, Pennsylvania
Balcony of the Monongahela House
Pittsburgh, Pennsylvania (a more extended address)
Alliance, Ohio
Cleveland, Ohio
Ravenna, Ohio
Hudson, Ohio
Painesville, Ohio
Ashtabula, Ohio
Conneaut, Ohio
Erie, Pennsylvania
Westfield, New York

☆ ☆ ☆

February 16, 1861

Remarks at Dunkirk, New York

Standing as I do, with my hand upon this staff, and under the folds of the American flag, I ASK YOU TO STAND BY ME SO LONG AS I STAND BY IT.

CW IV: 219–220 (220)

☆ ☆ ☆

February 16, 1861

Speech at Buffalo, New York

Your worthy Mayor has thought fit to express the hope that I may be able to relieve the country from its present—or I should say, its threatened difficulties. I am sure I bring a heart true to the work. [Tremendous applause.] For the ability to perform it, I must trust in that Supreme Being who has never forsaken this favored land, through the instrumentality of this great and intelligent people. Without that assistance I shall surely fail. With it I cannot fail. . . .

CW IV: 220–221

☆ ☆ ☆

Whistle-stops:

Batavia, New York
Clyde, New York
Syracuse, New York
Utica, New York
Little Falls, New York
Fonda, New York
Schenectady, New York

☆ ☆ ☆

Lincoln actually made three addresses in Albany. The first was a short address to the mayor; the second was a reply to the governor. Finally, he addressed the legislature.

February 18, 1861

Address to the Legislature at Albany, New York

Mr. President and Gentlemen of the Legislature of the State of New York: It is with feelings of great diffidence, and I may say with feelings of awe, perhaps greater than I have recently experienced, that I meet you here in this place. The history of this great State, the renown of those great men who have stood here, and spoke here, and been heard here, all crowd around my fancy, and incline me to shrink from any attempt to address you. . . . It is true that while I hold myself without mock modesty, the humblest of all individuals that have ever been elevated to the Presidency, I have a more difficult task to perform than any one of them. . . . In the mean time, if we have patience; if we restrain ourselves; if we allow ourselves not to run off in a passion, I still have confidence that the ***Almighty, the Maker of the Universe*** *will, through the instrumentality of this great and intelligent* *people, bring us through this as He has through all the other difficulties of our country.*

CW IV: 225–226

☆ ☆ ☆

Whistle-stops:

Troy, New York
Hudson, New York

☆ ☆ ☆

February 19, 1861

Remarks at Poughkeepsie, New York

It is with your aid, as the people, that I think we shall be able to preserve—not the country, for the country will preserve itself, [Cheers.] but the institutions of the country; [Great cheering.] those institutions which have made us free, intelligent and happy—the most free, the most intelligent and the happiest people on the globe. . . .

CW IV: 228–229

☆ ☆ ☆

Whistle-stops:

Fishkill, New York
Peekskill, New York
Astor House in New York City
Newark, New Jersey
Brooklyn, New York City
Reply to Mayor Fernando Wood at New York City
Balcony of City Hall, New York City
Jersey City, New Jersey

☆ ☆ ☆

February 21, 1861

Remarks at Newark, New Jersey

With my own ability I cannot succeed, without the sustenance of Divine Providence, and of this great, free, happy, and intelligent people. Without these I cannot hope to succeed; with them I cannot fail.

CW IV: 234

☆ ☆ ☆

Whistle-stop:
New Brunswick, New Jersey

☆ ☆ ☆

February 21, 1861

Address to the New Jersey Senate at Trenton, New Jersey

Mr. President and Gentlemen of the Senate of the State of New-Jersey: I am very grateful to you for the honorable reception. . . . Back in my childhood, the earliest days of my being able to read, I got hold of a small book, such a one as few of the younger members have ever seen, "Weem's Life of Washington." I remember all the accounts there given of the battle fields and struggles for the liberties of the country, and none fixed themselves upon my imagination so deeply as the struggle here at Trenton, New-Jersey. The crossing of the river; the contest with the Hessians; the great hardships endured at that time, all fixed themselves on my memory more than any single revolutionary event; and you all know, for you have all been boys, how these early impressions last longer than any others. I recollect thinking . . . that there must have been something more than common that those men struggled for. I am exceedingly anxious that that thing which they struggled for; that something even more than National Independence; that something that held out a great promise to all the people of the world to all time to come; I am exceedingly anxious that this Union, the Constitution, and the liberties of the people shall be perpetuated in accordance with the original idea for which that struggle was made, and I shall be most happy indeed if I shall be an humble instrument in the hands of the Almighty, and of this, his almost chosen people, for perpetuating the object of that great struggle. . . .

CW IV: 235–236

☆ ☆ ☆

Lincoln's addresses to the New Jersey legislature show the compelling personal power and persuasive logic that he used when facing an audience in a state he did not carry.

February 21, 1861

Address to the New Jersey General Assembly at Trenton, New Jersey

Mr. Speaker and Gentlemen: I have just enjoyed the honor of a reception by the other branch of this Legislature, and I return to you and them my thanks for the reception which the people of New-Jersey have given, through their chosen representatives, to me, as the representative, for the time being, of the majesty of the people of the United States. I appropriate to myself very little of the demonstrations of respect with which I have been greeted. I think little should be given to any man, but that it should be a manifestation of adherence to the Union and the Constitution. . . .

And if I do my duty, and do right, you will sustain me, will you not? [Loud cheers and cries of "Yes," "Yes," "We will."] Received, as I am, by the members of a Legislature the majority of whom do not agree with me in political sentiments, I trust that I may have their assistance in piloting the ship of State through this voyage, surrounded by perils as it is; for, if it should suffer attack now, there will be no pilot ever needed for another voyage.

CW IV: 236–237

☆ ☆ ☆

In the following address, Lincoln noted that he was standing near the "consecrated hall" where the Constitution and the Declaration of Independence were written. Lincoln included a phrase from Psalm 137:5-6:

February 21, 1861

Reply to Mayor Alexander Henry at Philadelphia, Pennsylvania

I have never asked anything that does not breathe from those walls. All my political warfare has been in favor of the teachings coming forth from that sacred hall. ***May my right hand forget its cunning and my tongue cleave to the roof of my mouth****, if ever I prove false to those teachings.*

CW IV: 238–239

☆ ☆ ☆

Whistle-stop:

Wilmington, Delaware

☆ ☆ ☆

The following speech is a good example of Lincoln expressing his sublime motives upon entering the presidency.

February 22, 1861

Speech in Independence Hall, Philadelphia, Pennsylvania

I am filled with deep emotion at finding myself standing here in the place where were collected together the wisdom, the patriotism, the devotion to principle, from which sprang the institutions under which we live. You have kindly suggested to me that in my hands is the task of restoring peace to our distracted country. . . . I have often pondered over the dangers which were incurred by the men who assembled here and adopted that Declaration of Independence—I have pondered over the toils that were endured by the officers and soldiers of the army, who achieved that Independence. (Applause.) I have often inquired of myself, what great principle or idea it was that kept this Confederacy so long together.

Lincoln begins with an eloquent summation of the birthright of America—an idea he'd embraced since boyhood. Realistic, he states the present dangers. Obviously, dark clouds obscure that glorious vision.

Now, my friends, can this country be saved upon that basis? If it can, I will consider myself one of the happiest men in the world if I can help to save it. If it can't be saved upon that principle, it will be truly awful. But, if this country cannot be saved without giving up that principle—I was about to say I would rather be assassinated on this spot than to surrender it. (Applause)

Now, in my view of the present aspect of affairs, there is no need of bloodshed and war. There is no necessity for it. I am not in favor of such a course, and I may say in advance, there will be no blood shed unless it be forced upon the Government. . . .

*I have said nothing but what I am willing to live by, and, in the pleasure of **Almighty God**, die by.*

CW IV: 240–241

☆ ☆ ☆

Immediately after finishing the speech above, Lincoln was accompanied to a platform outside where he took part in the flag-raising ceremony. The new flag had thirty-four stars, the last for the newest state, Kansas.

February 22, 1861

Speech at the Flag-raising before Independence Hall, Philadelphia, Pennsylvania

FELLOW CITIZENS:—I am invited and called before you to participate in raising above Independence Hall the flag of our country, with an additional star upon it. (Cheers.) I propose now, in advance of performing this very pleasant and complimentary duty, to say a few words. I propose to say that when that flag was originally raised here it had but thirteen stars. I wish to call your attention to the fact, that, under the blessing of God, each additional star added to that flag has given additional prosperity and happiness to this country until it has advanced to its present condition; and its welfare in the future, as well as in the past, is in your hands.

CW IV: 241–242 (241)

☆ ☆ ☆

Whistle-stops

Leaman Place, Pennsylvania
Lancaster, Pennsylvania

☆ ☆ ☆

After Pennsylvania's governor spoke of the country's general unease and the mammoth task before Lincoln, the president-elect made this response:

February 22, 1861

Reply to Governor Andrew J. Curtin at Harrisburg, Pennsylvania

I feel that, under God, in the strength of the arms and wisdom of the heads of these masses, after all, must be my support. [Immense cheering.] As I have often had occasion to say, I repeat to you—I am quite sure I do not deceive myself when I tell you I bring to the work an honest heart; I dare not tell you that I bring a head sufficient for it. [A voice—"we are sure of that."] If my own strength should fail, I shall at least fall back upon these masses, who, I think, under any circumstances will not fail.

CW IV: 243–244

☆ ☆ ☆

Later that day, Lincoln used the flag-raising event in Philadelphia as an illustration. His words reveal one secret of his leadership ability: Even as president, he realized he was but an instrument performing a small part of an important action.

February 22, 1861

Address to the Pennsylvania General Assembly at Harrisburg

. . . Our friends . . . provided a magnificent flag of the country. They had arranged it so that I was given the honor of raising it to the head of its staff [applause]; and when it went up, I was pleased that it went to its place by the strength of my own feeble arm. When, according to the arrangement, the cord was pulled and it flaunted gloriously to the wind without an accident, in the light [bright] glowing sun-shine of the morning, I could not help hoping that there was in the entire success of that beautiful ceremony, at least something of an omen of what is to come. . . . In the whole of that proceeding I was a very humble instrument. I had not provided the flag; I had not made the arrangement for elevating it to its place; I had applied but a very small portion of even my feeble strength in raising it. In the whole transaction, I was in the hands of the people who had arranged it, and if I can have the same generous co-operation of the people of this nation, I think the flag of our country may yet be kept flaunting gloriously.

CW IV: 244–245

☆ ☆ ☆

Perhaps the most striking feature of Lincoln's addresses along the whistle-stop tour to Washington was the consistency of his position. Regardless of the audience, whether they were sympathetic to the South or to the Union cause, Lincoln expressed the same convictions. He reminded people that the Union could only be preserved through their efforts. He did not plan on interfering with those states that currently allowed slavery, though he vigorously opposed its expansion. He saw no need for war—though if force was used against the government it would have no choice but to fight back.

February 26, 1861

Reply to Committee of Congress Reporting the Electoral Count

With deep gratitude to my countrymen for this mark of their confidence; with a distrust of my own ability to perform the required duty under the most favorable circumstances, now rendered doubly difficult by existing national perils; yet with a firm reliance on the strength of our free government, and the ultimate loyalty of the people to the just principles upon which it is founded, and above all an unshaken faith in the Supreme Ruler of nations, I accept this trust. Be pleased to signify my acceptance to the respective Houses of Congress.

CW IV: 246

☆ ☆ ☆

The following statement is a classic example of the tact and wisdom Abraham Lincoln exhibited when entering the tense environment of Washington, D.C., in which the institution of slavery existed. His tact was worth a great army, for both Maryland and Washington, D.C., remained in the Union.

At the beginning of his administration, Lincoln was mercilessly condemned by abolitionists for being soft on slavery. Had he not remained firm in the position of this reply to the mayor, he would have failed to win the cooperation to hold the state of Maryland. Had the well-meaning abolitionists had their way, the cause of emancipation would have been lost before Lincoln could rally the forces of a democratic people's government together.

February 27, 1861

Reply to Mayor James G. Berret in Washington, D.C.

. . . It is the first time in my life . . . that I have said anything publicly within a region of country where the institution of slavery exists, . . . very much of the ill feeling that has existed and still exists between the people of the section from whence I came and the people here, is owing to a misunderstanding between each other which unhappily prevails. I therefore avail myself of this opportunity to assure you, Mr. Mayor, and all the gentlemen present, that I have not now, and never have had, any other than as kindly feelings towards you as to the people of my own section. I have not now, and never have

had, any disposition to treat you in any respect otherwise than as my own neighbors. . . . I hope, in a word, when we shall become better acquainted—and I say it with great confidence—we shall like each other the more.
CW IV: 246–247

☆ ☆ ☆

The inaugural journey was over. Lincoln had reached out to people all along the way, and they responded to him. They appreciated his humility upon entry into office, his confidence in the common people, and his absolute dependence upon the Supreme Being for help.

Yet Lincoln still faced some distrust and hostility, not only from the South, but from those in the border states (see map on page 182) and often from newspapers in the North. Benjamin Thomas notes that a hostile press in New York snickered at Lincoln's social errors and dubbed him a "gorilla" and a "baboon."[3]

Because Lincoln admitted that he would need divine help to guide the country through such a difficult time, some biographers believe that Lincoln demonstrated a lack of self-confidence and personal leadership. However, his two secretaries later wrote a ten-volume history of the life of Abraham Lincoln in which they summarized the expressions of their president on this inaugural journey:

> From that morning when, standing amid the falling snowflakes on the railway car at Springfield, he asked the prayers of his neighbors in those touching phrases whose echo rose that night in invocations from thousands of family altars, to the memorable hour when on the steps of the National Capitol he humbled himself before his Creator in the sublime words of the second inaugural, there is not an expression known to have come from his lips or his pen but proves that he held himself answerable in every act of his career to a more august tribunal than any on earth.[4]

CHAPTER 14

PRESIDENT OF A DIVIDED HOUSE

Americans take for granted the peaceful transition of power between political parties following an election. In fact, this transfer of authority is much more remarkable than we realize. It first happened in 1800, when Thomas Jefferson defeated President John Adams, the incumbent. Jefferson was not a member of the Federalist party, as were Adams and George Washington. In his book *A New Birth of Freedom: Abraham Lincoln and the Coming of the Civil War*, Harry Jaffa writes of how extraordinary that election was:

> We know of no example before 1800 of a government in which the instruments of political power passed from one set of hands to those of their most uncompromisingly hostile political rivals and opponents because of a free vote. . . . To the best of our knowledge, this was the first time in the history of the world that such a thing had happened.[1]

Whereas in 1800 the party that failed to win the election was willing to step out of office, in 1860 the Southern factions that could not win the election by the casting of ballots simply refused to remain part of the Union. Abraham Lincoln would be inaugurated president of a nation, but a great portion of that country was in rebellion, choosing bullets to try to win what they could not gain through the ballot box.

☆ ☆ ☆

Eighty percent of all eligible voters cast their ballots in the election of 1860. Though Abraham Lincoln received an overwhelming majority of electoral votes, he received less than 40 percent of the popular vote. Six weeks before his inauguration, Alabama, Florida, Georgia, Louisiana, Mississippi, South Carolina, and Texas had seceded from the United States. Thus Lincoln was inaugurated president of a "divided house."

The division was apparent, not only in the South, but also between pro- and anti-Lincoln forces in the North. For example, in New York slavery had been illegal since 1827, but a constitutional amendment to grant suffrage to free African Americans went down in defeat, seven to one. Though Lincoln carried New York State, in New York City, the largest city of the land, strong resistance imposed a roadblock for the incoming administration.

And as in most political battles, many people remained neutral, choosing to play it safe and not get involved. Many Southerners did not support slavery but worried about what would happen to their region under Lincoln's administration; some Northerners were willing to let the difficulties over slavery continue if that would prevent them from having to send their sons to war.

Still others were ardent abolitionists who demanded that Lincoln outlaw slavery immediately. Without question, Lincoln hated slavery passionately. The ironic and irritating fact to President Lincoln was that many who were zealously aligned with him in their desire to free the slaves did not help him in his efforts. The abolitionists could not understand why, upon taking the oath of office, Lincoln did not emancipate the slaves. Yet as president, Lincoln was obligated to follow the rule of law. He had no constitutional authority to order the slaves' emancipation. That would take an amendment to the Constitution, which permitted slavery.

That also explains why Lincoln enforced the Runaway Slave Act that forced the return of fugitive slaves. Lincoln considered it an evil law; however, when he took the oath of office he promised to support the Constitution, which allowed slavery. He could not conquer lawlessness by breaking laws himself. If he would abstain from upholding one law, how could he enforce others? Instead, his strategy was, first, to uphold existing laws at all cost—including those with which he disagreed—and, second, lead a people's government in changing the Constitution to prohibit slavery.

Some abolitionists blasted Lincoln for being more concerned about saving the Union than freeing the slaves. But should a captain of a capsizing ship be more concerned about saving the life of his grandson on board or about saving the ship? It's a ridiculous question. He cannot save the grandson unless he saves the ship. If he saves the ship, his grandson will be unharmed.

And, as we'll explore further, it was critical that Lincoln gain the trust of the border states—such as Missouri and Kentucky—and prevent them from joining the Confederacy. This was possible only if he kept his pledge to uphold the Constitution, even those parts with which he disagreed.

When Lincoln took office, Congress was splintered into several factions that reflected the divisions within the country:

- the radically antislavery
- the antislavery
- those who would accept the idea of the right of states to secede
- those who wanted to remain neutral
- those who would accept slavery
- those who favored slavery

President Lincoln's immediate focus was on preserving the nation. To him, the Union was still a Union though undergoing a state of rebellion. This was true even though, across the Potomac in Arlington, Virginia, he could see a waving Confederate flag. Lincoln's task would be to heal the schism so that the nation would no longer be divided.

☆ ☆ ☆

On March 4, 1861, outgoing president James Buchanan met his successor at Willard's Hotel. Together, they were driven in a carriage to the Capitol, where the new president would be sworn in. Seated in the front row of dignitaries—an important figure of support—sat Stephen Douglas. When Lincoln arose to deliver his inaugural address, he found no place to lay his top hat and cane. In a kind gesture, Douglas reached out to hold them for the president during his speech.

The boy who read about his country by firelight, the young man in whose heart burned the love of liberty, the country lawyer, the man of destiny rose to the podium. He would accept the sacred trust of leadership and lead his people in answering the question that he would ask at Gettysburg: Could "any nation so conceived, and so dedicated . . . long endure?" His first address as president helped explain to his countrymen where he planned to take them.

March 4, 1861

First Inaugural Address—Final Text

Fellow citizens of the United States:

In compliance with a custom as old as the government itself, I appear before you to address you briefly, and to take, in your presence, the oath prescribed by the Constitution of the United States, to be taken by the President "before he enters on the execution of his office. . . ."

. . . "I have no purpose, directly or indirectly, to interfere with the institution of slavery in the States where it exists. I believe I have no lawful right to do so, and I have no inclination to do so." . . .

In our nation's history, no problem resulted in so much soul searching as the question that faced Lincoln as he stood at the podium with his hand on a Bible: Could he, should he, take the oath to enforce a Constitution that allowed slavery? Some could take the oath and the office, then disregard the oath. Not Lincoln. The acceptance of the oath was a momentous act, and he was acutely conscious of the fact that the Constitution clearly required the return of fugitive slaves. The most solid and sacred principle of government to Lincoln was that we must be a nation of law. He could not choose which laws to uphold and which to break. Detestable as a law requiring the return of fugitive slaves was, it must be enforced until the law itself could be changed.

Like an attorney in a courtroom, Lincoln answered the perplexing question as to why the South did not have the right to secede. First, he reviewed the rights of the states, laying out his reasoning regarding the federal government and the Constitutional rights of states:

"Resolved, *That the maintenance inviolate of the rights of the States, and especially the right of each State to order and control its own domestic institutions according to its own judgment exclusively, is essential to that balance of power on which the perfection and endurance of our political fabric depend; and we denounce the lawless invasion by armed force of the soil of any State or Territory, no matter under what pretext, as among the gravest of crimes." . . .*

I take the official oath to-day, with no mental reservations, and with no purpose to construe the Constitution or laws, by any hypercritical rules.

Having taken the oath to support the Constitution, he could not retract. Those words would cause him agonizing, sleepless nights. However, by his promise, he had a chance of holding the allegiance of the border states. And holding the Union together was clearly a top priority for Lincoln.

I hold, that in contemplation of universal law, and of the Constitution, the Union of these States is perpetual. Perpetuity is implied, if not expressed, in the fundamental law of all national governments. It is safe to assert that no government proper, ever had a provision in its organic law for its own termination. Continue to execute all the express provisions of our national Constitution, and the Union will endure forever—it being impossible to destroy it, except by some action not provided for in the instrument itself.

Again, if the United States be not a government proper, but an association of States in the nature of contract merely, can it, as a contract, be peaceably unmade, by less than all the parties who made it? One party to a contract may violate it—break it, so to speak; but does it not require all to lawfully rescind it? . . .

The Union is much older than the Constitution. It was formed in fact, by the Articles of Association in 1774. It was matured and continued by the Declaration of Independence in 1776. It was further matured and the faith of all the then thirteen States expressly plighted and engaged that it should be perpetual, by the Articles of Confederation in 1778. And finally, in 1787, one of the declared objects for ordaining and establishing the Constitution, was "to form a more perfect union."

But if destruction of the Union, by one, or by a part only, of the States, be lawfully possible, the Union is less *perfect than before the Constitution, having lost the vital element of perpetuity.*

It follows from these views that no State, upon its own mere motion, can lawfully get out of the Union,—that resolves *and* ordinances *to that effect are legally void; and that acts of violence, within any State or States, against the authority of the United States, are insurrectionary or revolutionary, according to circumstances.*

I therefore consider that, in view of the Constitution and the laws, the Union is unbroken; and, to the extent of my ability, I shall take care, as the Constitution itself expressly enjoins upon me, that the laws of the Union be faithfully executed in all the States. Doing this I deem to be only a simple duty on my part; and I shall perform it, so far as practicable, unless my rightful masters, the American people, shall withhold the requisite means, or, in some authoritative manner, direct the contrary. I trust this will not be regarded as a menace, but only as the declared purpose of the Union that it will *constitutionally defend, and maintain itself. . . .*

The Southern states that had seceded declared that the Constitution had been enacted as a compact of sovereign states that could leave the Union at their will. The federal government, they said, had only limited power granted it by the states. Senator John Calhoun of South Carolina was the exponent of this theory. On the surface, the argument sounded formidable. However, in this message, as well as in his July 4, 1861, message to a special session of Congress, Lincoln builds a solid case for a permanent union.

Plainly, the central idea of secession, is the essence of anarchy. A majority, held in restraint by constitutional checks, and limitations, and always changing easily, with deliberate changes of popular opinions and sentiments, is the only true sovereign of a free people. . . . The rule of a minority, as a permanent arrangement, is wholly inadmissable; . . .

This country, with its institutions, belongs to the people who inhabit it. Whenever they shall grow weary of the existing government, they can exercise their constitutional *right of amending it, or their* revolutionary *right to dismember, or overthrow it. I can not be ignorant of the fact that many worthy, and patriotic citizens are desirous of having the national constitution amended. While I make no recommendation of amendments, I fully recognize the rightful authority of the people over the whole subject, . . . and I should, under existing circumstances, favor, rather than oppose, a fair oppertunity being afforded the people to act upon it. . . .*

The Chief Magistrate derives all his authority from the people, and they have conferred none upon him to fix terms for the separation of the States. The people themselves can do this also if they choose; but the executive, as such, has nothing to do with it. His duty is to administer the present government, as it came to his hands, and to transmit it, unimpaired by him, to his successor.

Why should there not be a patient confidence in the ultimate justice of the people? Is there any better, or equal hope, in the world? In our present differences, is either party without faith of being in the right? If the

Almighty Ruler of nations, with his eternal truth and justice, be on your side of the North, or on yours of the South, that truth, and that justice, will surely prevail, by the judgment of this great tribunal, the American people.

By the frame of the government under which we live, this same people have wisely given their public servants but little power for mischief; and have, with equal wisdom, provided for the return of that little to their own hands at very short intervals.

While the people retain their virtue, and vigilence, no administration, by any extreme of wickedness or folly, can very seriously injure the government, in the short space of four years.

Having made the strongest arguments in his persuasive intellectual power, Lincoln lowered his tone, ceased to reason, and gently tugged the heartstrings of those who disagreed. He asked for time and quiet, unhurried contemplation.

My countrymen, one and all, think calmly and well, *upon this whole subject. Nothing valuable can be lost by taking time. . . . If it were admitted that you who are dissatisfied, hold the right side in the dispute, there still is no single good reason for precipitate action. Intelligence, patriotism, Christianity, and a firm reliance on Him, who has never yet forsaken this favored land, are still competent to adjust, in the best way, all our present difficulty.*

In your *hands, my dissatisfied fellow countrymen, and not in* mine, *is the momentous issue of civil war. The government will not assail* you. *You can have no conflict, without being yourselves the aggressors.* You *have no* ***oath registered in Heaven*** *to destroy the government, while* I *shall have the* ***most solemn one*** *to "preserve, protect and defend" it. . . .*

Some scholars suggest that Lincoln used religious phrases with rational rather than spiritual convictions. When he voiced the above-emphasized words, he was either speaking words of sincerity or the words of a hypocrite. When he said that his oath was registered in heaven, he was either emphasizing the solemnity with which he took the oath—or following in the tradition of Judas Iscariot, another hypocrite.

We are not enemies, but friends. We must not be enemies. Though passion may have strained, it must not break our bonds of affection. The mystic chords of memory, stretching from every battle-field, and patriot grave, to every living heart and hearthstone, all over this broad land, will yet swell the chorus of the Union, when again touched, as surely they will be, by the better angels of our nature.

CW IV: 262–271, Final Text (262–266, 268–271)

The words were momentous: "I take the official oath to-day, with no mental reservations, and with no purpose to construe the Constitution or laws, by *any hypercritical rules*" (emphasis mine). Those words would have resounding implications in his policies regarding slavery. Representing a serious trust, the words would cause him agonizing criticism. He would stand tall, firmly committed to law and obedience to the Constitution, and lead a people's government.

☆ ☆ ☆

A number of states, including New York, Pennsylvania, Massachusetts, Illinois, Minnesota, and Oregon, sent delegations to meet with the newly sworn-in president.

March 5, 1861

Reply to Pennsylvania Delegation

We should bear this in mind, and act in such a way as to say nothing insulting or irritating. I would inculcate this idea, so that we may not, like Pharisees, set ourselves up to be better than other people.

CW IV: 273–274 (273)

The Pharisees, who often were in conflict with Christ, were proud of their rigid laws and felt superior to other persons.

☆ ☆ ☆

The day after his inauguration, Lincoln received word from Fort Sumter off the South Carolina coast that Major Robert Anderson had supplies for no more than six weeks. If more supplies were not sent, he and his troops would have to abandon the fort. The highly respected general in chief of the Army, Winfield Scott, and most advisors reasoned that it was too late to save the fort and advised surrender. President Lincoln put his foot down; the whole foot at one time, as one would do who had "learned to walk on plowed ground." He would not surrender.

Lincoln hoped to resolve the situation peacefully. However, the

Confederate authorities would not accept a federal presence at the fort under any terms. When Anderson refused to evacuate, Confederate troops began firing on the fort. Two days later, Anderson and his men surrendered. The Civil War had begun.

☆ ☆ ☆

Elmer Ellsworth was an infantry-drilling expert who studied law in the Lincoln-Herndon law office. Lincoln had become attached to him as though he were a son, taking him along on the inaugural journey. When Confederate troops advanced into Alexandria and were within sight of Washington, Ellsworth became angered by the sight of a Confederate flag flying atop a hotel. He ran in and cut it down but was killed by the hotel's owner as he headed back down the stairs. Ellsworth was one of the very first casualties of the war, causing Lincoln sorrow that merely previewed the constant bereavement that would become his daily burden.

May 25, 1861

To Ephraim D. and Phoebe Ellsworth

To the Father and Mother of Col. Elmer E. Ellsworth:

My dear Sir and Madam, In the untimely loss of your noble son, our affliction here, is scarcely less than your own. So much of promised usefulness to one's country, and of bright hopes for one's self and friends, have rarely been so suddenly dashed, as in his fall. In size, in years, and in youthful appearance, a boy only, his power to command men, was surpassingly great. This power, combined with a fine intellect, an indomitable energy, and a taste altogether military, constituted in him, as seemed to me, the best natural talent, in that department, I ever knew. And yet he was singularly modest and deferential in social intercourse. My acquaintance with him began less than two years ago; yet through the latter half of the intervening period, it was as intimate as the disparity of our ages, and my engrossing engagements, would permit. To me, he appeared to have no indulgences or pastimes; and I never heard him utter a profane, or an intemperate word. What was conclusive of his good heart, he never forgot his parents. The honors he labored for so laudably, and, in the sad end, so gallantly gave his life, he meant for them, no less than for himself.

In the hope that it may be no intrusion upon the sacredness of your sorrow, I have ventured to address you this tribute to the memory of my young friend, and your brave and early fallen child.

May God give you that consolation which is beyond all earthly power. Sincerely your friend in a common affliction—A. Lincoln

CW IV: 385–386

☆ ☆ ☆

Though Lincoln's opponent in two Senate races and one presidential race, Stephen Douglas backed Lincoln from the time he realized he himself did not have the support to be elected president. Once Lincoln was in office, Douglas was a tireless proponent of holding the Union together. On April 25, 1861, Douglas gave a "Preserve the Flag" address to the Illinois legislature, which united Illinois and encouraged thousands to enlist in the Union army. Not long after, he fell ill with typhoid fever. When he died on June 3, Lincoln draped the White House in black and called for national mourning.

It is to Douglas's credit that he gave his last efforts to helping his lifetime antagonist—and to Lincoln's that he was able to reach out, even to his adversaries, and gain their support in the mammoth task of preserving the Union.

☆ ☆ ☆

During the first four months of Lincoln's administration, his critics (including members of his cabinet) continually badgered the president to lay out his policies in dealing with the Confederacy. Meanwhile, he was quietly producing a masterpiece. Fittingly it was presented in Special Session to Congress on July 4 in his first year as president. This truly great address offers many succinctly crafted statements for students interested in government and especially the constitutional questions of the secession. Given to a truly "divided house" nation, Lincoln expressed his feelings to those at the heart of the rebellion and sounded forth to all generations of all nations the birthright of America.

July 4, 1861

Message to Congress in Special Session

Fellow-citizens of the Senate and House of Representatives:

This issue embraces more than the fate of these United States.

It presents to the whole family of man, the question, whether a constitutional republic, or a democracy—a government of the people, by the same people—can, or cannot, maintain its territorial integrity, against its own domestic foes. It presents the question, whether discontented individuals, too few in numbers to control administration, according to organic law, in any case, can always, upon the pretences made in this case, or on any other pretences, or arbitrarily, without any pretence, break up their Government, and thus practically put an end to free government upon the earth. It forces us to ask: "Is there, in all republics, this inherent, and fatal weakness?" "Must a government, of necessity, be too strong *for the liberties of its own people, or too* weak *to maintain its own existence?"*

Lincoln the attorney had a keen ability to make precise statements, cutting to the heart of an argument. The quote emphasized above is a question relevant to Americans today anxious to preserve our liberties in the face of new enemies. Lincoln had succinctly stated the dilemma: In wartime, a democratic government must somehow avoid two extremes: either being too strong to respect the liberties of its people or too weak to forcefully defend them.

For Lincoln, this challenge was playing out dramatically in Baltimore just forty miles from the White House. Maryland was a key state in the defense of the Union, for rather than seceding with other slave states, Maryland had declared its neutrality. It was an important route for federal troops coming to the defense of Washington or marching south to confront Confederate troops. However, Maryland was teeming with anti-Union forces dedicated to blowing up bridges, uprooting train tracks, and disrupting the military's progress in any way possible. Lincoln's government had the difficult task of protecting the rights of its citizens in that state—many of whom were actively supporting the enemy.

The situation was exasperating for President Lincoln. The city was falling into utter lawlessness—marching troops were fired upon, telegraph lines were cut, and supplies were torched. The chief of the Baltimore police department urged that railroad bridges north of Baltimore be burned in order to prevent more federal troops from entering the city.

Convinced he must take strong action, Lincoln reluctantly moved to suspend habeas corpus, a protection of Americans' civil liberties designed to prevent someone from being unlawfully detained or held without given cause. The Constitution (Article 1, Section 9) prevents the suspension of habeas corpus except "in cases of Rebellion or Invasion [when] the public safety may require it." Lincoln's decision did not sit well with Roger Taney, then chief justice of the Supreme Court.

William Rehnquist, who served as the court's chief justice from 1986 to 2005, wrote an account of the long-running battle between Lincoln and Taney in his book *All the Laws but One: Civil Liberties in Wartime*, a title taken from Lincoln's July Fourth address. In his book, Rehnquist says that the Constitution was silent as to which branch of the government might exercise the authority to suspend the writ but that "the writ, which had been fashioned 'with such extreme tenderness of the citizens' liberty,' could, as interpreted by Taney, allow 'all the laws, but one, to go unexecuted, and the government itself go to pieces, lest that one be violated.'"

Rehnquist added: "Here was Lincoln the advocate at his very best. There was no reference to the difficult constitutional issue but only the posing of a starkly simple question that seemed to admit of but one answer."[2]

In his July 4 speech, President Lincoln noted the hypocrisy of citizens who would demand their habeas corpus rights while rebelling against their government and recklessly breaking other laws in the process. He asked:

> . . . *Are all the laws,* but one, *to go unexecuted, and the government itself go to pieces, lest that one be violated? Even in such a case, would not the official oath be broken, if the government should be overthrown, when it was believed that disregarding the single law, would tend to preserve it?* . . .
>
> *In a word, the people will save their government, if the government itself, will do its part, only indifferently well.* . . .
>
> *With rebellion thus sugar-coated, they have been drugging the public mind of their section for more than thirty years; and, until at length, they have brought many good men to a willingness to take up arms against the government.* . . .
>
> . . . *They make the point, that the one, because it is a minority, may rightfully do, what the others, because they are a majority, may not rightfully do. These politicians are subtle, and profound, on the rights of minorities. They are not partial to that power which made the Constitution, and speaks from the preamble, calling itself "We, the People."* . . .

Lincoln answered those who defended the right of the Southern states to secede.

Our adversaries have adopted some Declarations of Independence; in which, unlike the good old one, penned by Jefferson, they omit the words "all men are created equal." Why? They have adopted a temporary national constitution, in the preamble of which, unlike our good old one, signed by Washington, they omit "We, the People," and substitute "We, the deputies of the sovereign and independent States." Why? Why this deliberate pressing out of view, the rights of men, and the authority of the people?

This is essentially a People's contest. On the side of the Union, it is a struggle for maintaining in the world, that form, and substance of government, whose leading object is, to elevate the condition of men—to lift artificial weights from all shoulders—to clear the paths of laudable pursuit for all—to afford all, an unfettered start, and a fair chance, in the race of life. Yielding to partial, and temporary departures, from necessity, this is the leading object of the government for whose existence we contend.

"Elevate the condition of men"—this was President Lincoln's vision from boyhood to his last breath. It was his vision of our American birthright, entrusted to our country to give leadership to all the nations of the world. He continued:

Our popular government has often been called an experiment. Two points in it, our people have already settled—the successful establishing, *and the successful* administering *of it. One still remains—its successful* maintenance *against a formidable [internal] attempt to overthrow it. It is now for them to demonstrate to the world, that those who can fairly carry an election, can also suppress a rebellion—that ballots are the rightful, and peaceful, successors of bullets; and that when ballots have fairly, and constitutionally, decided, there can be no successful appeal, back to bullets; that there can be no successful appeal, except to ballots themselves, at succeeding elections. Such will be a great lesson of peace; teaching men that what they cannot take by an election, neither can they take it by a war—teaching all, the folly of being the beginners of a war.*

Lincoln concluded with words of confidence and strength, trusting in Providence for help:

It was with the deepest regret that the Executive found the duty of employing the war-power, in defense of the government, forced upon him. He could but perform this duty, or surrender the existence of the government. No compromise, by public servants, could, in this case, be a cure; not that compromises are not often proper, but that no popular government can long survive a marked precedent, that those who carry an election, can only save the government from immediate destruction, by giving up the main point, upon which the people gave the election. The people themselves, and not their servants, can safely reverse their own deliberate decisions. . . . In full view of his great responsibility, he has, so far, done what he has deemed his duty. You will now, according to your own judgment, perform yours. He sincerely hopes that your views, and your action, may so accord with his, as to assure all faithful citizens, who have been disturbed in their rights, of a certain, and speedy restoration to them, under the Constitution, and the laws.

And having thus chosen our course, without guile, and with pure purpose, let us renew our ***trust in God****, and go forward without fear, and with manly hearts.*

CW IV: 421–441 (426, 430, 432–433, 436–441)

It was indeed appropriate that this speech with its lofty American ideals was delivered on the Fourth of July, 1861.

☆ ☆ ☆

Barely four months after the Inauguration, in the latter part of July of 1861, an overconfident Northern army advanced to the battle at Manassas Junction, Virginia. Urged on with confident cries of "On to Richmond," they were decisively defeated and driven back into Washington. There were two battles of Manassas, the other a year later, and both were called Bull Run. We turn to Benjamin Thomas to give the desolate picture:

> Beaten soldiers dropped exhausted in the streets, slumped down on the steps of houses, or staggered on like sleepwalkers. . . . Looking out of the White House windows, Lincoln could see it all.
>
> The President pieced together the story of the rout—coats, hats, boots, and canteens thrown aside; haversacks spilling shirts,

socks, and tins of jam along the road; broken wagons, abandoned guns and rifles, the wild panic of flight. . . .

The enemy did not pursue in the heavy rain. . . .

Horace Greeley wrote Lincoln that he had just passed his seventh sleepless night. What could he do to help? "If it is best for the country and for mankind that we make peace with the rebels at once and on their own terms, do not shrink even from that."

Lincoln had no thought of peace on Confederate terms, but he knew now that this war would not be won in any summer excursion. Walt Whitman, with a poet's sensitivity, understood how the catastrophe at Bull Run must have afflicted Lincoln. "But the hour, the day, the night pass'd," he wrote, "and whatever returns, a day, a night like that can never again return. The President, recovering himself, begins that very night—sternly, rapidly sets about the task of reorganizing his forces, and placing himself in position for future and surer work. If there was nothing else of Abraham Lincoln for history to stamp him with, it is enough to send him with his wreath to the memory of all future time, that he endured that hour, that day, bitterer than gall—indeed a crucifixion day—that it did not conquer him—that he unflinchingly stemm'd it, and resolv'd to lift himself and the Union out of it."[3]

☆ ☆ ☆

During this horrible time, Lincoln issued the first of many proclamations, calling on all Americans to join him in interceding to their heavenly Father for assistance. His reminder that the "fear of the LORD is the beginning of wisdom" is found in Job 28:28, Psalm 111:10, and Proverbs 9:10. He also reminded them that God, in Hebrews 4:16, invites us to come before His throne of grace.

August 12, 1861

Proclamation of a National Fast Day

By the President of the United States of America:

A Proclamation.

Whereas a joint Committee of both Houses of Congress has waited on the President of the United States, and requested him to "recommend a day of public humiliation, prayer and fasting, to be observed by the people of the United States with religious solemnities, and the offering of fervent supplications to Almighty God for the safety and welfare of these States, His blessings on their arms, and a speedy restoration of peace:"—

And whereas it is fit and becoming in all people, at all times, to acknowledge and revere the **Supreme Government of God**; to bow in humble submission to his chastisements; to confess and deplore their sins and transgressions in the full conviction that the **fear of the Lord is the beginning of wisdom**; and to pray, with all fervency and contrition, for the pardon of their past offences, and for a blessing upon their present and prospective action:

And whereas, when our own beloved Country, once, by the **blessing of God**, united, prosperous and happy, is now afflicted with faction and civil war, it is peculiarly fit for us to recognize the **hand of God** in this terrible visitation, and in sorrowful remembrance of our own faults and crimes as a nation and as individuals, to humble ourselves before Him, and to pray for His mercy,—to pray that we may be spared further punishment, though most justly deserved; that our arms may be blessed and made effectual for the re-establishment of law, order and peace, throughout the wide extent of our country; and that the inestimable boon of civil and religious liberty, earned under His guidance and blessing, by the labors and sufferings of our fathers, may be restored in all its original excellence:—

Therefore, I, Abraham Lincoln, President of the United States, do appoint the last Thursday in September next, as a day of humiliation, prayer and fasting for all the people of the nation. And I do earnestly recommend to all the People, and especially to all ministers and teachers of religion of all denominations, and to all heads of families, to observe and keep that day according to their several creeds and modes of worship, in all humility and with all religious solemnity, to the end that the united prayer of the nation may ascend to the **Throne of Grace** and bring down plentiful blessings upon our Country.

In testimony whereof, I have hereunto set my hand, and caused the Seal of the United States to be affixed, this 12th. [L.S.] day of August A.D. 1861, and of the Independence of the United States of America the 86th.

By the President: ABRAHAM LINCOLN

WILLIAM H. SEWARD, Secretary of State.

CW IV: 482–483

In the early years of the war, Lincoln received many more discouraging reports from the battlefield. On several other occasions he issued proclamations urging his countrymen to humble themselves before the Almighty and seek His mercy. It is clear from his writings that he also never lost sight of America's strengths and held fast to her ideals. The advantages the American system gives to the average worker was a theme he turned to repeatedly, including in his first annual message to Congress.

In December, he gave Congress what we now call the State of the Union Address. With the overwhelming burden of the Civil War that was not going well, we would assume that war would make up the main part of the address. The president's annual message, however, reminds us of the ocean of administrative detail that was his as the chief executive officer. The entire address fills eighteen pages in *The Collected Works.*

December 3, 1861

Annual Message to Congress

Fellow Citizens of the Senate and House of Representatives:

In the midst of unprecedented political troubles, we have cause of great gratitude to God for unusual good health, and most abundant harvests.

President Lincoln then discussed many issues, including:

- commerce with other nations
- railroad construction
- protection of American vessels against pirates
- Supreme Court vacancies
- relations with Native American tribes
- natural resources in the territories
- a colonization plan for emancipated slaves

Having spoken briefly on all these topics and more, Lincoln turned to the issues of civil unrest. First, he spoke of the improved situation in Maryland. His tough stance had yielded good results.

Maryland was made to seem *against the Union. Our soldiers were assaulted, bridges were burned, and railroads torn up, within her limits; and we were many days, at one time, without the ability to bring a single regiment over her soil to the capital. Now, her bridges and railroads are repaired and open to the government; she already gives seven regiments to the cause of the Union and none to the enemy. . . .*

These three States of Maryland, Kentucky, and Missouri, neither of which would promise a single soldier at first, have now an aggregate of not less than forty thousand in the field. . . . After a somewhat bloody struggle of months, winter closes on the Union people of western Virginia, leaving them masters of their own country.

President Abraham Lincoln ended the address looking past the difficulties of the present to a great American future.

The struggle of today, is not altogether for today—it is for a vast future also. With a reliance on Providence, all the more firm and earnest, let us proceed in the great task which events have devolved upon us.

CW V: 35–53 (35, 49–50, 53)

☆ ☆ ☆

Two letters Lincoln wrote to heads of state in early 1862 give us a glimpse into Lincoln's diplomacy skills. The first was written to a grief-stricken Queen Victoria after her husband, Prince Albert, died at age forty-three. Interestingly, just that fall the prince had helped defuse a tense situation, when the Union had angered the British by stopping a British ship that was carrying Confederate emissaries overseas.

February 1, 1862

To Queen Victoria

To Her Majesty Victoria,
Queen of the United Kingdom
of Great Britain and Ireland,

Great and Good Friend: By a letter from your son, His Royal Highness, the Prince of Wales, which has just been received, I am informed of the overwhelming affliction which has fallen upon Your Majesty, by the untimely death of His Royal Highness the late Prince Consort, Prince Albert, of Saxe Coburg. This condolence may not be altogether ineffectual, since we are sure it emanates from motives and natural affection. I do not dwell upon it, however, because I know that the ***Divine hand that has wounded, is the only one that can heal****: And so, commending Your Majesty and the*

Prince Royal, the Heir Apparent, and all your afflicted family to the tender mercies of God, I remain Your Good Friend, Abraham Lincoln.

CW V: 117–118

Lincoln offered a beautiful sentiment appropriate for an expression of sorrow. The emphasized words above could be a paraphrase of any of these Scriptures: "I wound, and I heal: neither is there any that can deliver out of my hand" (Deuteronomy 32:39); "He maketh sore, and bindeth up: he woundeth, and his hands make whole" (Job 5:18); and "He hath torn, and he will heal us; he hath smitten, and he will bind us up" (Hosea 6:1).

☆ ☆ ☆

During such a dark time, the King of Siam perhaps offered Lincoln some comic relief by offering to supply a stock of elephants to be raised in America. Lincoln graciously demurred, while thanking him for the other gifts he had sent.

February 3, 1862

To the King of Siam

Great Good Friend: I have received Your Majesty's two letters. . . .

I have also received in good condition the royal gifts . . . a sword of costly materials and exquisite workmanship; a photographic likeness of Your Majesty and of Your Majesty's beloved daughter; and also two elephants' tusks of length and magnitude such as indicate that they could have belonged only to an animal which was a native of Siam.

I appreciate most highly Your Majesty's tender of good offices in forwarding to this Government a stock from which a supply of elephants might be raised on our own soil. This Government would not hesitate to avail itself of so generous an offer if the object were one which could be made practically useful in the present condition of the United States.

Meantime, wishing for Your Majesty a long and happy life, and for the generous and emulous People of Siam the highest possible prosperity, I commend both to the blessing of ***Almighty God****. Your Good Friend,* Abraham Lincoln.

CW V: 125–126

☆ ☆ ☆

Early in 1862, Abraham and Mary Lincoln were hit with a heartbreaking personal loss. Eleven-year-old Willie died, probably of several maladies, in the White House on February 20. The funeral, officiated by Rev. Phineas Gurley, was held in the East Room of the White House. Both Abraham and Mary were devastated.

Coping with the death of another son would have been difficult enough, but Lincoln also had to deal with a war that wasn't going well and the continued badgering from partisan groups. Amazingly, Lincoln did not crumble but actually emerged from this period of anguish with increased strength.

Biographer Nathaniel W. Stephenson recounts how the president patiently faced the conflicts and the raging partisan groups. When Congress was dismissed in midyear, all admitted that the president was having his way. Stephenson writes:

> Out of this strange period of intolerable confusion, a gigantic figure had at last emerged. The outer and the inner Lincoln had fused. He was now a coherent personality, masterful in spite of his gentleness, with his own peculiar fashion of self-reliance, having a policy of his own devising, his colors nailed upon the masthead.[4]

CHAPTER 15

THE DIVINE WILL

If John Bunyan had been writing about Lincoln in the style of *Pilgrim's Progress*, he would have told of the young pilgrim who drove an oxen-drawn wagon out of the wilderness, lingering for a time in the City of Skepticism. There he absorbed the philosophies of distinguished writers who dismissed Abe's early faith as passé. Cynical questions quickly became stubbornly rooted. Bunyan would have noted that the ideas implanted in the City of Skepticism plagued Lincoln, and in later years made the wading of the River of Sorrow doubly difficult.

As a child, Abe Lincoln had been unable to understand the milk sickness plague that took his mother and her aunt and uncle, three of the very few persons he knew. His only other relative, other than his father, was his sister, Sarah, and she died in childbirth just before he turned nineteen.

When he and Mary lost their son Edward, it would have been quite natural for Lincoln to become bitter. Fortunately, at just that time, he came upon Dr. Smith and his book, *The Christian's Defense* (see chapter 7). His faith began to revive as he read the Bible and began attending the church Smith led.

By the time Lincoln reached the presidency, he seemed firmly convinced that God was guiding him. Therefore, taking the oath of the presidency was a solemn trust. With the patriotic flame ignited from childhood guiding his steps, he was committed to leading his country to the greatness of a "birthright" of democracy that would spread to other nations of the world. He stated that he considered himself to be an instrument of a Divine Hand.

Occasionally in his writings Lincoln used the word *eternal*, a word he didn't use lightly, since it implies metaphysical concepts and the sovereignty of God. He was conscious of the report that he would make someday to his own Maker. That view explains, at least in part, his decision in February 1862 to delay by a few weeks the execution of a New York man who had received the death penalty. Lincoln wanted to give him time to prepare for the "awful change" that awaited him. He wrote: "It becomes my painful duty to admonish the prisoner that, relinquishing all expectation of pardon by human authority, he refer himself alone to the mercy of the 'common God and Father of all men.'"[1]

At that time, Abraham and Mary Lincoln were enduring a succession of losses of their own. The sickening tragedy of war struck them in the first days of the conflict, when one of the first casualties was young Colonel E. E. Ellsworth, who had been studying law in the Lincoln-Herndon law firm and had come to Washington on the inaugural train (see chapter 14). Three months later came the fatality of Colonel Edward Baker, after whom Abraham and Mary had named their second son. Elected to the U.S. Senate by the people of Oregon, Baker was the only sitting senator killed in the Civil War, struck down at the Battle of Ball's Bluff.

As detailed in the last chapter, the Lincolns' third son, William, died on February 20, 1862. And only Lincoln could comfort Mary in the loss of a brother, a brother-in-law, and other members of the Todd family as they died wearing uniforms of gray. The nation, grieving over the steady stream of casualties, could not fully realize the bitter gall in the cup of their leader.

The first Battle of Manassas, also called Bull Run, had been a disheartening defeat (see chapter 14). A year later, there was an even more discouraging loss at the same Manassas Junction. As an expected victory turned into bitter defeat because of discord among his commanders, Lincoln was utterly distraught. A footnote in *The Collected Works* reads: "Lincoln seems to have plumbed to his lowest depths, and was reported by Attorney General Bates to have 'seemed wrung by the bitterest anguish . . . he felt almost ready to hang himself.'"[2]

On July 22, 1862, Lincoln read the first draft of the Emancipation Proclamation to his cabinet. One cabinet member warned Lincoln that it would cost him the next election. Certainly it would spark riots.

Old dragons raised their heads with old cynical questions. Willie's death, in particular, caused Lincoln and his wife psychological and emotional torture.

☆ ☆ ☆

We don't have detailed records of Lincoln's thoughts during this time. Yet undoubtedly in the silence of the long nights, from every creak of the furniture, every stirring of air, there pressed the question—*Why?*

Is there a God who sees the daily casualty lists?

Perhaps there is a creator God, but does He care? Does He see the terrible suffering, the amputated limbs, the widows and orphans?

Could it be that the skeptics and infidels were right? Eleven years earlier when his son Eddy died, Lincoln had fought his way through the tears in his personal sorrows and clutched the promises of God that the spirit survives the body.

The pain was renewed with Willie's death and only compounded by overwhelming national problems. Tens of thousands of men were being butchered—for what? It was an absolutely needless, suicidal war as a divided nation fought itself. If one side was in the right, wouldn't God intervene on its behalf? In this war, the tide seemed to turn in favor of one side, only to revert to the other.

The doubts of his young manhood surely echoed again through his mind: How can a God of omnipotent power and omniscient wisdom allow this carnage to go on?

☆ ☆ ☆

Francis Carpenter was the young artist commissioned to paint the historic signing of the Emancipation Proclamation. He later remembered:

> Passing through the main hall of the domestic apartment on one of those days, I met [Lincoln], clad in a long morning wrapper, pacing back and forth a narrow passage leading to one of the windows, his hands behind him, great black rings under his eyes, his head bent forward upon his breast—altogether such a picture of the effects of sorrow, care, and anxiety as would have melted the hearts of the worst of his adversaries, who so mistakenly applied to him the epithets of tyrant and usurper.[3]

Undaunted, President Lincoln stood when a lesser man would have folded. He would have been well aware of a few men profiled in the Bible who had stood up to unyielding pressure. He knew of seventeen-year-old

Joseph, who kept his faith despite constant mistreatment and unjust imprisonment. He also remembered Job, who lost his family and all his possessions. Covered with repulsive sores and ostracized from his village to a pile of ashes, Job endured his testing and emerged like precious metal refined in the furnace.

In at least three speeches given on the inaugural journey between Springfield and Washington, Lincoln mentioned the "God who has never forsaken our land." In his inaugural address, he had rallied support with the words: "Intelligence, patriotism, Christianity, and a firm reliance on Him, who has never yet forsaken this favored land, are still competent to adjust, in the best way, all our present difficulty."[4]

As Lincoln had led his people into the terrible conflict, he had been confident that God would not forsake the Union. Yet now it seemed as if the God upon whom he had depended was not helping them. *Had his assurance that God would not forsake His people been idle words?*

Abraham Lincoln could have retreated to the thinking of his days as a skeptic and argued that God was either unwilling or incapable of helping the cause of the Union. Instead, rising in faith to a God who cares, he rejected the reasoning that the Almighty was unconcerned, concluding instead that we humans do not always understand God's will.

Previously, he had asked what the will of God was. Now he accepted the Almighty's will with a new understanding that we humans—like Joseph and Job—cannot always understand it.

President Lincoln was leaving the shaky ground of believing that God would help His people because they were right and arriving on the solid ground of accepting the will of God even when he could not understand it. He was beginning to sort out the great themes of the Second Inaugural. In that great address, Lincoln would have the nerve—*yes, the nerve*—to dare express that the North might share some of the guilt over the slavery question. Lincoln would say that it is characteristic of people to see the sins of others more than their own.

☆ ☆ ☆

In the quiet of the night Lincoln sat at his desk. As he pondered all that was going on—his grief over the death of his son, the struggle over how to handle the Emancipation Proclamation, and the infighting of generals that was causing disastrous defeats—Lincoln faced the great question: *What is the will of God?*

The lonely, embattled man then wrote:

September 1862

Meditation on the Divine Will

The will of God prevails. In great contests each party claims to act in accordance with the will of God. Both may *be, and one* must *be wrong. God can not be* for, *and* against *the same thing at the same time. In the present civil war it is quite possible that God's purpose is something different from the purpose of either party—and yet the human instrumentalities, working just as they do, are of the best adaptation to effect His purpose. I am almost ready to say this is probably true—that God wills this contest, and wills that it shall not end yet. By his mere quiet power, on the minds of the now contestants, He could have either* saved *or* destroyed *the Union without a human contest. Yet the contest began. And having begun He could give the final victory to either side any day. Yet the contest proceeds.*

CW V: 403–404

After Lincoln's assassination, one of his secretaries, John Hay, found the "Meditation on the Divine Will," seen by no other mortal while President Lincoln lived.

John Hay and John Nicolay, Lincoln's other secretary, give us a glimpse into Lincoln's intentions when he sat down to write this short piece.

> It is a paper which Mr. Lincoln wrote in September, 1862, while his mind was burdened with the weightiest question of his life, the weightiest with which this century has had to grapple. Wearied with all the considerations of law and of expediency with which he had been struggling for two years, he retired within himself and tried to bring some order in his thoughts by rising above the wrangling of men and of parties, and pondering the relations of human government to the Divine. In this frame of mind, absolutely detached from any earthly considerations, he wrote this meditation. It has never been published. It was not written to be seen of men. It was penned in the awful sincerity of a perfectly honest soul trying to bring itself into closer communion with its Maker.[5]

Considering his long struggle toward faith in the Bible and in a God who in justice and righteousness controls events, this "Meditation on the Divine Will" is an epochal personal experience. Lincoln was alone with no human companion for solace, and this spiritual experience, along with his unusual capacity for growth, lifted him to renewed vigor.

The piece also hints at a change in Lincoln's spiritual perspective—from seeing all events as predetermined by a distant and inscrutable God to recognizing God's active involvement in history. Lincoln scholar Dr. Ronald White writes:

> Historians and biographers have continued to use Lincoln's engagement with fatalism as a young man as the main rubric to understand his religious thought as president. This approach, static in its engagement with a changing Lincoln, fails to do justice to the growth and change in Lincoln's thinking, especially during the Civil War. If Lincoln was drawn to a doctrine of necessity in the 1840's, the ideas and words in the Meditation on the Divine Will give evidence of a quite different perspective on the nature of God's involvement in history. Instead of the appeal to some power in the handbill of 1846, Lincoln writes in the Meditation on the Divine Will of God's purpose and that God wills, language growing from an understanding of a purposeful God who acts in history.[6]

Lincoln, after the Second Battle of Bull Run, voiced not fatalism or resignation but a desire to discern the often inscrutable will of God in human affairs.

As Lincoln had learned, when our frail minds become so sure of what is right, we are baffled when things do not work out. From now on, Lincoln would often advise Americans to stop, take a deep breath, and reexamine their assumptions.

When we study the teachings of the Lord Jesus, we see that Lincoln was emphasizing something of great importance to the Master. In His parables and teachings, Jesus makes it clear that humans tend to become comfortable in thinking things are all right when they are not.

> Of the ten virgins, five were certain they had sufficient oil though they did not. (Matthew 25:1-13)

The man with one talent buried it, considering it the best thing to do. (Matthew 25:24-30)

Both the sheep and the goats were surprised to learn the truth about themselves. (Matthew 25:31-46)

The man who had no wedding garment did not realize that it was expected. (Matthew 22:11-13)

The Pharisee was certain God was happy with him. (Luke 18:11-12)

People often follow the wrong leaders; the blind follow the blind. (Matthew 15:14)

Likewise, many people in the North were strongly and *rightfully* opposed to slavery but were unwilling to acknowledge their own shortcomings. In recognizing the fallacy of their thinking—and his own—Lincoln had emerged as a stronger, more capable leader.

CHAPTER 16

THE MILITARY

One of Lincoln's great struggles during the Civil War years was to find military leadership with the will and boldness to fight the Confederacy aggressively.

> Lincoln's chief military problem was to find a general equal to the hard task the North faced in the Civil War. Though its resources were far in excess of those of the South, they were largely offset by the different roles of the two contestants. The North in the end had to do nothing less than conquer a large area defended by brave armies commanded by Robert E. Lee with a staff of superb generals, some of the best this nation has produced. Great superiority in man power and munitions was needed; but it was not sufficient. It was a case of Napoleon's maxim of the necessity of the man.[1]

Kenneth P. Williams begins his five-volume study, *Lincoln Finds a General: A Military Study of the Civil War*, with that observation. He continues:

> Three years of war passed before the historic day in March, 1864 when the experienced and modest Grant met Lincoln, also experienced and equally modest. Behind the General were notable successes; behind the President were months of disappointment with generals who had been unequal to the hard task of conducting offensive operations against the Confederate army commanded by Lee, and who had even missed good chances of

shortening the war by destroying Lee's army on his two ventures across the Potomac.[2]

Though for years finding the right commander in the field proved to be an elusive goal, Lincoln was notably successful in stimulating his subordinates to act above themselves. His challenge was to discipline and praise, pull antagonists together, and squelch rebellion within the military ranks. Though he rode herd over a cabinet of diverse views, though he fought constant battles with a recalcitrant Congress, and though newsmen made it difficult to get his ideas through to the people, his most exasperating challenge was to nudge the military commanders to victories.

☆ ☆ ☆

Lincoln viewed Zachary Taylor, who had led the United States during the Mexican War, as a model military man. When Taylor had run for the presidency, Lincoln had campaigned diligently for him because he embodied the traits that Lincoln deeply respected, such as willingness to promote the honor and reputation of other officers rather than one's own ego. We get a sense of what Lincoln looked for in his military men from the tribute he gave the former president when Taylor died. Lincoln gave this eulogy on July 25, 1850, in Chicago.

July 25, 1850

Eulogy on Zachary Taylor

. . . *He was never beaten, and never retreated. In* all, *the odds was greatly against him; in each, defeat seemed inevitable; and yet* in all, *he triumphed. Wherever he has led, while the battle still raged, the issue was painfully doubtful; yet in* each *and* all, *when the din had ceased, and the smoke had blown away, our country's flag was still seen, fluttering in the breeze.*

Gen. Taylor's battles were not distinguished for brilliant military manoeuvers; but in all, he seems rather to have conquered by the exercise of a sober and steady judgment, coupled with a dogged incapacity to understand that defeat was possible. His rarest military trait, was a combination of negatives—absence of excitement *and absence of* fear. *He could not be* flurried, *and he could not be* scared.

In this eulogy, Lincoln speaks quite frankly regarding the seriousness of life and death. He refers to our Maker, an appropriate title for Deity for the occasion. (See the chart on page 258 for Lincoln's usage of the term.) He also reminds his listeners that the humble will be exalted (Matthew 23:12; Luke 14:11, 18:14).

Yet, under all circumstances, trusting to our Maker, and through his wisdom and beneficence, to the great body of our people, we will not despair, nor despond. . . .

*But he is gone. The conqueror at last is conquered. The fruits of labor, his name, his memory and example, are all that is left us—his example, verifying the great truth, that "***he that humbleth himself, shall be exalted***" teaching, that to serve one's country with a singleness of purpose, gives assurance of that country's gratitude, secures its best honors, and makes "a dying bed, soft as downy pillows are."*

The death of the late President may not be without its use, in reminding us, that we, *too, must die. Death, abstractly considered, is the same with the high as with the low; but practically, we are not so much aroused to the contemplation of our own mortal natures, but the fall of* many *undistinguished, as that of* one *great, and well known, name. By the latter, we are forced to muse, and ponder, sadly.*

CW II: 83–90 (87, 89–90)

☆ ☆ ☆

May 13, 1862

Speech to the Twelfth Indiana Regiment

It has not been customary heretofore, nor will it be hereafter, for me to say something to every regiment passing in review. It occurs too frequently for me to have speeches ready on all occasions. As you have paid such a mark of respect to the Chief Magistrate, it appears proper that I should say a word or two in reply.

Your Colonel has thought fit, on his own account and in your name, to say that you are satisfied with the manner in which I have performed my part in the difficulties which have surrounded the nation. For your kind expressions I am extremely grateful, but, on the other hand, I assure you that the nation is more indebted to you, and such as you, than to me. It is upon the brave hearts and strong arms of the people of the country that our reliance has been placed in support of free government and free institutions.

For the part that you and the brave army of which you are a part have, under Providence, performed in this great struggle, I tender more thanks—greatest thanks that can be possibly due—and especially to this regiment, which has been the subject of good report. The thanks of the nation will follow you, and may ***God's blessing rest upon you*** *now and forever. I hope that upon your return to your homes you will find your friends and loved ones well and happy. I bid you farewell.*

CW V: 213

☆ ☆ ☆

Today with reconnaissance from air and long-distance cameras and with intricate military intelligence, we can hardly imagine how difficult it was to know the location of an enemy battalion during the Civil War. This letter to General Boyle reveals some of the difficulty. Lincoln uses the word *Babel,* found in Genesis 11:9, to describe a confusing situation.

September 12, 1862

To Jeremiah T. Boyle

Gen. Boyle—

Your despatch of last evening received. Where is the enemy which you dread in Louisville? How near to you? What is Gen. Gilbert's opinion? With all possible respect for you, I must think Gen. Wright's military opinion is the better. He is as much responsible for Louisville, as for Cincinnati. . . . For us here, to control him there on the ground would be a ***Babel*** *of confusion which would be utterly ruinous. Where do you understand Buell to be? and what is he doing?*

A. Lincoln

CW V: 416

☆ ☆ ☆

Five days later, Generals McClellan and Lee led their troops in the Battle of Antietam, the bloodiest day of combat with 23,100 casualties. No clear victor emerged from the conflict.

☆ ☆ ☆

Although Lincoln had fallen out of the habit of church attendance as a young man, by this point, he had recognized its importance. He encouraged the servicemen to worship each Sunday as well.

November 15, 1862

Order for Sabbath Observance

The President, Commander-in-Chief of the Army and Navy, desires and enjoins the orderly **observance of the Sabbath** by the officers and men in the military and naval service. The importance for man and beast of the prescribed weekly rest, the sacred rights of Christian soldiers and sailors, a becoming deference to the best sentiment of a Christian people, and a due regard for the **Divine will**, demand that Sunday labor in the Army and Navy be reduced to the measure of strict necessity.

The discipline and character of the national forces should not suffer, nor the cause they defend be imperiled, by the profanation of the day or name of the **Most High**. "At this time of public distress"—adopting the words of Washington in 1776—"men may find enough to do in the service of **God** and their country without abandoning themselves to vice and immorality." The first General Order issued by the Father of his Country after the Declaration of Independence, indicates the spirit in which our institutions were founded and should ever be defended: *"The General hopes and trusts that every officer and man will endeavor to live and act as becomes a* **Christian soldier** *defending the dearest rights and liberties of his country."*

ABRAHAM LINCOLN.

CW V: 497–498

☆ ☆ ☆

General Rosecrans had informed Lincoln of a victory in the Battle of Murfreesboro. Because he had so often been disappointed with officers who did not possess the fighting instinct, Lincoln was quick to give encouragement and credit for success. Lincoln did not often use the expression "God bless you," so the use of the term to Rosecrans was purposeful.

January 5, 1863

To William S. Rosecrans

Major General W. S. Rosecrans

Your despatch announcing retreat of enemy has just reached here. ***God bless you****, and all with you! Please tender to all, and accept for yourself, the Nation's gratitude for yours, and their, skill, endurance, and dantless courage. A. LINCOLN*

CW VI: 39

☆ ☆ ☆

Lincoln's personal relationships to his military officers were exceptional. General Hooker was a particularly talented officer, with corresponding serious faults. Lincoln's letter to the general is a classic example of a clear, nonconfrontational statement of a problem.

January 26, 1863

To Joseph Hooker

Major General Hooker:

I have placed you at the head of the Army of the Potomac. Of course I have done this upon what appear to me to be sufficient reasons. And yet I think it best for you to know that there are some things in regard to which, I am not quite satisfied with you. I believe you to be a brave and a skilful soldier, which, of course, I like. I also believe you do not mix politics with your profession, in which you are right. You have confidence in yourself, which is a valuable, if not an indispensable quality. You are ambitious, which, within reasonable bounds, does good rather than harm. But I think that during Gen. Burnside's command of the Army, you have taken counsel of your ambition, and thwarted him as much as you could, in which you did a great wrong to the country, and to a most meritorious and honorable brother officer. I have heard, in such way as to believe it, of your recently saying that both the Army and the Government needed a Dictator. Of course it was not for this, but in spite of it, that I have given you the command. Only those generals who gain successes, can set up dictators. What I now ask of you is military success, and I will risk the dictatorship. The government will support you to the utmost of it's ability, which is neither more nor less than it has done and will do for all commanders. I much fear that the spirit which you have aided to infuse into the Army, of criticising their Commander, and withholding confidence from him, will now turn upon you. I shall assist you as far as I can, to put it down. Neither you, nor Napoleon, if he were alive again, could get any good out of an army, while such a spirit prevails in it.

And now, beware of rashness. Beware of rashness, but with energy, and sleepless vigilance, go forward, and give us victories.

Yours very truly   A. Lincoln

CW VI: 78–79

☆ ☆ ☆

Because Lincoln needed more officers than had come up through West Point, he had granted direct commissions to some. One so appointed was John A. McClernand, a Democrat whom he knew well from his New Salem days. McClernand's commander, General Ulysses S. Grant, was unhappy when McClernand had a newspaper article published in which he took credit that Grant did not believe he deserved. Grant then relieved him of his duties.[3] McClernand's friends sent the president a letter saying how many in the field were unhappy with Grant's decision to relieve McClernand of his command. With the tact and wisdom that he used with all his generals, Lincoln wrote the unhappy general, including a phrase from Hebrews 12:1, in which the Christian life is compared to a race run before many witnesses. Though Lincoln was hurt by the situation, he could not interfere with a field decision made by his field commander.

August 12, 1863

To John A. McClernand

I doubt whether your present position is more painful to you than to myself. Grateful for the patriotic stand so early taken by you in this life-and-death struggle of the nation, I have done whatever has appeared practicable to advance you and the public interest together. . . .

*My belief is that the permanent estimate of what a general does in the field, is fixed by the "**cloud of witnesses**" who have been with him in the field; and that relying on these, he who has the right needs not to fear.*

Your friend as ever
A. Lincoln

CW VI: 383

☆ ☆ ☆

Lincoln was mindful, not only of the demands on military leadership, but the sacrifices that common soldiers were making in the war effort.

Lincoln had been invited to speak again at the Cooper Union Auditorium in the week following his Gettysburg Address. Reluctantly, he turned down the opportunity to address the audience at the place that had been so important in catapulting him into the presidency (see chapter 12). However, he did draft remarks in which he recognized the soldiers' sacrifices.

December 2, 1863

To George Opdyke and Others

Honor to the Soldier, and Sailor everywhere, who bravely bears his country's cause. Honor also to the citizen who cares for brother in the field, and serves, as he best can, the same cause—honor to him, only less than to him, who braves, for the common good, the storms of heaven and the storms of battle.

Your Obt. Servt.
A. LINCOLN
CW VII: 32

☆ ☆ ☆

A footnote in *The Collected Works* contains a letter from Colonel Richard M. Edwards.[4] He explains that he, along with about twenty other men, had become loyal to the Union after having held positions in Tennessee's Confederate state legislature. They were concerned that the oath they had taken in that legislature would prevent them from serving in the Union. Lincoln agreed that Edwards and others loyal to the Union should be allowed to serve.

February 5, 1864

To Edwin M. Stanton

Submitted to the Sec. Of War. On principle I dislike an oath which requires a man to swear he has *not done wrong. It rejects the* ***Christian principle of forgiveness*** *on terms of repentance. I think it is enough if the man does no wrong* hereafter. *A. LINCOLN*
CW VII: 169

☆ ☆ ☆

Ulysses S. Grant, a West Point graduate, had fought under General Zachary Taylor during the Mexican War. At the start of the Civil War, Illinois' governor appointed him commander of an undisciplined volunteer regiment. He impressed his superiors, particularly Lincoln, with his effective leadership and aggressive fighting spirit. He is credited with securing the first significant Union victories, and despite a humiliating setback at Shiloh, he came back and led his men to triumph in Vicksburg and Chattanooga. Lincoln made the following remarks when he presented Ulysses S. Grant with a commission as lieutenant general.

March 9, 1864

Speech to Ulysses S. Grant

The nation's appreciation of what you have done, and it's reliance upon you for what remains to do, in the existing great struggle, are now presented with this commission, constituting you Lieutenant General in the Army of the United States. With this high honor devolves upon you also, a corresponding responsibility. As the country herein trusts you, so, under God, it will sustain you. I scarcely need to add that with what I here speak for the nation goes my own hearty personal concurrence.

CW VII: 234

Note the beautiful exchange of letters between the commander in chief and General Grant.

April 30, 1864

Ulysses S. Grant
Lieutenant General Grant,

Not expecting to see you again before the Spring campaign opens, I wish to express, in this way, my entire satisfaction with what you have done up to this time, so far as I understand it. The particulars of your plans I neither know, or seek to know. You are vigilant and self-reliant; and, pleased with this, I wish not to obtrude any constraints or restraints upon you. While I am very anxious that any great disaster, or the capture of our men in great numbers, shall be avoided, I know these points are less likely to escape your attention than they would be mine. If there is anything wanting which is within my power to give, do not fail to let me know it.

And now with a brave Army, and a just cause, may ***God sustain you****.*

Yours very truly.
A. Lincoln

CW VII: 324

May 1, 1864

General Grant's Reply to Lincoln's Letter

"Your very kind letter of yesterday is just received. The confidence you express for the future, and satisfaction with the past, in my military administration is acknowledged with pride. It will be my earnest endeavor that you, and the country, shall not be disappointed. . . .

Indeed since the promotion which placed me in command of all the Armies, and in view of the great responsibility, and importance of success, I have been astonished at the readiness with which every thing asked for has been yielded without even an explanation being asked. Should my success be less than I desire, and expect, the least I can say is, the fault is not with you."

CW VII: 324–325 (footnote)

☆ ☆ ☆

Not only did Lincoln freely express his gratitude to his military officers, he was open with the soldiers about what their sacrifices meant to the country. Following are speeches to three different Ohio regiments returning to their homes:

August 18, 1864

Speech to the One Hundred Sixty-Fourth

SOLDIERS—You are about to return to your homes and your friends . . . I wish it might be more generally and universally understood what the country is now engaged in. We have, as all will agree, a free Government, where every man has a right to be equal with every other man. In this great struggle, this form of Government and every form of human right is endangered if our enemies succeed. . . . There is involved in this struggle the question whether your children and my children shall enjoy the privileges we have enjoyed. . . . There may be some irregularities in the practical application of our system. It is fair that each man shall pay taxes in exact proportion to the value of his property; but if we should wait before collecting a tax to adjust the taxes upon each man in exact proportion with every other man, we should never collect any tax at all. There may be mistakes made sometimes; things may be done wrong while the officers of the Government do all they can to prevent mistakes. But I beg of you, as citizens of this great Republic, not to let your minds be carried off from the great work we have before us. This struggle is too large for you to be diverted from it by any small matter. When you return to your homes rise up to the height of a generation of men worthy of a free Government, and we will carry out the great work we have commenced. I return to you my sincere thanks, soldiers, for the honor you have done me this afternoon.

CW VII: 504–505

August 22, 1864

Speech to One Hundred Sixty-sixth Ohio Regiment

I suppose you are going home to see your families and friends. . . . It is not merely for to-day, but for all time to come that we should perpetuate for our children's children this great and free government, which we have enjoyed all our lives. I beg you to remember this, not merely for my sake, but for yours. I happen temporarily to occupy this big White House. I am a living witness that any one of your children may look to come here as my father's child has. It is in order that each of you may have through this free government which we have enjoyed, an open field and a fair chance for your industry, enterprise and intelligence; that you may all have equal privileges in the race of life, with all its desirable human aspirations. It is for this the struggle should be maintained, that we may not lose our birth-right—not only for one, but for two or three years. The nation is worth fighting for, to secure such an inestimable jewel.

CW VII: 512

August 31, 1864

Speech to One Hundred Forty-eighth Ohio Regiment

Whenever I appear before a body of soldiers, I feel tempted to talk to them of the nature of the struggle in which we are engaged. . . . We are striving to maintain the government and institutions of our fathers, to enjoy them ourselves, and transmit them to our children and our children's children forever. . . .

But this government must be preserved in spite of the acts of any man or set of men. It is worthy your every effort. Nowhere in the world is presented a government of so much liberty and equality. To the humblest and poorest amongst us are held out the highest privileges and positions.

The present moment finds me at the White House, yet there is as good a chance for your children as there was for my father's.

Again, I admonish you not to be turned from your stern purpose of defending your beloved country and its free institutions by any arguments urged by ambitious and desiring men, but stand fast to the Union and the old flag. Soldiers, I bid you God-speed to your homes.

CW VII: 528–529

Lincoln was also profuse in his thanks to the military leaders as they ended their tours of duty.

September 3, 1864

Order of Thanks to David G. Farragut and Others

The national thanks are tendered by the President to Admiral Farragut and Major General Canby for the skill and harmony with which the recent operations in Mobile Harbor, and against Fort Powell, Fort Gaines, and Fort Morgan, were planned and carried into execution. Also, to Admiral Farragut and Major General Granger, under whose immediate command they were conducted, and to the gallant commanders on sea and land, and to the sailors and soldiers engaged in the operations, for their energy and courage, which, under the blessing of Providence, have been crowned with brilliant success, and have won for them the applause and thanks of the nation.

Abraham Lincoln

CW VII: 532–533

September 3, 1864

Order of Thanks to William T. Sherman and Others

The national thanks are herewith tendered by the President to Major General William T. Sherman, and the gallant officers and soldiers of his command before Atlanta, for the distinguished ability, courage, and perseverance displayed in the campaign in Georgia, which, under Divine favor, has resulted in the capture of the City of Atlanta. The marches, battles, sieges, and other military operations that have signalized this campaign must render it famous in the annals of war, and have entitled those who have participated therein to the applause and thanks of the nation.

Abraham Lincoln

CW VII: 533

☆ ☆ ☆

Lincoln understood the tremendous sacrifice made by the thousands of soldiers who fought in the Civil War, and he understood that thousands of families were paying a heavy price too. One of the most poignant letters attributed to Lincoln (though most probably written by John Hay) came near the end of the Civil War. When Lincoln signed it, this masterpiece became his.

The Collected Works states that the information given to President Lincoln when he wrote this letter was later found to be incorrect, but the fact that it was two sons instead of five who died in combat does not diminish the beautiful expression of sympathy.

November 21, 1864

To Mrs. Lydia Bixby

Dear Madam,—I have been shown in the files of the War Department a statement of the Adjutant General of Massachusetts, that you are the mother of five sons who have died gloriously on the field of battle.

I feel how weak and fruitless must be any words of mine which should attempt to beguile you from the grief of a loss so overwhelming. But I cannot refrain from tendering to you the consolation that may be found in the thanks of the Republic they died to save.

I pray that our ***Heavenly Father*** *may assuage the anguish of your bereavement, and leave you only the cherished memory of the loved and lost, and the solemn pride that must be yours, to have laid so costly a sacrifice upon the altar of Freedom. Yours, very sincerely and respectfully,*

A. Lincoln.

CW VIII: 116–117

CHAPTER 17

A NATION UNSHACKLED

In his First Inaugural Address, Lincoln made a heartfelt plea for the South to put the idea of secession on hold. The passionate president concluded his speech by declaring that he was "loath to close":

> We are not enemies, but friends. We must not be enemies. Though passion may have strained, it must not break our bonds of affection.

As president-elect, Abraham Lincoln made many whistle-stop speeches to thousands of his countrymen in a long, circuitous route that ended in Washington, D.C. (see chapter 13), a city in which slaves were bought and sold on auction blocks. The sight of these auctions had always been personally repulsive to Lincoln. Yet if he had behaved as a hard-liner abolitionist, he would have lost the war before it started, because the border states would have joined the Confederacy, making victory beyond reach.

The abolitionists (and many people yet today) failed to understand this dynamic. Almost from his first day in office, leaders from a number of Christian groups urged the president to free the slaves.

The *New York Tribune* printed a report of the visitation of a delegation of Progressive Friends, which presented him with a resolution, adopted during the group's annual meeting, that urged him to emancipate the slaves.

June 20, 1862

On Remarks to a Delegation of Progressive Friends

Wm. Barnard addressed the President in a few words, expressing sympathy for him in all his embarrassments, and an earnest desire that he might, under divine guidance, be led to free the slaves and thus save the nation from destruction. In that case, nations yet unborn would rise up to call him blessed and, better still, he would secure the blessing of God.

The President responded very impressively, saying that he was deeply sensible of his need of Divine assistance. He had sometime thought that perhaps he might be an instrument in God's hands of accomplishing a great work and he certainly was not unwilling to be. Perhaps, however, God's way of accomplishing the end which the memorialists have in view may be different from theirs. It would be his earnest endeavor, with a firm reliance upon the Divine arm, and seeking light from above, to do his duty in the place to which he had been called.

CW V: 278–279 (279)

The *Cincinnati Daily Gazette* reported on an exchange between Lincoln and some Presbyterian church leaders.

July 17, 1862

Remarks to Committee of Reformed Presbyterian Synod

Mr. Lincoln then replied. As to the moral character of the institution of Slavery, and as to its political bearing on the institutions of this or any other Nation, he said there was, between him and the committee, no difference of sentiment. He went on to say:

Had Slavery no existence among us, and were the question asked shall we adopt such an institution? we should agree as to the reply which should be made. If there be any diversity in our views it is not as to whether we should receive Slavery when free from it, but as to how we may best get rid of it already amongst us. Were an individual asked whether he would wish to have a wen* on his neck, he could not hesitate as to the reply; but were it asked whether a man who has such a wen should at once be relieved of it by the application of the surgeon's knife, there might be diversity of opinion, perhaps the man might bleed to death, as the result of such an operation.

"Feeling deeply my responsibility to my country and to that **God to whom we all owe allegiance**, I assure you I will try to do my best, and so may God help me."

CW V: 327

Lincoln's challenge was to explain to the antislavery forces that, while he was in full agreement with their desire to end slavery, he could not

*An abnormal growth or a cyst protruding from a surface esp. of the skin.

immediately free the slaves without endangering the republic—and its Constitution. While he took no immediate action to free the slaves, his lawyer's mind was constantly wrestling with the issue.

He began by recommending a most logical idea: offering full compensation for slaves through the federal treasury. If such legislation had passed, it might have saved the lives of 600,000 men and millions of dollars spent maintaining two fighting armies. It also would have spared the ravaging of Southern plantations and property. Though it would not have much chance of acceptance, Lincoln urged acceptance with all his presidential power.

Lincoln submitted a draft of a bill to Congress to compensate any State that abolished slavery, but slaveholders had gone too far and refused to consider the plan.

July 14, 1862

To the Senate and House of Representatives

Fellow citizens of the Senate, and House of Representatives:

Herewith is the draft of a Bill to compensate any State which may abolish slavery within it's limits, the passage of which, substantially as presented, I respectfully, and earnestly recommend.

Be it enacted by the Senate and House of Representatives of the United States of America, in Congress assembled, That whenever the President of the United States shall be satisfied that any State shall have lawfully abolished slavery within and throughout such State, either immediately, or gradually, it shall be the duty of the President, assisted by the Secretary of the Treasury, to prepare and deliver to such State, an amount of six per cent interest bearing bonds, of the United States, equal to the aggregate value, at ———dollars per head, of all the slaves within such State, as reported by the census of the year One thousand, eight hundred and sixty——— the whole amount for any one State, to be delivered at once, if the abolishment be immediate, or, in equal annual instalments, if it be gradual—interest to begin running on each bond at the time of it's delivery, and not before.

CW V: 324

The president then introduced his ideas of the black race colonizing in some other part of the world, asking them where they would be most happy. Lincoln expressed the biblical principle that man is created by and related to his Creator, and that fact gives worth and dignity.[1]

August 14, 1862

Address on Colonization to a Deputation of Negroes

There is much to encourage you. For the sake of your race you should sacrifice something of your present comfort for the purpose of being as grand in that respect as the white people. It is a cheering thought throughout life that something can be done to ameliorate the condition of those who have been subject to the hard usage of the world. It is difficult to make a man miserable while he feels he is worthy of himself, and claims kindred to the great God who made him. In the American Revolutionary war sacrifices were made by men engaged in it; but they were cheered by the future. Gen. Washington himself endured greater physical hardships than if he had remained a British subject. Yet he was a happy man, because he was engaged in benefiting his race—something for the children of his neighbors, having none of his own.

CW V: 370-75 (373)

By rejecting the proposition of compensation, the Southern plantation owners would lose their total investment in slaves, their plantations would be torn up, and most tragically for them, they would lose their sons. The dollar cost of redemption of slaves was far less than the purchase of military arms and the keeping of the armies in the fields. Compensation was a sensible idea! It would have stopped the flow of blood and the numbers of widows and fatherless from rising. There would have been no battlefield deaths or amputations. The Southern plantations would have been spared the waste and destruction, and we in our generation would not have known the legacy of bitterness that has been ours.

Still, to no one's surprise the South rejected the idea, but it is difficult to understand how antislavery, well-meaning people in the North were so dedicated to immediate emancipation that they could not even consider Lincoln's idea of compensation.

☆ ☆ ☆

One of the loudest antislavery voices was that of newspaper editor Horace Greeley, whose articles were read nationwide. In the summer of 1862 he published an editorial called "The Prayer of Twenty Millions." In it, he upbraided the president for fighting against the evil of slavery while refusing to enact legislation to forbid it. Furthermore, he predicted that freeing the slaves would weaken the Confederacy. What Greeley didn't know was that Lincoln had already drafted (and read to his cabinet) a preliminary emancipation proclamation.

Lincoln was terribly concerned about the evils of slavery, yet he viewed the situation in light of all other challenges facing the Union. Chief among the considerations—and not fully appreciated by the great mass of readers—was that a proclamation of emancipation would infuriate the border states of Missouri, Kentucky, Maryland, West Virginia, and Delaware. If they turned against the Union, all would be forfeited, and what the twenty million desired so ardently would be lost. Lincoln gave careful study to his reply to Greeley, for he knew the impact it could have.

August 22, 1862

To Horace Greeley

Hon. Horace Greely: Executive Mansion,
Dear Sir Washington, August 22, 1862.

I have just read yours of the 19th. addressed to myself through the New-York Tribune. If there be in it any statements, or assumptions of fact, which I may know to be erroneous, I do not, now and here, controvert them. If there be in it any inferences which I may believe to be falsely drawn, I do not now and here, argue against them. If there be perceptable in it an impatient and dictatorial tone, I waive it in deference to an old friend, whose heart I have always supposed to be right.

As to the policy I "seem to be pursuing" as you say, I have not meant to leave any one in doubt.

I would save the Union. I would save it the shortest way under the Constitution. The sooner the national authority can be restored; the nearer the Union will be "the Union as it was." If there be those who would not save the Union, unless they could at the same time save *slavery, I do not agree with them. If there be those who would not save the Union unless they could at the same time* destroy *slavery, I do not agree with them. My paramount object in this struggle* is *to save the Union, and is* not *either to save or to destroy slavery. If I could save the Union without freeing* any *slave I would do it, and if I could save it by freeing* all *the slaves I would do it; and if I could save it by freeing some and leaving others alone I would also do that. What I do about slavery, and the colored race, I do because I believe it helps to save the Union; and what I forbear, I forbear because I do* not *believe it would help to save the Union. I shall do* less *whenever I shall believe what I am doing hurts the cause, and I shall do* more *whenever I shall believe doing more will help the cause. I shall try to correct errors when shown to be errors; and I shall adopt new views so fast as they shall appear to be true views.*

I have here stated my purpose according to my view of official *duty; and I intend no modification of my oft-expressed* personal *wish that all men every where could be free. Yours, A. L*INCOLN

CW V: 388–389

Many abolitionists simply would not acknowledge the extremely difficult balancing act in which Lincoln was engaged. As an attorney, Lincoln had been admired for his ability to cut to the heart of a question. As a war president, he quickly understood that, for the Union to be successful, the border states, all of which permitted slavery, must remain neutral.

AMERICA IN 1861

These states created a wide swath of neutral ground separating the North from the South. Over four years of intense fighting, the North and

South both seemed to be gaining ground at different times, yet had the border states sided with the South, the tide would quickly have turned in favor of the Confederacy.

And what was the price for keeping the states within the Union? Lincoln promised to do nothing to interfere with slavery within their borders. Naturally, it was a difficult promise to keep and his critics screamed, but Lincoln kept his word, convinced that failing to do so would have far more severe consequences. Yet what Greeley did not fully understand was how intensely Lincoln had been agonizing over how to end the slaves' captivity.

☆ ☆ ☆

The state of Missouri was the epitome of the divided nation. Holding to a neutral position, it was torn asunder by powerful protagonists. What made matters excruciatingly difficult for Lincoln was that the antislavery forces in Missouri had splintered over such issues as:

- whether a specific general ought to be relieved;
- the work of Enrolled Militia in Missouri;
- who should be allowed to vote in an election.

One can hardly imagine how such disputes gnawed upon Lincoln.

A Missouri statewide convention drafted proposals and appointed several emissaries, including Charles D. Drake, to present them to President Lincoln. Lincoln wrote a carefully worded reply.

October 5, 1863

To Charles D. Drake and Others

It is easy to conceive that all these shades of opinion, and even more, may be sincerely entertained by honest and truthful men. Yet, all being for the Union, by reason of these differences, each will prefer a different way of sustaining the Union. At once sincerity is questioned, and motives are assailed. Actual war coming, blood grows hot, and blood is spilled. Thought is forced from old channels into confusion. Deception breeds and thrives. Confidence dies, and universal suspicion reigns. . . . Strong measures, deemed indispensable but harsh at best, such men make worse

by mal-administration. Murders for old grudges, and murders for pelf *, *proceed under any cloak that will best cover for the ocasion.*
CW VI: 499–504 (500)

Later in this letter, the president acknowledged his frustration with those who abused their administrative authority, who "contrary to the Great Prayer, were led into temptation." In fact, the Missouri situation almost made Lincoln throw up his hands. Biographer David Donald writes:

> Lincoln no longer believed that he could solve the Missouri question to anyone's satisfaction, including his own. He had, he told Attorney General Bates, "no friends in Missouri." The whole issue reminded him of a lesson he had learned as a boy when he was plowing. "When he came across stumps too deep and too tough to be torn up, and too wet to burn," he said, "he plowed round them."[2]

☆ ☆ ☆

To a delegation of Christians from several denominations, Lincoln explained in a dissertation of nearly six pages why he had not yet issued an emancipation proclamation.

September 13, 1862

Reply to Emancipation Memorial Presented by Chicago Christians of All Denominations

I am approached with the most opposite opinions and advice, and that by religious men, who are equally certain that they represent the Divine will. I am sure that either the one or the other class is mistaken in that belief, and perhaps in some respects both. I hope it will not be irreverent for me to say that if it is probable that God would reveal his will to others, on a point so connected with my duty, it might be supposed he would reveal it directly to me; for, unless I am more deceived in myself than I often am, it is my earnest desire to know the will of Providence in this matter. And if I can learn what it is I will do it! . . . *Why, the rebel soldiers are praying with a great deal more earnestness, I fear, than our own troops, and expecting God to favor their side. . . .*

What good *would a proclamation of emancipation from me do, especially as we are now situated? . . . Would* my word *free the slaves, when I*

*Money, riches.

cannot even enforce the Constitution in the rebel States? Is there a single court, or magistrate, or individual that would be influenced by it there? . . . for I am told that whenever the rebels take any black prisoners, free or slave, they immediately auction them off! . . . For instance, when, after the late battles at and near Bull Run, an expedition went out from Washington under a flag of truce to bury the dead and bring in the wounded, and the rebels seized the blacks who went along to help and sent them into slavery, . . .

The president then summarized his understanding of the Chicago group's resolution (or memorial) to him, acknowledging the truth of the principles it outlined.

. . . That the memorial contained facts, principles, and arguments which appealed to the intelligence of the President and to his faith in ***Divine Providence****; that he could not deny that the* ***Bible*** *denounced oppression as one of the highest of crimes, and threatened* ***Divine judgments*** *against nations that practice it; that our country had been exceedingly guilty in this respect, both at the North and South; that our just punishment has come by a slaveholder's rebellion; that the virus of secession is found wherever the virus of slavery extends, and no farther; so that there is the amplest reason for expecting to avert* ***Divine judgments*** *by putting away the sin, and for hoping to remedy the national troubles by striking at their cause.*

We observed, further, that we freely admitted the probability, and even the certainty, that ***God*** *would reveal the path of duty to the President as well as to others, provided he sought to learn it in the appointed way; but, as according to his own remark, Providence wrought by means and not miraculously, it might be, God would use the suggestions and arguments of other minds to secure that result.*

A few paragraphs later, Lincoln refers to 2 Thessalonians 3:10, which says able-bodied men should not expect to eat unless they also work. However, the arming of black soldiers was another matter. Lincoln knew the fifty thousand Union soldiers from the border states would resent the arming of black men. All would be lost should they, out of anger, desert the Union and join the rebels.

They should be welcomed and fed, and then, according to ***Paul's doctrine****, that they who eat must work, be made to labor and to fight for their liberty and ours.*

If we were to arm them, I fear that in a few weeks the arms would be in the hands of the rebels; and indeed thus far we have not had arms enough to equip our white troops. I will mention another thing, though it meet only your scorn and contempt: There are fifty thousand bayonets in the Union armies from the Border Slave States. It would be a serious matter if, in consequence of a proclamation such as you desire, they should go over to the rebels. I do not think they all would—not so many indeed as a year ago, or as six months ago—not so many to-day as yesterday. Every day increases their Union feeling.

And I can assure you that the subject is on my mind, by day and night, more than any other. Whatever shall appear to be ***God's will I will do****.*

CW V: 419–425 (419–423, 425)

Unbeknownst to those Chicagoans—in fact, to everyone outside his cabinet—Lincoln had at last decided the time had come to issue an order freeing the slaves in the rebel states. While he was determined to issue the preliminary emancipation proclamation he'd read to his cabinet that July, he wanted to wait for a significant Union military victory before doing so. When the Northern troops defeated the Confederate troops in the Battle of Antietam—and stopped Lee's first invasion into the North—on September 17, Lincoln determined the time had come.

September 22, 1862

Preliminary Emancipation Proclamation

That on the first day of January in the year of our Lord, one thousand eight hundred and sixty-three, all persons held as slaves within any state, or designated part of a state, the people whereof shall then be in rebellion against the United States shall be then, thenceforward, and forever free; . . .

CW V: 433-436 (434)

The following document, though not in *The Collected Works*, was recorded by Salmon Chase, secretary of the treasury, in his diary of the cabinet meeting in which the president announced that he had written the Preliminary Emancipation Proclamation, though he did not announce the proclamation at that time:

> Gentlemen:
>
> [Y]ou all remember that, several weeks ago, I read to you an Order I had prepared on this subject, which, on account of objections made by some of you, was not issued. Ever since then, my mind has been much occupied with this subject, and I have thought all along that the time for acting on it might very probably come, I think the time has come now. . . . When the rebel army was at Fredricksburg, I determined, as soon as it should be driven out of Maryland, to issue a Proclamation of Emancipation such as I thought most likely to be useful. I said nothing to any one, but I made the promise to myself, and to my **Maker**. I have got you together to hear what I have written down. I do not wish your advice about the main matter—for that I have determined for myself.[3]

While Lincoln informed his cabinet of his decision to issue the proclamation, he was not asking them whether or not they thought he should. He was merely inviting their input on the details.

Instead, he had determined to announce that if the rebels did not end their fighting and rejoin the Union by January 1, 1863, all slaves in the rebellious South would be freed. Many people, even today, do not understand why President Lincoln proclaimed freedom to all slaves in the states that were in rebellion, where in most cases federal laws were not in authority. Why didn't he proclaim at the same time freedom to slaves in the border states where federal laws were in control?

Because the Constitution allowed slavery, President Lincoln had no legal power to free slaves. There was no way for him to make a proclamation that contradicted the Constitution, but as commander in chief, he had legal power to declare all slaves free within the states that were in rebellion, since they were subject to military control.

While it may seem odd that declaring emancipation in territory still occupied by the enemy would be effective, the proclamation was a powerful psychological tool, encouraging slaves in rebellion. Lincoln's clear vision and ridiculous-sounding policy brought the war to a hastened end.

Yet many of Lincoln's friends and opponents thought it was a bad move. In his book *The Emancipation Proclamation*, historian John Hope Franklin explains what Lincoln was up against.

> If the Proclamation transformed the war into a crusade against slavery, thousands of ardent supporters of the Union would no longer be interested; and confidence in Lincoln, who had declared that the preservation of the Union was the paramount issue, would be undermined.
>
> As early as July the Postmaster General, Montgomery Blair . . . had predicted that a proclamation to free the slaves would cost the Republicans the fall elections. . . . In the weeks that followed the announcement of his emancipation policy he was depressed by the loud critics who predicted ruin for the Republicans. The war Democrats insisted that he had betrayed the original aims of the War. The radical Republicans condemned him for the conservative course he was pursuing. . . .
>
> In New York the Democrats were especially vigorous in their attack on the Proclamation. It was a proposal "for the butchery of women and children, for scenes of lust and rapine, and of arson and murder."[4]

☆ ☆ ☆

Of course, Lincoln also received praise for this bold act. Just a few days after the release of the Preliminary Emancipation Proclamation, a large crowd gathered at the White House to serenade the president and celebrate his decision to issue the proclamation. After rousing music and speeches, the president himself briefly addressed the crowd.

September 24, 1862

Reply to Serenade in Honor of Emancipation Proclamation

Fellow-Citizens: I appear before you to do little more than acknowledge the courtesy you pay me, and to thank you for it. I have not been distinctly informed why it is this occasion you appear to do me this honor, though I suppose it is because of the proclamation. I was about to say, I suppose I understand it. What I did, I did after very full deliberation, and under a very heavy and solemn sense of responsibility.

I can only trust in God I have made no mistake. I shall make no attempt on this occasion to sustain what I have done or said by any comment. It is now for the country and the world to pass judgment on it, and, may be, take action upon it. I will say no more upon this subject. In my position I am environed with difficulties.
CW V: 438–9

Not surprisingly, the South refused to surrender, so Lincoln prepared to enact the Emancipation Proclamation on January 1, 1863. Francis B. Carpenter was given permission to reside in the White House while completing a painting of the signing of the Emancipation Proclamation. Often, during the terrible days of the Battle of the Wilderness, Lincoln could hardly sleep. Carpenter was a firsthand observer of the president's ordeal and gave a written story of the signing of the document:

> Mr. Lincoln took a pen, dipped it in ink, moved his hand to the place for the signature, held it a moment, and then removed his hand and dropped the pen. After a little hesitation he again took up the pen and went through the same movement as before. Mr. Lincoln then turned to Mr. Seward, and said:
>
> "I have been shaking hands since nine o'clock this morning, and my right arm is almost paralyzed. If my name ever goes into history it will be for this act, and my whole soul is in it. If my hand trembles when I sign the Proclamation, all who examine the document hereafter will say, 'He hesitated.'" He then turned to the table, took up the pen again, and slowly, firmly wrote that "Abraham Lincoln" with which the whole world is now familiar. He looked up, smiled, and said: "That will do."[5]

January 1, 1863

Emancipation Proclamation by the President of the United States of America:

Whereas, on the twentysecond day of September, in the year of our Lord one thousand eight hundred and sixty two, a proclamation was issued by the President of the United States, containing, among other things, the following, towit:

"That on the first day of January, in the year of our Lord one thousand eight hundred and sixty-three, all persons held as slaves within any State or designated part of a State, the people whereof shall then be in rebellion against the

United States, shall be then, thenceforward, and forever free; and the Executive Government of the United States, including the military and naval authority thereof, will recognize and maintain the freedom of such persons, and will do no act or acts to repress such persons, or any of them, in any efforts they may make for their actual freedom.

"That the Executive will, on the first day of January aforesaid, by proclamation, designate the States and parts of States, if any, in which the people thereof, respectively, shall then be in rebellion against the United States; and the fact that any State, or the people thereof, shall on that day be, in good faith, represented in the Congress of the United States by members chosen thereto at elections wherein a majority of the qualified voters of such State shall have participated, shall, in the absence of strong countervailing testimony, be deemed conclusive evidence that such State, and the people thereof, are not then in rebellion against the United States."

Now, therefore I, Abraham Lincoln, President of the United States, by virtue of the power in me vested as Commander-in-Chief, of the Army and Navy of the United States in time of actual armed rebellion against authority and government of the United States, and as a fit and necessary war measure for suppressing said rebellion, do, on this first day of January, in the year of our Lord one thousand eight hundred and sixty three, and in accordance with my purpose so to do publicly proclaimed for the full period of one hundred days, from the day first above mentioned, order and designate as the States and parts of States wherein the people thereof respectively, are this day in rebellion against the United States, the following, towit:

Arkansas, Texas, Louisiana, (except the Parishes of St. Bernard, Plaquemines, Jefferson, St. Johns, St. Charles, St. James[,] Ascension, Assumption, Terrebonne, Lafourche, St. Mary, St. Martin, and Orleans, including the City of New-Orleans) Mississippi, Alabama, Florida, Georgia, South-Carolina, North-Carolina, and Virginia, (except the fortyeight counties designated as West Virginia, and also the counties of Berkley, Accomac, Northampton, Elizabeth-City, York, Princess Ann, and Norfolk, including the cities of Norfolk & Portsmouth [)]; and which excepted parts are, for the present, left precisely as if this proclamation were not issued.

And by virtue of the power, and for the purpose aforesaid, I do order and declare that all persons held as slaves within said designated States, and parts of States, are, and henceforward shall be free; and that the Executive government of the United States, including the military and naval authorities thereof, will recognize and maintain the freedom of said persons.

And I hereby enjoin upon the people so declared to be free to abstain from all violence, unless in necessary self-defence; and I recommend to them that, in all cases when allowed, they labor faithfully for reasonable wages.

And I further declare and make known, that such persons of suitable condition, will be received into the armed service of the United States to garrison forts, positions, stations, and other places, and to man vessels of all sorts in said service.

And upon this act, sincerely believed to be an act of justice, warranted by the Constitution, upon military necessity, I invoke the considerate judgment of mankind, and the gracious favor of **Almighty God**.

In witness whereof, I have hereunto set my hand and caused the seal of the United States to be affixed.

Done at the City of Washington, this first day of January, in the year of our Lord one thousand eight hundred and sixty three, and of the Independence of the United States of America the eighty-seventh.

By the President: ABRAHAM LINCOLN

WILLIAM H. SEWARD, Secretary of State

CW VI: 28–31—THE EMANCIPATION

In 1871 the original document of the Emancipation Proclamation was burned in the Chicago fire. Fortunately, a facsimile had been made.

The reactions on that first day of 1863 were mixed. Biographer Stephen Oates writes:

> From New York to Chicago, Democratic papers smeared the proclamation as a "wicked, atrocious, and revolting deed" which would unleash hordes of "negro barbarians." "It is impudent and insulting to God as to man, . . . for it declares those 'equal' whom God created unequal." . . . a storm of anti-Negro, anti-Lincoln protest rolled over the land, with rumbles of riot and disunion in parts of the Midwest. And there was trouble in the army as well. Correspondents who traveled with Union forces claimed that hardly one soldier in ten approved of emancipation; they reported that white soldiers cursed "niggers" with an "unreasoning hatred" and swore that they weren't going to fight to free any slaves.[6]

Many in the South had feared that emancipation would result in a massive revolt among the slaves. However, Lincoln urged the slaves to avoid unnecessary violence and work for wages. He also promised to allow them to enlist in the U.S. armed forces.

Yet Americans were still anxious to hear more about what this act would mean. James C. Conkling was an old friend and mayor of Springfield who had written to Lincoln, inviting him to address a mass meeting in that city. Undoubtedly, Lincoln would have liked to make the trip to visit old friends and his townspeople. However, rather than making the long journey, Lincoln wrote a speech for Conkling to read, covering all the arguments about the emancipation proclamation and the use of colored soldiers in army ranks.

August 26, 1863

To James C. Conkling

Peace does not appear so distant as it did. I hope it will come soon, and come to stay; and so come as to be worth the keeping in all future time. It will then have been proved that, among free men, there can be no successful appeal from the ballot to the bullet; and that they who take such appeal are sure to lose their case, and pay the cost. And then, there will be some black men who can remember that, with silent tongue, and clenched teeth, and steady eye, and well-poised bayonet, they have helped mankind on to this great consummation; while, I fear, there will be some white ones, unable to forget that, with malignant heart, and deceitful speech, they have strove to hinder it.

Still let us not be over-sanguine of a speedy final triumph. Let us be quite sober. Let us diligently apply the means, never doubting that a ***just God, in his own good time, will give us the rightful result****. Yours very truly A. Lincoln*

CW VI: 406–410 (410)

☆ ☆ ☆

Robert Lincoln thought the following fragment probably was written about the same time as the Springfield letter to James Conkling. It expresses many of the same ideas and ends in similar fashion.

August 26, 1863

Fragment

You began the war, and you can end it. If questions remain, let them be solved by peaceful means—by courts, and votes. This war is an appeal, by you, from the ballot to the sword; and a great object with me has been to teach the futility of such appeal—to teach that what is decided by the ballot, can not be reversed by the sword—to teach that there can be no successful appeal from a fair election, but to the next election. . . .

The prospects of the Union have greatly improved recently; still, let us not be over-sanguine of a speedy final triumph. Let us diligently apply the means, never doubting that a **just God**, *in his own good time, will give us the rightful result.*

CW VI: 410–411

☆ ☆ ☆

Lincoln had exempted a few areas of the South, mostly those under Union control, from the Proclamation. Tennessee was the only state exempted, and that was because Andrew Johnson was serving as the Lincoln-appointed military governor of the state. As a U.S. senator, Andrew Johnson had been the only senator from a secession state who remained loyal to the Union. Though a onetime slave owner, Johnson was a stalwart proponent of Lincoln's policies.

September 11, 1863

To Andrew Johnson

Private

Hon. Andrew Johnson: Executive Mansion,
My dear sir: Washington

I see that you have declared in favor of emancipation in Tennessee, for which, may **God bless you**. *Get emancipation into your new State government—Constitution—and there will be no such word as fail for your case.*

The raising of colored troops I think will greatly help every way.

Yours very truly. A. Lincoln

CW VI: 440

☆ ☆ ☆

After all the struggle to assure passage of the Emancipation Proclamation, Lincoln must have been particularly gratified by the response of many African-Americans. Francis B. Carpenter, the artist who completed the painting of the signing of the Emancipation Proclamation, remembered one such event this way:

> On the Fourth of July an unprecedented event was witnessed in Washington. By special consent of the President, the White House grounds were granted to the colored people of the city for a grand Sunday-school festival, and never did they present a busier or more jubilant scene. Inside the grounds a platform was erected, upon which accommodations were placed for speakers. Around this were rows of benches, which, during the greater part of the day, were not only well filled but crowded. . . . From the thick-leaved branches of the trees were suspended swings, of which all, both old and young, made abundant use. . . . No celebration of the day presented a greater appearance of enjoyment and success.[7]

The Baltimore guests presented the president with an elegant copy of the Holy Bible. Carpenter continued:

> The volume was of the usual pulpit size, bound in violet-colored velvet. The corners were bands of solid gold, and carved upon a plate also of gold, not less than one fourth of an inch think. Upon the left-hand cover, was a design representing the President in a cotton-field knocking the shackles off the wrists of a slave, who held one hand aloft as if invoking blessings upon the head of his benefactor—at whose feet was a scroll upon which was written "Emancipation"; upon the other cover was a similar plate bearing the inscription:
>
> "To Abraham Lincoln, President of the United States, the friend of Universal Freedom. From the loyal colored people of Baltimore, as a token of respect and gratitude. Baltimore, July 4th, 1864."[8]

Lincoln's written response follows.

September 7, 1864

Reply to Loyal Colored People of Baltimore upon Presentation of a Bible

So far as able, within my sphere, I have always acted as I believed to be right and just; and I have done all I could for the good of mankind generally. In letters and documents sent from this office I have expressed myself better than I now can. In regard to this ***Great Book****, I have but to say, it is the best gift God has given to man.*

All the good the ***Saviour*** *gave to the world was communicated through this book. But for it we could not know right from wrong. All things most desirable for man's welfare, here and hereafter, are to be found portrayed in it. To you I return my most sincere thanks for the very elegant copy of the great Book of God which you present.*

CW VII: 542

CHAPTER 18

APPEALING TO THE ALMIGHTY

When Lincoln arrived in Washington, he described himself as an instrument of the Almighty. The year 1862 was perhaps the most difficult and draining of Lincoln's life, as he buried a son, dealt with the endless ups and downs of a war, and determined to issue the Emancipation Proclamation.

If his "Meditation on the Divine Will" was an inward reflection of his turning to God during this unmitigated crisis, there were outward signs that his faith was becoming more and more important to him as well. He and Mary attended Sunday morning services at the capital city's New York Avenue Presbyterian Church, where the sermons of Dr. Phineas Gurley appealed to Lincoln's zest for literature and good reasoning.

The history of the Presbyterian Church in Washington that Lincoln attended contains an additional interesting detail:

> It was discovered quite by accident that he was a frequent attendant at the mid-week prayer meeting. He had made an agreement with Dr. Gurley that he would slip into the pastor's study by the side door and that the glass paneled door leading to the lecture room was to be left ajar so that he might inconspicuously share the inspiration of the meeting and pray with the church for the things nearest its heart.[1]

Despite these connections to this church, Lincoln did not become a member of it either. Yet his lack of membership in a particular church or denomination was perhaps an advantage. People of all faiths revered him. One author tells of a Jewish woman's meeting with the president:

> [A rabbi] had occasion to accompany a poor Jewish woman to the White House and beseech the President to pardon her wayward son who had deserted. She told her story in Yiddish, of which the President did not understand a word. But Abraham Lincoln only saw before him a mother imploring him for the life of her child; and as he listened to her unintelligible and yet agonizing plea, the tears coursed down his cheeks.[2]

☆ ☆ ☆

In fact, from the beginning of the Civil War, Lincoln had urged his countrymen to seek the mercy of their heavenly Father, just as this poor mother had appealed to him for compassion. (See pages 149–150, which includes Lincoln's first such proclamation, released just after the shocking Union defeat at Manassas Junction [Bull Run] in August 1861.)

From our first Continental Congress, government officials have urged Americans to seek divine assistance through prayer and then to express their gratitude to God. Lincoln's secretary of state, William H. Seward, wrote some of the calls to thanksgiving, including this first one. As there was no radio, newspapers covered presidential statements.

The following order applied only to the District of Columbia.

November 27, 1861

Order for Day of Thanksgiving

The Municipal authorities of Washington and Georgetown in this District, have appointed tomorrow, the 28th. instant, as a day of thanksgiving, the several Departments will on that occasion be closed, in order that the officers of the government may partake in the ceremonies. ABRAHAM LINCOLN.

CW V: 32

☆ ☆ ☆

Several letters make clear that Lincoln was aware of, and grateful for, the support and prayers of religious groups throughout the nation. Samuel Tobey was a leading member of the Society of Friends.

March 19, 1862

To Samuel B. Tobey

Dr. Samuel Boyd Tobey: Washington

My dear Sir: A domestic affliction, of which doubtless you are informed, has delayed me so long in making acknowledgment for the very kind and appropriate letter, signed, on behalf, and by direction of a Meeting of the Representatives of the Society of Friends for New-England, held at Providence, Rhode Island the 8th. of second month 1862, by Samuel Boyce, clerk, and presented to me by yourself and associates. Engaged, as I am, in a great war, I fear it will be difficult for the world to understand how fully I appreciate the principles of peace, inculcated in this letter, and everywhere, by the Society of Friends. Grateful to the good people you represent for their prayers in behalf of our common country, I look forward hopefully to an early end of war, and return of peace.

Your obliged friend

A. Lincoln

CW V: 165

Abraham Hart, president of the Congregation Hope of Israel, had written Lincoln, enclosing a copy of a prayer.

May 13, 1862

To Abraham Hart

My dear Sir Permit me to acknowledge the receipt of your communication of April 23d containing a copy of a Prayer recently delivered at your Synagogue, and to thank you heartily for your expressions of kindness and confidence. I have the honor to be Your Obt. Servt

CW V: 212

May 13, 1862

Response to Evangelical Lutherans

Gentlemen: I welcome here the representatives of the Evangelical Lutherans of the United States. I accept with gratitude their assurances of the sympathy and support of that enlightened, influential, and loyal class of my fellow-citizens in an important crisis which involves, in my judgment, not only the civil and religious liberties of our own dear land, but in a large degree the civil and religious liberties of mankind in many countries and through many ages. . . . You all may recollect that in taking up the sword thus forced into our hands this Government appealed to the prayers of the pious and the good, and declared that it placed its whole dependence upon the favor of God. I now humbly and reverently, in your presence, reiterate the acknowledgment of that dependence, not doubting that, if it shall please the Divine Being who determines the destinies of nations that this shall remain a united people, they will, humbly seeking the Divine guidance, make their prolonged national existence a source of new benefits to themselves and their successors, and to all classes and conditions of mankind.

CW V: 212–213

☆ ☆ ☆

Though in the western theater of the war Ulysses S. Grant and the other generals were making progress by early 1862, Lincoln had been quite disappointed with General George McClellan, for he had shown little aggressiveness on the eastern front, jeopardizing the defense of Washington, D.C. In this period of frustrating perplexities, Lincoln nonetheless called on Americans to express their gratitude to God.

April 10, 1862

Proclamation of Thanksgiving for Victories

By the President of the United States of America.

It has pleased **Almighty God** to vouchsafe signal victories to the land and naval forces engaged in suppressing an internal rebellion, and at the same time to avert from our country the dangers of foreign intervention and invasion.

It is therefore recommended to the People of the United States that, at their next weekly assemblages in their accustomed places of public worship which shall occur after notice of this proclamation shall have been received, they especially acknowledge and render thanks to our **Heavenly Father** for these inestimable blessings; that they then and there implore spiritual consolations in behalf of all who have been brought into affliction by the casualties and calamities of sedition and civil war, and that they reverently invoke the **Divine Guidance** for our national counsels, to the end that they may speedily result in the restoration of peace, harmony, and unity throughout our borders, and hasten the establishment of fraternal relations among all the countries of the earth.

In witness whereof, I have hereunto set my hand and caused the seal of the United States to be affixed.

Done at the City of Washington, this tenth day of April, in the year of our Lord one thousand eight hundred and sixty-two, and of the Independence of the United States the eighty-sixth.

By the President: ABRAHAM LINCOLN

WILLIAM H. SEWARD, Secretary of State

CW V: 185–186

☆ ☆ ☆

Despite their good intentions, many Christian leaders came to the White House either to ask the president to do something for them or to adopt their viewpoint on an issue—usually slavery. Yet at least one Christian leader seemed to come with the sole purpose of praying for the president and supporting him in any way she could.

Eliza P. Gurney was a respected Quaker minister, and her late husband had also been a Quaker minister. Her poems, exhortations, and notes, filled with devotional light, encouragement, and scriptural exhortation, were published in 1884.

Having been promised an interview with the president, she and three friends waited two days in wet weather for their appointment.

When at last she met the president, Eliza expressed her feelings by quoting Scripture, uttering words of encouragement, and delivering a sincere exhortation. A summary of her address is recorded in her published book.[3] At the end of their meeting, Mrs. Gurney knelt "and uttered a short but most beautiful, eloquent and comprehensive prayer that light and wisdom might be shed down from on high, to guide our President."[4]

The president wrote a letter thanking her for her support. In it, he used a phrase from 1 Peter 4:12 in which the apostle speaks of the "fiery trial" that believers in God should expect to experience. The excerpt below ends with a reference drawn from Psalm 67:4.

October 26, 1862

Reply to Eliza P. Gurney

*I am glad of this interview, and glad to know that I have your sympathy and prayers. We are indeed going through a great trial—a **fiery trial**. In the very responsible position in which I happen to be placed, being a humble instrument in the hands of our **Heavenly Father**, as I am, and as we all are, to work out his great purposes, I have desired that all my works and acts may* *be according to his will, and that it might be so, I have sought his aid—but if after endeavoring to do my best in the light which he affords me, I find my efforts fail, I must believe that for some purpose unknown to me, He wills it otherwise. If I had had my way, this war would never have been commenced; If I had been allowed my way this war would have been ended before this, but we find it still continues; and we must believe that He permits it for some wise purpose of his own, mysterious and unknown to us; and though with our limited understandings we may not be able to comprehend it, yet we cannot but believe, that* ***he who made the world still governs*** *it.*

CW V: 478

If there is any question of the impact Gurney's visit made on the president, it was answered in a second letter Lincoln sent her two years later.

September 4, 1864

To Eliza P. Gurney

My esteemed friend.

I have not forgotten—probably never shall forget—the very impressive occasion when yourself and friends visited me on a Sabbath forenoon two years ago. Nor has your kind letter, written nearly a year later, ever been forgotten. In all, it has been your purpose to strengthen my reliance on God. I am much indebted to the good christian people of the country for their constant prayers and consolations; and to no one of them, more than to yourself.

In the next paragraph, President Lincoln states his resignation to the will of God in spite of his inability to understand. Notice the word *ordains.* God ordains His purposes, though we humans cannot understand. For the same feeling and expression of ideas, see chapter 15, "The Divine Will."

The purposes of the ***Almighty*** *are perfect, and must prevail, though we erring mortals may fail to accurately perceive them in advance. We hoped for a happy termination of this terrible war long before this; but God knows best, and has ruled otherwise. We shall yet acknowledge His wisdom and our own error therein. Meanwhile we must work earnestly in the* ***best light He gives us, trusting that so working still conduces to the great ends He ordains. Surely He intends some great good to follow this mighty convulsion, which no mortal could make, and no mortal could stay****.*

Your people—the Friends—have had, and are having, a very great trial. On principle, and faith, opposed to both war and oppression, they can only practically oppose oppression by war. In this hard dilemma, some have chosen one horn and some the other. For those appealing to me on conscientious grounds, I have done, and shall do, the best I could and can, in my own conscience, under my oath to the law. That you believe this I doubt not; and believing it, I shall still receive, for our country and myself, your earnest prayers to our ***Father in Heaven****. Your sincere friend*

A. Lincoln.

CW VII: 535

☆ ☆ ☆

Like Eliza Gurney, Caleb Russell and Sallie Fenton were from a branch of the Society of Friends. They wrote President Lincoln expressing their approval for the "Proclamation of Prospective Emancipation." Among some church groups, it was common to use the illustration of Aaron and Hur holding up the hands of Moses in prayer (see Exodus 17:10-12). In their letter to the president, Russell and Fenton had written: "At this very late period we can do but very little more, than bear our testimony on favor of justice and liberty and like Aaron and Him [Hur] of old would gladly hold up thy hands as they did the hands of Moses." The president responded:

January 5, 1863

To Caleb Russell and Sallie A. Fenton

It is most cheering and encouraging for me to know that in the efforts which I have made and am making for the restoration of a righteous peace to our country, I am upheld and sustained by the good wishes and ***prayers of God's people****.*

In his letter to Russell and Fenton, President Lincoln opened his heart in a powerful and most meaningful sentiment. Brilliant minds both in and out of government were his contemporaries: the philosopher Ralph Waldo Emerson, great ministers such as Phillips Brooks and Henry Ward Beecher, the editor Horace Greeley, and an enlightenment movement led by Theodore Parker. Lincoln read all of them, listened to them, but wrote:

No one is more deeply than myself aware that without His favor our highest wisdom is but as foolishness and that our most strenuous efforts would avail nothing in the shadow of His displeasure.

Acknowledging the pauperism of human brains in solving the problems of the nation, Lincoln was akin to the apostle Paul when he entered Corinth, the great cultural center of Grecian glory. Facing the mighty center of idolatry, the apostle Paul had nothing to trust of his own wisdom and talent. His total reliance was upon God. The apostle, paraphrasing from Isaiah 29:14, wrote in 1 Corinthians 1:19-20: "For it is written, I will destroy the wisdom of the wise, and will bring to nothing the understanding of the prudent. Where is the wise? where is the scribe? where is the disputer of this world? hath not God made foolish the wisdom of this world?"

President Lincoln led the nation in the spirit of the apostle, acknowledging "our highest wisdom is but as foolishness." He would mine every good idea from every intellect, while thoroughly recognizing that "our most strenuous efforts would avail nothing in the shadow of His displeasure."

Lincoln concluded his letter to Caleb Russell and Sallie Fenton:

I am conscious of no desire for my country's welfare, that is not in consonance with His will, and of no plan upon which we may not ask His blessing. It seems to me that if there be one subject upon which all good men may unitedly agree, it is imploring the gracious favor of the ***God of Nations*** *upon the struggles our people are making for the preservation of their* ***precious birthright*** *of civil and religious liberty.*

Very truly, Your friend A. Lincoln.

CW VI: 39–40

As he closed his letter, Lincoln returned to the analogy of American liberty as a birthright given by God. The early Hebrew concept of birthright comes from the story of Esau and Jacob (Genesis 25:21-34) and is consistent with Lincoln's ideas of liberty being a gift from the Creator to man. With this birthright, Lincoln believed, comes the sacred responsibility of propagating it to all mankind.

☆ ☆ ☆

March 30, 1863

Proclamation Appointing a National Fast Day by the President of the United States of America

Whereas, the Senate of the United States, devoutly recognizing the Supreme Authority and just Government of Almighty God, in all the affairs of men and of nations, has, by a resolution, requested the President to designate and set apart a day for National prayer and humiliation:

And whereas it is the duty of nations as well as of men, to own their dependence upon the overruling power of God, to confess their sins and transgressions, in humble sorrow, yet with assured hope that genuine repentance will lead to mercy and pardon; and to recognize the sublime truth, announced in the Holy Scriptures and proven by all history, that those nations only are blessed whose God is the Lord:

And, insomuch as we know that, by His divine law, nations like individuals are subjected to punishments and chastisements in this world, may we not justly fear that the awful calamity of civil war, which now desolates the land, may be but a punishment, inflicted upon us, for our presumptuous sins, to the needful end of our national reformation as a whole People? We have been the recipients of the choicest bounties of Heaven. We have been preserved, these many years, in peace and prosperity. We have grown in numbers, wealth and power, as no other nation has ever grown. But we have forgotten God. We have forgotten the gracious hand which preserved us in peace, and multiplied and enriched and strengthened us; and we have vainly imagined, in the deceitfulness of our hearts, that all these blessings were produced by some superior wisdom and virtue of our own. Intoxicated with unbroken success, we have become too self-sufficient to feel the necessity of redeeming and preserving grace, too proud to pray to the God that made us!

The confession that America has "forgotten God," echoes several Old Testament Scriptures that decry how Israel turned aside from God. (See, for example, Deuteronomy 32:18; Jeremiah 2:32, 3:21, 13:25, 18:15; Ezekiel 23:35; Hosea 8:14.)

In his writings, Lincoln often spoke of God as our Maker, the one to whom we must someday give an account. For instance, in a letter to his stepbrother about his father's approaching death, Lincoln left his father to "a merciful Maker" (see chapter 7, page 55). When giving his eulogy for President Taylor, he spoke of man's need to trust his Maker (see chapter 16, page 165). In his diary, Salmon Chase recorded these words from Lincoln: "I made the promise to myself, and to my Maker" (see chapter 17, page 187).

In the next paragraph, Lincoln acknowledged America may have offended God, similar to the situation described in 2 Chronicles 28:13.

It behooves us then, to humble ourselves before the *offended Power*, to confess our national sins, and to pray for clemency and forgiveness.

Now, therefore, in compliance with the request, and fully concurring in the views of the Senate, I do, by this my proclamation, designate and set apart Thursday, the 30th. day of April, 1863, as a day of national humiliation, fasting and prayer. And I do hereby request all the People to abstain, on that day, from their ordinary secular pursuits, and to unite, at their several places of public worship and their respective homes, in keeping the day **holy to the Lord**, and devoted to the humble discharge of the religious duties proper to that solemn occasion.

All this being done, in sincerity and truth, let us then rest humbly in the hope authorized by the **Divine teachings**, that the united cry of the Nation will be heard on high, and answered with blessings, no less than the pardon of our national sins, and the restoration of our now divided and suffering Country, to its former happy condition of unity and peace.

In witness whereof, I have hereunto set my hand and caused the seal of the United States to be affixed.

Done at the City of Washington, this thirtieth day of March, in the year of our Lord one thousand eight hundred and sixty-three, and of the Independence of the United States the eighty seventh.

By the President: Abraham Lincoln

William H. Seward, Secretary of State

CW VI: 155–156

☆ ☆ ☆

In the following proclamation, Lincoln established the last Thursday in November for Thanksgiving, setting the precedent for the holiday we still celebrate today.

On taking office, President Lincoln said he depended on divine assistance for the impossible task ahead. He emphasized that without it, human efforts would fail. When he issued the following proclamation, the

Union armies had won recent victories at Vicksburg and at Gettysburg, but Lincoln was realistic. He knew that disheartening setbacks were likely ahead—and the final outcome was still unclear.

In this beautiful Proclamation of Thanksgiving, we read the words of a man who, regardless of the threatening clouds that filled the horizon, marched ahead in faith that God would yet work out His will.

October 3, 1863

Proclamation of Thanksgiving By the President of the United States of America.

The year that is drawing toward its close, has been filled with the blessings of fruitful fields and healthful skies. To these bounties, which are so constantly enjoyed that we are prone to forget the source from which they come, others have been added, which are of so extraordinary a nature, that they cannot fail to penetrate and soften even the heart which is habitually insensible to the ever watchful providence of Almighty God. In the midst of a civil war of unequalled magnitude and severity, which has sometimes seemed to foreign States to invite and to provoke their aggression, peace has preserved with all nations, order has been maintained, the laws have been respected and obeyed, and harmony has prevailed everywhere except in the theatre of military conflict; while that theatre has been greatly contracted by the advancing armies and navies of the Union. Needful diversions of wealth and of strength from the fields of peaceful industry to the national defence, have not arrested the plough, the shuttle or the ship; the axe has enlarged the borders of our settlements, and the mines, as well of iron and coal as of the precious metals, have yielded even more abundantly than heretofore. Population has steadily increased, notwithstanding the waste that has been made in the camp, the siege and the battle-field; and the country, rejoicing in the consciousness of augmented strength and vigor, is permitted to expect continuance of years with large increase of freedom. No human counsel hath devised nor hath any mortal hand worked out these great things. They are the gracious gifts of the Most High God, who, while dealing with us in anger for our sins, hath nevertheless remembered mercy.

The Hebrew prophet Habakkuk wrote, "In wrath remember mercy" (Habakkuk 3:2). Though President Lincoln substituted the word *anger* for *wrath*, the prayer is the same, that in the time of retribution for sin God be inclined to mercy.

It has seemed to me fit and proper that they should be solemnly, reverently and gratefully acknowledged as with one heart and one voice by the whole American People. I do therefore invite my fellow citizens in every part of the United States, and also those who are at sea and those who are sojourning in foreign lands, to set apart and observe the last Thursday of November next, as a day of **Thanksgiving and Praise to our beneficent Father** who dwelleth in the Heavens. And I recommend to them that while offering up the ascriptions justly due to Him for such singular deliverances and blessings, they do also, with humble penitence for our national perverseness and disobedience, commend to His tender care all those who have become widows, orphans, mourners or sufferers in the lamentable civil strife in which we are unavoidably engaged, and fervently implore the interposition of the **Almighty Hand** to heal the wounds of the nation and to restore it as soon as may be consistent with the **Divine purposes** to the full enjoyment of peace, harmony, tranquillity and Union.

In testimony whereof, I have hereunto set my hand and caused the Seal of the United States to be affixed.

Done at the City of Washington, this Third day of October, in the year of our Lord one thousand eight hundred and sixty-three, and of the Independence of the United States the Eighty-eighth.

Abraham Lincoln

CW VI: 496–497

☆ ☆ ☆

President Lincoln's frequent and passionate proclamations calling upon Americans to seek God's guidance and mercy show that he clearly saw no hope for the nation's survival without God's help.

October 24, 1863

Remarks to Baltimore Presbyterian Synod

Gentlemen of the Baltimore Synod: I can only say that in this case, as in many others, I am profoundly grateful for the support given me in every field of labor in which it can be given, and which has ever been extended to me by the religious community of the country. I saw before taking my position here that I was to have an administration, if it could be called such, of extraordinary difficulty, and it seems to me that it was ever present with me as an extraordinary matter that in the time of the greatest diffi-

culty that this country had ever experienced, or was likely to experience, the man who, at the least of it, gave poor promise of ability, was brought out for duty at that time. I was early brought to the living reflection that there was nothing in the arms of this man, however there might be in others, to rely upon for such difficulties, and that without the direct assistance of the Almighty I was certain of failing. I sincerely wish that I was a more devoted man than I am. Sometimes in my difficulties I have been driven to the last resort to say God is still my only hope. It is still all the world to me.

CW VI: 535–536 (536)

☆ ☆ ☆

December 7, 1863

Announcement of Union Success in Tennessee

Reliable information being received that the insurgent force is retreating from East Tennessee, under circumstances rendering it probable that the Union forces can not hereafter be dislodged from that important position; and esteeming this to be of high national consequence, I recommend that all loyal people do, on receipt of this, informally assemble at their places of worship and tender special homage and gratitude to Almighty God, for this great advancement of the national cause.

A. Lincoln

CW VII: 35

☆ ☆ ☆

During the war, an area or territory might be under military control for various reasons. Churches in such situations sometimes created problems, as the following two documents make clear.

Oliver D. Filley and several others in St. Louis had petitioned the president for the release of Rev. Dr. Samuel McPheeter and the restoration of his pastoral rights. Lincoln makes clear that the government must not be in the business of running churches; it simply does not have that authority. In the first paragraph below, Lincoln quotes from a letter he had sent to General Samuel Curtis, in which he had made this same point.

December 22, 1863

To Oliver D. Filley

'I must add that the U.S. government must not, as by this order, undertake to run the churches. When an individual, in a church or out of it, becomes dangerous to the public interest, he must be checked; but the churches, as such must take care of themselves. . . .'

I have never interfered, nor thought of interfering as to who shall or shall not preach in any church; nor have I knowingly, or believingly, tolerated any one else to so interfere by my authority.

CW VII: 85–86

Lincoln quoted from that same order when writing Edwin M. Stanton, his secretary of war, a few months later. Stanton's department had given Bishop Edward Ames control and possession of Methodist churches in Memphis and New Orleans—which clearly contradicted Lincoln's earlier pledges that his government would not interfere with church affairs.

February 11, 1864

To Edwin M. Stanton

My dear Sir

In January 1863, the Provost-Marshal at St. Louis, having taken the control of a certain church from one set of men and given it to another, I wrote Gen. Curtis on the subject, as follows:

"The U.S. Government must not, as by this order, undertake to run the churches. When an individual, in a church or out of it, becomes dangerous to the public interest, he must be checked; but the churches, as such, must take care of themselves. It will not do for the U.S. to appoint trustees, Supervisors, or other agents for the churches."

CW VII: 178–179

☆ ☆ ☆

Americans supported their troops, not only through prayer, but through charitable contributions such as to the Sanitary Commission. Sanitary Fairs, held in cities all over the country, raised money for sick and injured soldiers and for the improvement of military camp conditions. Since more soldiers died of disease than in battle, the fairs were critically important.

Lincoln supported the Commission's efforts and even spoke at a few of the Sanitary Fairs, including those in Washington, D.C. and Philadelphia.

March 18, 1864

Remarks at Closing of Sanitary Fair, Washington, D. C.

Ladies and Gentlemen: *I appear to say but a word. This extra-ordinary war in which we are engaged falls heavily upon all classes of people, but the most heavily upon the soldier. For it has been said,* ***all that a man hath will he give for his life****; and while all contribute of their substance the soldier puts his life at stake, and often yields it up in his country's cause. The highest merit, then, is due to the soldier. [Cheers.]*

In Job 2:4, Satan argues that a person will give up everything to ensure his heart continues pumping blood and his lungs breathe air. Using the soldiers as an example, Lincoln dismissed that thought.

In this extraordinary war extraordinary developments have manifested themselves, such as have not been seen in former wars; and amongst these manifestations nothing has been more remarkable than these fairs for the relief of suffering soldiers and their families.

CW VII: 253–254

Lincoln's address at the Sanitary Fair in Philadelphia was received with great emotion.

June 16, 1864

Speech at Great Central Sanitary Fair, Philadelphia, Pennsylvania

War, at the best, is terrible, and this war of ours, in its magnitude and in its duration, is one of the most terrible. It has deranged business, totally in many localities, and partially in all localities. It has destroyed property, and ruined homes; it has produced a national debt and taxation unprecedented, at least in this country. It has carried mourning to almost every home, until it can almost be said that the "heavens are hung in black." Yet it continues . . . The Sanitary Commission, with all its benevolent labors, the Christian Commission, with all its Christian and benevolent labors . . . have contributed to the comfort and relief of the soldiers.

CW VII: 394–396 (394)

☆ ☆ ☆

September 3, 1864

Proclamation of Thanksgiving and Prayer

The signal success that Divine Providence has recently vouchsafed to the operations of the United States fleet and army in the harbor of Mobile and the reduction of Fort-Powell, Fort-Gaines, and Fort-Morgan, and the glorious achievements of the Army under Major General Sherman in the State of Georgia, resulting in the capture of the City of Atlanta, call for devout acknowledgement to the Supreme Being in whose hands are the destinies of nations. It is therefore requested that on next Sunday, in all places of public worship in the United-States, thanksgiving be offered to Him for His mercy in preserving our national existence against the insurgent rebels who so long have been waging a cruel war against the Government of the United-States, for its overthrow; and also that prayer be made for the Divine protection to our brave soldiers and their leaders in the field, who have so ofen and so gallantly perilled their lives in battling with the enemy; and for blessing and comfort from the Father of Mercies to the sick, wounded, and prisoners, and to the orphans and widows of those who have fallen in the service of their country, and that he will continue to uphold the Government of the United-States against all the efforts of public enemies and secret foes. ABRAHAM LINCOLN

CW VII: 533–534

October 20, 1864

Proclamation of Thanksgiving
By the President of the United States of America:
A Proclamation.

It has pleased Almighty God to prolong our national life another year, defending us with his guardian care against unfriendly designs from abroad, and vouchsafing to us in His mercy many and signal victories over the enemy, who is of our own household. It has also pleased our Heavenly Father to favor as well our citizens in their homes as our soldiers in their camps and our sailors on the rivers and seas with unusual health. He has largely augmented our free population by emancipation and by immigration, while he has opened to us new sources of wealth, and has crowned the labor of our working men in every department of industry with abundant rewards. Moreover, He has been pleased to animate and inspire our minds and hearts with fortitude, courage and resolution sufficient for the great trial of civil war into which we have been brought by our adherence as a nation to the cause of Freedom and Humanity, and to afford to us reasonable hopes of an ultimate and happy deliverance from all our dangers and afflictions.

Now, therefore, I, Abraham Lincoln, President of the United States, do, hereby, appoint and set apart the last Thursday in November next as a day, which I desire to be observed by all my fellow-citizens wherever they may then be as a day of Thanksgiving and Praise to **Almighty God the beneficent Creator and Ruler of the Universe**. And I do farther recommend to my fellow-citizens aforesaid that on that occasion they do reverently humble themselves in the dust and from thence offer up penitent and fervent prayers and supplications to the **Great Disposer** of events for a return of the inestimable blessings of Peace, Union and Harmony throughout the land, which it has pleased him to assign as a dwelling place for ourselves and for our posterity throughout all generations.

In testimony whereof, I have hereunto set my hand and caused the seal of the United States to be affixed.

Done at the city of Washington this twentieth day of October, in the year of our Lord one thousand eight hundred and sixty four, and, of the Independence of the United States the eighty-ninth. ABRAHAM LINCOLN

By the President:

WILLIAM H. SEWARD, Secretary of State.

CW VIII: 55–56

CHAPTER 19

SECURING AMERICA'S BIRTHRIGHT

In the midst of the chaos and momentous events of his presidency, Lincoln continued to speak frequently about America's birthright and her responsibilities to the Creator. In fact, the great addresses of his presidency—beginning and ending with his inaugural addresses but also including his annual addresses to Congress and the Gettysburg Address—stand as a testament to Lincoln's deepest beliefs and his ability to keep a fractured nation from dividing permanently. Lincoln labored diligently on these speeches, giving each individuality and literary quality.

The Constitution requires the president to address the country on the state of the union. In Lincoln's day, these were given in December and called the Annual Address. In his Second Annual Address to Congress, delivered in December 1862, Lincoln urged his countrymen to be grateful to God for His mercies. He then acknowledged the deep divisions within the country but urged Americans to work toward reconciliation.

Though Lincoln's Second Annual Address to Congress is not well known, it is a literary masterpiece. In it President Lincoln used a passage from the book of Ecclesiastes to lay out his conception of the great purposes of America. The passage chosen is not commonly known, causing one to appreciate Lincoln's receptive mind to literature. Ecclesiastes is philosophy, a soliloquy by Solomon regarding the meaning of life. In an eight-verse poem, the book's writer describes the endless repetition of time, and from the poem Lincoln lifted a sentence (in italics below) that had arrested his mind possibly years before using it.

Vanity of vanities, saith the Preacher, vanity of vanities; all is vanity.

What profit hath a man of all his labour which he taketh under
the sun?

One generation passeth away, and another generation cometh:
but the earth abideth for ever.

The sun also ariseth, and the sun goeth down,
and hasteth to his place where he arose.

The wind goeth toward the south, and turneth about unto
the north;
it whirleth about continually,
and the wind returneth again according to his circuits.

All the rivers run into the sea; yet the sea is not full;
unto the place from whence the rivers come, thither they
return again.

All things are full of labour; man cannot utter it:
the eye is not satisfied with seeing, nor the ear filled with
hearing.

The thing that hath been, it is that which shall be;
and that which is done is that which shall be done:
and there is no new thing under the sun.

Ecclesiastes 1:2-9

December 1, 1862

Annual Message to Congress

Fellow-citizens of the Senate and House of Representatives:

Since your last annual assembling another year of health and bountiful harvests has passed. And while it has not pleased the ***Almighty*** *to bless us with a return of peace, we can but press on, guided by the best light He gives us, trusting that in His own good time, and wise way, all will yet be well.*

Lincoln proceeded with eight pages of discussion of national problems before using his text from Ecclesiastes:

A nation may be said to consist of its territory, its people, and its laws. The territory is the only part which is of certain durability. "One genera-

tion passeth away, and another generation cometh, but the earth abideth forever." It is of the first importance to duly consider, and estimate, this ever-enduring part. That portion of the earth's surface which is owned and inhabited by the people of the United States, is well adapted to be the home of one national family; and it is not well adapted for two, or more. Its vast extent, and its variety of climate and productions, are of advantage, in this age, for one people, whatever they might have been in former ages. Steam, telegraphs, and intelligence, have brought these, to be an advantageous combination, for one united people. . . .

"Physically speaking, we cannot separate. We cannot remove our respective sections from each other, nor build an impassable wall between them. . . .

Can aliens make treaties, easier than friends can make laws? Can treaties be more faithfully enforced between aliens, than laws can among friends? Suppose you go to war, you cannot fight always; and when, after much loss on both sides, and no gain on either, you cease fighting, the identical old questions, as to terms of intercourse, are again upon you." . . .

Our national strife springs not from our permanent part; not from the land we inhabit; not from our national homestead. There is no possible severing of this, but would multiply, and not mitigate, evils among us. In all its adaptations and aptitudes, it demands union, and abhors separation. In fact, it would, ere long, force reunion, however much of blood and treasure the separation might have cost.

And picking up his scriptural text:

Our strife pertains to ourselves—to the passing generations of men; and it can, without convulsion, be hushed forever with the passing of one generation.

With these words, Lincoln acknowledges the possibility of disaster for America: that this great nation with unlimited potential could lose its power and influence within a single generation. With this literary exposé from Ecclesiastes for background, Lincoln unveiled to Congress a resolution and articles amendatory to the Constitution of the United States concerning the abolition of slavery. His proposal: States that would abolish slavery before 1900 would receive compensation. He provided more details:

Is it doubted, then, that the plan I propose, if adopted, would shorten the war, and thus lessen its expenditure of money and of blood? Is it doubted that it would restore the national authority and national prosperity, and perpetuate both indefinitely? Is it doubted that we here—Congress and Executive—can secure its adoption? Will not the good people respond to a united, and earnest appeal from us? Can we, can they, by any other means, so certainly, or so speedily, assure these vital objects? We can succeed only by concert. It is not "can any *of us* imagine *better?" but "can we all do better?" Object whatsoever is possible, still the question recurs "can we do better?" The* **dogmas** *of the quiet past, are inadequate to the stormy present. The occasion is piled high with difficulty, and we must rise with the occasion. As our case is new, so we must think anew, and act anew. We must disenthrall our selves, and then we shall save our country. . . .*

Lincoln used his rare ability to select the precise word. The dictionary defines *dogma* as "something held as an established opinion, especially: a definite authoritative tenet."[1] *Disenthrall* is to free ourselves from ideas that have held us "captivated" or "spellbound." In a great paragraph, Lincoln pierces the layers of surface thinking and easy conclusions.

The letter to Philemon in the New Testament provides a good illustration of *disenthrallment.* The apostle Paul wrote to a friend who was the owner of a runaway slave. Philemon had his dogma regarding property rights. It would seem natural for the apostle with his strong Christian faith and convictions to awaken the conscience of his friend. But Paul stopped, stepped back, and shook off his "enthrallment" with his own convictions against slavery. In friendship, he asked Philemon to issue freedom to a runaway slave, charging it to the apostle's account. The beautiful spirit of the apostle won his friend. Abraham Lincoln also used disenthrallment as a powerful personal weapon.

Lincoln's words, "the occasion is piled high with difficulty," were an understatement, for the Union had gone through a disastrous year with more sacrifice and bloodshed on the horizon. Like Churchill speaking during the dark hours of World War II, Lincoln stood undaunted with an inward confidence that could only come from a God-inspired faith.

Fellow-citizens, we *cannot escape history. We of this Congress and this administration, will be remembered in spite of ourselves. No personal significance, or insignificance, can spare one or another of us. The fiery trial through which we pass, will light us down, in honor or dishonor, to the latest generation. We* say *we are for the Union. The world will not forget that we say this. We know how to save the Union. The world knows we do know how to save it. We—even* we here*—hold the power, and bear the responsibility. In* giving *freedom to the* slave, *we* assure *freedom to the* free *—honorable alike in what we give, and what we preserve. We shall nobly save, or meanly lose, the last best, hope of earth. Other means may succeed; this could not fail. The way is plain, peaceful, generous, just—a way which, if followed, the world will forever applaud, and God must forever bless.*

Abraham Lincoln

CW V: 518–537 (518, 527–529, 537)

We might summarize Lincoln's phrase "last best hope of earth" this way:

Last: after centuries of tyranny

Best: for if a people's government will not work, nothing will. The black man would keep his chains, and the weaker men of every generation would be destined for serfdom as they have since Adam.

Hope: Webster's dictionary gives the meaning in classical usage as "ground or source of happy expectation." Lincoln had solid confidence that in the Creator's plan, when His creatures cooperate in a "People's Government," there is good government.

☆ ☆ ☆

The Union's situation in early summer 1863 was a precarious one. From Vicksburg, a natural citadel on a high bluff along the Mississippi, the Confederates controlled all water traffic. For months, General Grant and his soldiers had doggedly kept a choke-hold siege, but they were unable to take the city.

Meanwhile, Robert E. Lee was fully cognizant that his armies need not defeat the Union. Rather, they must discourage the North so that peace advocates would cry to end the conflict, allowing the South to secede. Thus, he was determined to make an excursion into Pennsylvania in a valiant attempt to win a victory—perhaps even take a city like Harrisburg or Philadelphia—and in so doing, demoralize the North.

Lincoln recognized the seriousness of this threat. Adding to the danger,

Lincoln was, by this point, utterly frustrated with his generals. Not knowing what else do, on Sunday morning, June 28, he appointed George Gordon Meade his fifth commanding general. Meade, a West Point graduate, was still bothered by two bullet wounds taken at Frayser's Farm. Enlisted men knew him as a "snapping turtle," but they respected and trusted him.

Two great armies took positions in and around the sleepy little town of Gettysburg. Not surprisingly, as the Union generals considered the import of their decisions, some of them advised retreat, but ultimately they decided to dig in and fight. To follow the action as closely as possible, Lincoln spent most of his time in the telegraph office.

For three days, from July 1 to July 3, the two armies fought. Tens of thousands paid the "last full measure"; estimates of the total casualties vary, but some are as high as fifty thousand.

In the telegraph office, Lincoln had reason to celebrate that Independence Day: The Union Army had defeated Lee's forces. President Abraham Lincoln announced the good news to the country:

July 4, 1863, 10:00 A.M.

Announcement of News from Gettysburg

The President announces to the country that news from the Army of the Potomac, up to 10 P.M. of the 3rd. is such as to cover that Army with the highest honor, to promise a great success to the cause of the Union, and to claim the condolence of all for the many gallant fallen. And that for this, he especially desires that on this day, **He whose will, not ours, should ever be done**, be everywhere remembered and reverenced with profoundest gratitude.

ABRAHAM LINCOLN

CW VI: 314

That same day, General Grant announced victory at Vicksburg. Following the announcement of July 4, President Lincoln issued a proclamation of thanksgiving to God for these significant Union victories.

July 15, 1863

Proclamation of Thanksgiving

By the President of the United States of America.

It has pleased Almighty God to hearken to the supplications and prayers of an afflicted people, and to vouchsafe to the army and the navy of the United States victories on land and on the sea so signal and so effective as to furnish reasonable grounds for augmented confidence that the Union of these States will be maintained, their constitution preserved, and their peace and prosperity permanently restored. But these victories have been accorded not without sacrifices of life, limb, health and liberty incurred by brave, loyal and patriotic citizens. Domestic affliction in every part of the country follows in the train of these fearful bereavements. It is meet and right to recognize and confess the presence of the Almighty Father and the power of His Hand equally in these triumphs and in these sorrows:

Now, therefore, be it known that I do set apart Thursday the 6th. day of August next, to be observed as a day for National Thanksgiving, Praise and Prayer, and I invite the People of the United States to assemble on that occasion in their customary places of worship, and in the forms approved by their own consciences, render the homage due to the Divine Majesty, for the wonderful things he has done in the Nation's behalf, and invoke the influence of **His Holy Spirit** to subdue the anger, which has produced, and so long sustained a needless and cruel rebellion, to change the hearts of the insurgents, to guide the counsels of the Government with wisdom adequate to so great a national emergency, and to visit with tender care and consolation throughout the length and breadth of our land all those who, through the vicissitudes of marches, voyages, battles and sieges, have been brought to suffer in mind, body or estate, and finally to lead the whole nation, through the paths of repentance and submission to the **Divine Will**, back to the perfect enjoyment of Union and fraternal peace.

In witness whereof, I have hereunto set my hand and caused the seal of the United States to be affixed.

Done at the city of Washington, this fifteenth day of July, in the year of our Lord one thousand eight hundred and sixty-three, and of the Independence of the United States of America the eighty-eighth.

By the President: ABRAHAM LINCOLN

WILLIAM H. SEWARD, Secretary of State.

CW VI: 332–333

☆ ☆ ☆

Unfortunately, after winning at Gettysburg, General Meade did not follow up by cutting off General Lee's escape route back into Confederate lines. Because of this timid approach, Lee's battered and beaten forces lived to fight another day. The Union Army failed to deliver a knockout punch, so the war would drag on.

☆ ☆ ☆

President Lincoln was invited to make "a few appropriate remarks" at the dedication of the cemetery at Gettysburg on November 19, 1863. The main address would be made by Edward Everett, the former president of Harvard and a famed orator.

Tormented by telegraph reports and night visions of young men falling in battle, President Abraham Lincoln stepped upon the battlefield with its ghastly sights. While the grieving public and the critical press could not imagine Lincoln's thoughts, Walt Whitman provides a glimpse of the mental anguish the president must have felt:

> I saw battle-corpses, myriads of them,
> And the white skeletons of young men, I saw them,
> I saw the debris and debris of all the slain soldiers of the war,
> But I saw they were not as was thought,
> They themselves were fully at rest, they suffer'd not,
> The living remain'd and suffer'd, the mother suffer'd,
> And the wife and the child and the musing comrade suffer'd,
> And the armies that remain'd suffer'd.[2]

The tall, wearied man from the White House "suffer'd." What could a mortal man of dust say amidst the fallen? As Lincoln prepared his remarks for the dedication of the Soldiers National Cemetery in Gettysburg, he envisioned the bodies that a few months before were husbands, sweethearts, and fathers, full of life with dreams of tomorrow.

Words are empty, useless in the presence of life-and-death realities. Words make mockery of tears and heartaches. The president could only draw his thoughts from the words of the Eternal God. He began with the psalm of Moses, "From everlasting to everlasting, thou art God. . . . The days of our years are threescore years and ten; and if by reason of strength they be fourscore" (Psalm 90:2, 10). The final text of his speech appears below.

November 19, 1863

Address Delivered at the Dedication of the Cemetery at Gettysburg

Four score and seven years ago our fathers brought forth on this continent, a new nation, conceived in Liberty, and dedicated to the proposition that all men are created equal.

Now we are engaged in a great civil war, testing whether that nation, or any nation so conceived and so dedicated, can long endure. We are met on a great battle-field of that war. We have come to dedicate a portion of that field, as a final resting place for those who here gave their lives that that nation might live. It is altogether fitting and proper that we should do this.

But, in a larger sense, we can not dedicate—we can not consecrate—we can not hallow—this ground. The brave men, living and dead, who struggled here, have consecrated it, far above our poor power to add or detract. The world will little note, nor long remember what we say here, but it can never forget what they did here. It is for us the living, rather, to be dedicated here to the unfinished work which they who fought here have thus far so nobly advanced. It is rather for us to be here dedicated to the great task remaining before us—that from these honored dead we take increased devotion to that cause for which they gave the last full measure of devotion—that we here highly resolve that these dead shall not have died in vain—that this nation, ***under God****, shall have a new birth of freedom—and that government of the people, by the people, for the people, shall not perish from the earth.*

CW VII: 17–23 (23)

The ideas expressed had been long in writing. Under the inspiration of the hour, he added two words. He could not, nor would have wanted to leave them out. To the words written out on his manuscript, he inserted "under God." Those words were added to the copies Lincoln made after the address.

Lincoln historian Louis Warren commented on the significance of the phrase "a new birth of freedom": "The nation 'that was conceived in liberty' that the 'fathers brought forth' and that was 'dedicated to the proposition that all men are created equal,' now, under God, shall have 'a new birth of freedom.' Lincoln was conscious that a nation 'conceived in liberty' by its very nature, periodically, must be rejuvenated, rededicated, and even reborn if it were to survive."[3]

☆ ☆ ☆

Newspaper reactions to Lincoln's speech were largely positive. Many newspapers and periodicals, such as the *Columbus (Ohio) State Journal* and *Harpers New Monthly Magazine*, noted the simple eloquence of the speech and the emotional response it elicited from the audience at the cemetery dedication. A few reporters failed to grasp the significance of Lincoln's address.[4]

James Randall comments:

> In the voluminous literature covering Lincoln's address one finds less appreciation of its larger world significance than minute inspection of its most trivial detail. What did the President wear? . . . Did he ride his horse awkwardly or well? What kind of chair was provided for the nation's Chief on the platform?"[5]

Unfortunately Randall's statement is true. Many are fascinated by the background and countless details surrounding this address, yet they glibly recite Lincoln's words, which have so much meaning, even for Americans today.

☆ ☆ ☆

President Lincoln returned from Gettysburg at 1:10 a.m. the following morning. He had contracted a mild case of smallpox and went immediately to bed. While recovering, he had to prepare his Third Annual Message to Congress, which he would deliver in less than three weeks.

December 8, 1863

Annual Message to Congress

Fellow citizens of the Senate and House of Representatives:

Another year of health, and of sufficiently abundant harvests has passed. For these, and especially for the improved condition of our national affairs, our renewed, and profoundest gratitude to God is due.

While discussing the national problems of slavery, military problems, and foreign relationships, he made this remark regarding Indian tribes:

Sound policy and our imperative duty to these wards of the government demand our anxious and constant attention to their material well-being, to their progress in the arts of civilization, and above all, to that moral training which, under the blessing of ***Divine Providence****, will confer upon them the elevated and sanctifying influences, the hopes and consolation of the* ***Christian faith****. . . .*

Hence, our chiefest care must still be directed to the army and navy, who have thus far borne their harder part so nobly and well. And it may be esteemed fortunate that in giving the greatest efficiency to these indispensable arms, we do also honorably recognize the gallant men, from commander to sentinel, who compose them, and to whom, more than to others, the world must stand indebted for the home of freedom disenthralled, ***regenerated****, enlarged, and perpetuated.*

CW VII: 36-56 (36, 48, 53)

The term *regenerated* is an important New Testament word, one with which Lincoln spoke with familiarity. In the New Testament, it is used in its noun form in Titus 3:5.

Three weeks after his Gettysburg Address with its call for a "new birth of freedom," Lincoln called the world to recognize America, "the home of freedom disenthralled, regenerated, enlarged, and perpetuated."

CHAPTER 20

AN ENDURING LEGACY

Given Lincoln's stature in America today, it's hard to imagine that six months after Gettysburg, his political image was so low that Lincoln did not expect to be reelected. Yet the nation was demoralized by the very heavy cost in human life.

The victories at Gettysburg and at Vicksburg were a turning point in the war. Certainly, the nation had been relieved by the turning back of General Robert E. Lee in his campaign into Pennsylvania, but the Confederacy was far from willing to quit. General Grant was slowly, but powerfully, pushing his way toward Richmond, the Confederacy's capital, but the costs in sacrifice and blood were very high. On July 18, 1864, Lincoln issued a call for 500,000 additional volunteers to strengthen the depleted troops. A war-weary public increasingly demanded an end to the conflict, even if it meant continued slavery.

The Democrats nominated General George McClellan as their 1864 presidential candidate. Early that year, it was still unclear whom the Republicans would nominate. One of Lincoln's cabinet members, Secretary of the Treasury Salmon Chase, made it known that he was willing to be considered. At about this time, Lincoln wrote a memorandum for his cabinet. Though a kind and agreeable person, Lincoln did command a tight ship and demanded a perfect spirit of cooperation among the members of his cabinet.

July 14, 1864

Memorandum Read to Cabinet

I must myself be the judge, how long to retain in, and when to remove any of you from, his position. It would greatly pain me to discover any of you endeavoring to procure anothers removal, or, in any way to prejudice him before the public. Such endeavor would be a wrong to me; and much worse, a wrong to the country. My wish is that on this subject, no remark be made, nor question asked, by any of you, here or elsewhere, now or hereafter.

CW VII: 439

Less than three months before the election, Lincoln's defeat was so probable that he wrote the following and asked his cabinet members to sign the back of the sheet without reading it.

August 23, 1864

Memorandum Concerning His Probable Failure of Re-election

This morning, as for some days past, it seems exceedingly probable that this Administration will not be re-elected. Then it will be my duty to so co-operate with the President elect, as to save the Union between the election and the inauguration; as he will have secured his election on such ground that he can not possibly save it afterwards.

CW VII: 514

This most unusual action shows the mellow spirit of the president in spite of the improbability of his reelection.

Fortunately, by November the Union armies under Grant were making good progress, and it became clear to the public that the long ordeal would soon be over. On Election Day, November 8, 1864, Lincoln won a second term. Three days later, he retrieved the sealed paper from his desk and read the note to his cabinet.

☆ ☆ ☆

On the evening of his reelection, Lincoln greeted some of his supporters.

November 8, 1864

Response to a Serenade

I am ***thankful to God*** *for this approval of the people. But while deeply grateful for this mark of their confidence in me, if I know my heart, my gratitude is free from any taint of personal triumph. I do not impugn the motives of any one opposed to me. It is no pleasure to me to triumph over any one; but I give thanks to the* ***Almighty*** *for this evidence* *of the people's resolution to stand by free government and the rights of humanity.*

CW VIII: 96

November 10, 1864

Response to a Serenade

It has long been a grave question whether any government, not too *strong for the liberties of its people, can be strong* enough *to maintain its own existence, in great emergencies.*

On this point the present rebellion brought our republic to a severe test; and a presidential election occurring in regular course during the rebellion added not a little to the strain. If the loyal people, united, *were put to the utmost of their strength by the rebellion, must they not fail when* divided, *and partially paralized, by a political war among themselves?*

But the election was a necessity. . . .

But the election, along with its incidental, and undesirable strife, has done good too. It has demonstrated that a people's government can sustain a national election, in the midst of a great civil war. Until now it has not been known to the world that this was a possibility. It shows also how sound, *and how* strong *we still are. . . . Gold is good in its place; but living, brave, patriotic men, are better than gold. . . .*

While I am deeply sensible to the high compliment of a re-election; and duly grateful, as I trust, to ***Almighty God*** *for having directed my countrymen to a right conclusion, as I think, for their own good, it adds nothing to my satisfaction that any other man may be disappointed or pained by the result.*

May I ask those who have not differed with me, to join with me, in this same spirit towards those who have?

And now, let me close by asking three hearty cheers for our brave soldiers and seamen and their gallant and skilful commanders.

CW VIII: 100–101

☆ ☆ ☆

Despite the heavy emotional toll Lincoln's first term had cost him, the president never lost his love of telling funny stories or playing jokes. Noah Brooks, a reporter and close friend of Lincoln's, was often in Lincoln's office when other visitors stopped by and was sometimes brought in on the fun. Shortly after the 1864 election, Lincoln called Noah Brooks to him and wrote out the following story.

December 6, 1864

Story Written for Noah Brooks

THE PRESIDENT'S LAST, SHORTEST, AND BEST SPEECH.

On thursday of last week two ladies from Tennessee came before the President asking the release of their husbands held as prisoners of war at Johnson's Island. They were put off till friday, when they came again; and again put off to saturday. At each of the interviews one of the ladies urged that her husband was a religious man. On saturday the President ordered the release of the prisoners, and then said to this lady "You say your husband is a religious man; tell him when you meet him, that I say I am not much of a judge of religion, but that, in my opinion, the religion that sets men to rebel and fight against their government, because, as they think, that government does not sufficiently help *some* men to eat their bread on the sweat of *other* men's faces is not the sort of religion upon which people get to heaven!"

Noah Brooks, writing his recollections for *Harper's New Monthly Magazine*, added the following:

"To this the President signed his name at my request, by way of joke, and added for a caption, 'The President's Last, Shortest, and Best Speech.'"

CW VIII: 154–155

☆ ☆ ☆

The war was finally winding to a close. Lincoln's fourth and final annual message was filled with consideration of the problems the nation would face as it began to heal and rebuild.

December 6, 1864

Fourth Annual Message to Congress

Fellow-citizens of the Senate and House of Representatives:

Again the blessings of health and abundant harvests claim our profoundest gratitude to Almighty God. . . .

Thus it is hoped that with the return of domestic peace the country will be able to resume with energy and advantage its former high career of commerce and civilization. . . .

Lincoln used this speech to urge Congress to pass a constitutional amendment banning slavery, which the House had recently rejected.

At the last session of Congress a proposed amendment of the Constitution abolishing slavery throughout the United States, passed the Senate, but failed for lack of the requisite two-thirds vote in the House of Representatives. Although the present is the same Congress, and nearly the same members, and without questioning the wisdom or patriotism of those who stood in opposition, I venture to recommend the reconsideration and passage of the measure at the present session.

One of the most distressing problems facing the president was the willingness of many not only to allow the return of slavery but to reenslave persons formerly held under bondage. In reference to the revolting idea, Lincoln stated:

If the people should, by whatever mode or means, make it an Executive duty to re-enslave such persons, another, and not I, must be their instrument to perform it.

In stating a single condition of peace, I mean simply to say that the war will cease on the part of the government, whenever it shall have ceased on the part of those who began it.

CW VIII: 136–152 (136, 149, 152)

☆ ☆ ☆

Perhaps Lincoln's greatest legacy, and one that he witnessed just prior to being sworn in for a second term, was the passage of the thirteenth amendment to the Constitution. Although the House had rejected it once, Lincoln continued lobbying vigorously for the amendment until Congress passed it.

February 1, 1865

Resolution Submitting the Thirteenth Amendment to the States

Thirty-Eighth Congress of the United States of America;

At the *second* Session,

Begun and held at the City of Washington, on Monday, the *fifth* day of December, one thousand eight hundred and sixty-*four*.

A RESOLUTION

Submitting to the legislatures of the several States a proposition to amend the Constitution of the United States.

Resolved by the Senate and House of Representatives of the United States of America in Congress assembled, (two-thirds of both houses concurring), That the following article be proposed to the legislatures of the several States as an amendment to the constitution of the United States, which, when ratified by three-fourths of said Legislatures, shall be valid, to all intents and purposes, as a part of the said Constitution, namely: Article XIII. Section 1. Neither slavery nor involuntary servitude, except as a punishment for crime whereof the party shall have been duly convicted, shall exist within the United States, or any place subject to their jurisdiction. Section 2. Congress shall have power to enforce this article by appropriate legislation.

SCHUYLER COLFAX

Speaker of the House of Representatives.[1]

H. HAMLIN

Vice President of the United States, and President of the Senate.

Approved, February 1. 1865. ABRAHAM LINCOLN

CW VIII: 253

☆ ☆ ☆

Just one month later, Lincoln delivered a speech to the joint committee of Congress that had been appointed to officially inform him of his election to a second term as president. He had been the first president since Andrew Jackson to win reelection.

March 1, 1865

Reply to Notification Committee

Having served four years in the depths of a great, and yet unended national peril, I can view this call to a second term, in nowise more flatteringly to myself, than as an expression of the public judgment, that I may better finish a difficult work, in which I have labored from the first, than could any one less severely schooled to the task.

In this view, and with assured reliance on that **Almighty Ruler** who has so graceously sustained us thus far; and with increased gratitude to the generous people for their continued confidence, I accept the renewed trust, with it's yet onerous and perplexing duties and responsibilities.

Please communicate this to the two Houses of Congress.

CW VIII: 326–327

Referring to the above, Thurlow Weed wrote: "The reply to the Committee of Congress, informing of your re-election, is not only the neatest but the most pregnant and effective use to which the English Language was ever put."[2]

☆ ☆ ☆

The war had lasted four years. Except for a decisive turn in favor of the Union, Lincoln would have lost the election, and the new administration would likely have made a settled peace, with the South becoming a sovereign state with legalized slavery. Abraham Lincoln's name would not be known except as a footnote of one who tried and failed. How long the black man would have been in chains, who could know? And the nation would not have heard the masterpiece of the Second Inaugural Address.

In the Gettysburg Address, President Lincoln stated the unique purpose of our government, along with its peculiar privilege and greatness. He also said that loyalty and sacrifice were necessary conditions to maintaining our form of government. At Gettysburg, Lincoln expressed his concern that the American experiment in people's government would endure. The heartfelt words of this address will live as long as the Stars and Stripes wave.

The Second Inaugural Address recognizes that one of the challenges of a democracy is that men—good, thinking men—are different and will disagree. This address is the epitome of all Lincoln had written before and beautifully expresses his understanding of the American birthright, which he believed could lift and bless all mankind. Demonstrating again his ability to select the right quotation, President Lincoln uses a relatively unfamiliar verse, Psalm 19:9, to express his feelings that God's judgments are proper.

March 4, 1865

Second Inaugural Address

. . . Neither party expected for the war, the magnitude, or the duration, which it has already attained. Neither anticipated that the cause *of the conflict might cease with, or even before, the conflict itself should cease. Each looked for an easier triumph, and a result less fundamental and astounding. Both read the same Bible, and pray to the same God; and each invokes His aid against the other. It may seem strange that any men should dare to ask a just God's assistance in wringing their* ***bread from the sweat of other***

men's faces; *but let us* ***judge not that we be not judged****. The prayers of both could not be answered; that of neither has been answered fully. The Almighty has His own purposes.* ***"Woe unto the world because of offences! for it must needs be that offences come; but woe to that man by whom the offence cometh!"*** *If we shall suppose that American Slavery is one of those offences which, in the providence of God, must needs come, but which, having continued through His appointed time, He now wills to remove, and that He gives to both North and South, this terrible war, as the woe due to those by whom the offence came,* ***shall we discern therein any departure from those divine attributes which the believers in a Living God always ascribe to Him?*** *Fondly do we hope—fervently do we pray—that this mighty scourge of war may speedily pass away. Yet, if God wills that it continue, until all the wealth piled by the bond-man's two hundred and fifty years of unrequited toil shall be sunk, and until every drop of blood drawn with the lash, shall be paid by another drawn with the sword, as was said three thousand years ago, so still it must be said* ***"the judgments of the Lord, are true and righteous altogether."***

With malice toward none; with charity for all; with firmness in the right, as God gives us to see the right, let us strive on to finish the work we are in; to bind up the nation's wounds; to care for him who shall have borne the battles, and for his widow, and his orphan—to do all which may achieve and cherish a just, and a lasting peace, among ourselves, and with all nations.

CW VIII: 332–333

The Second Inaugural is like a sermon and is full of allusions from the following Scripture:

> Bread from the sweat of other men's faces. (Genesis 3:19)
> Judge not, that ye be not judged. (Matthew 7:1)
> Woe unto the world because of offences! For it must needs be that offences come; but woe to that man by whom the offence cometh! (Matthew 18:7; Luke 17:1)
> The judgments of the LORD are true and righteous altogether. (Psalm 19:9); (For a comment to Thurlow Weed regarding the selection of this verse, see page 236.)
> The phrase *Living God* is used in Scripture to differentiate between a god of wood or stone and a powerful God, one who responds to the appeals of His people.[3]

In his own life, Lincoln had progressed from a young man of uncertain faith through a dark tunnel in which he struggled to find and know the will of God. In this Second Inaugural Address, his faith glows in triumph, for he has witnessed the actions of a Living God.

Elton Trueblood wrote:

> If there has ever been any doubt about Lincoln's conception of God being personal, the Second Inaugural dispels that doubt. He refers with ambiguity to the "Living God." This is far removed from any philosophical system which sees God as an impersonal force. God, as envisaged in the Second Inaugural, is personal because He has a "will", and "living" because He makes a difference in contemporary history. The personal understanding of God's will separates Lincoln's thinking from the fatalism which sometimes is discussed in his youthful speculations.[4]

☆ ☆ ☆

As President Abraham Lincoln concluded the inaugural address for his second term, he bent low and kissed the Bible upon which he had taken his presidential oath. His hand was placed upon verses marked by pencil:

> None shall be weary nor stumble among them;
> none shall slumber nor sleep;
> Neither shall the girdle of their loins be loosed,
> nor the latchet of their shoes be broken:
> Whose arrows are sharp,
> And all their bows bent,
> their horses' hoofs shall be counted like flint,
> and their wheels like a whirlwind.
>
> Isaiah 5:27-28

Without knowing the context of this passage, this seems like a puzzling choice. The choice of this unusual passage of Scripture speaks again of Lincoln's rare acquaintance with the Bible. In the Old Testament, Jehovah God used people and even animals such as the great fish and the lions in the stories of Jonah and Daniel. In order to perform His will, He made use of nations, not only Israel but at times Israel's enemies. Verse 26, which immediately precedes the passage highlighted by pencil, reads: "[God] will lift up a banner to the nations from afar, and will whistle to them from the end of the earth" (NKJV). The Lord is summoning one of Israel's enemies to carry out His commands. In poetic language, the response was so energetic that "none shall slumber nor sleep." Their weapons were ready and "their horses' hoofs like flint."

America, by honoring God, would experience the benefits of divine blessings, great successes, and unusual progress. The context of these verses relates to nations that worshipped gods other than Jehovah. Though Lincoln knew God called only Israel his "chosen people," the president considered the American nation an "almost chosen people" (see part 3 opening page) with the privilege and responsibility of leading other nations to follow the precepts of the Divine Architect that they might also be blessed.

Most politicians test the wind before making unpopular statements, especially when quoting from the Bible. This was not Lincoln's practice. Like a Hebrew prophet, he expressed in the Second Inaugural Address what he felt needed to be said, realizing that truth, forcefully stated, is not always palatable. In his quotation of Psalm 19:9, he spoke, not as a politician, but as a statesman sincerely attempting to move his audience.

☆ ☆ ☆

Thurlow Weed was a prominent New York political boss and advisor whom Lincoln had consulted during his 1860 campaign. In the letter below, Lincoln responds to Weed's praise for his Second Inaugural.

March 15, 1865

To Thurlow Weed

My dear Sir,

Every one likes a compliment. Thank you for yours on my little notification speech, and on the recent Inaugural Address. I expect the latter to wear as well as—perhaps better than—any thing I have produced; but I believe it is not immediately popular. ***Men are not flattered by being shown that there has been a difference of purpose between the Almighty and them.*** *To deny it, however, in this case, is to deny that there is a God governing the world. It is a truth which I thought needed to be told; and as whatever of humiliation there is in it, falls most directly on myself, I thought others might afford for me to tell it. Yours truly A. LINCOLN*

CW VIII: 356

☆ ☆ ☆

We have seen many pictures of Abraham Lincoln in this book: the boy by firelight, the young orator at the Lyceum podium, the fiery debater challenging Douglas, the towering intellectual at Cooper Union. We've seen him embodying the spirit of government of, by, and for the people at Gettysburg and as the world statesman promoting malice toward none and charity for all at his second inauguration.

There is one more great picture, given us by biographers James Randall and Richard Current. They describe him as he walked though the streets of the evacuated Confederate capitol, Richmond, Virginia, on April 5, 1865. The tall man in his overcoat and top hat was recognized by many. As he walked along, he was greeted warmly by former slaves and soldiers alike.

> His appearance among the people of what had been, until so recently, the enemy capital, deeply moved a Boston newspaper correspondent, who wrote: "He came among them unheralded, without pomp or parade. He walked through the streets as if he were only a private citizen, and not the head of a mighty nation. He came not as a conqueror, not with bitterness in his heart, but with kindness. He came as a friend, to alleviate sorrow and suffering—to rebuild what had been destroyed."[5]

☆ ☆ ☆

General Robert E. Lee surrendered to General Ulysses S. Grant in Appomattox Court House, Virginia, on April 9. One month and five days after President Lincoln had so beautifully summed up the meaning of four years of costly devastation in his Second Inaugural Address, the war came to a weary end.

April 11, 1865

Last Public Address

We meet this evening, not in sorrow, but in gladness of heart. The evacuation of Petersburg and Richmond, and the surrender of the principal insurgent army, give hope of a righteous and speedy peace whose joyous expression can not be restrained. In the midst of this, however, ***He, from***

Whom all blessings flow*, must not be forgotten. A call for a national thanksgiving is being prepared, and will be duly promulgated.*

CW VIII: 399–405 (399–400)

From a White House porch, a serenading crowd asked the president: "What music would you like?" His answer: "Dixie."[6]

☆ ☆ ☆

"Let there be Malice toward none, Charity for all."

Will the America of the future—
will this vast, rich Union ever realize
what itself cost,
back there
after all?

Walt Whitman from *Leaves of Grass*,
preface note to 2nd annex (1891)

CONCLUSION

THE FAITH OF ABRAHAM LINCOLN

In his Second Inaugural Address, President Lincoln spoke of "the believers in a Living God." Did President Lincoln include himself in that body? Did he look to a "Living God" for wisdom, guidance, and assistance?

As I read the entire *Collected Works* over many years, I realized that Lincoln's own words illuminate the journey he made from doubt to trust in a personal God. Based on my reading of Lincoln's writings, I submit the following four conclusions.

1. Lincoln had a great capacity to grow—whether as a public speaker, an attorney, a legislator, or commander in chief. Biographers attest to Lincoln's ability to face personal deficiencies and make improvements. His life is a study of growth in character, intellect, leadership traits, and spiritual development.

Clearly his early childhood reading of the Bible anchored him through the difficult years and gave him depth and resilience as he piloted the Ship of State through the stormy seas. Many politicians have quoted Scripture, but few as extensively as Lincoln.

2. The preponderance of Lincoln's statements points to the development of a personal faith. Barring evidence to the contrary, we owe him acceptance of his word. Public statements, private letters, notes to friends, and documents meant only for his own eyes all speak in unified harmony of a growing faith in the God of the Bible. How can we question the preponderance of his written record?

3. In his First Inaugural Address, Lincoln took a purposeful oath before God. Though religious statements may be accepted as political rhetoric, Lincoln went beyond that in his conclusion to the First Inaugural Address:

> In your hands, my Dissatisfied fellow countrymen, and not in mine, is the momentous issue of civil war. The government will not assail you. You can have no conflict, without being yourselves the aggressors. You have no oath registered in Heaven to destroy the government, while I shall have the most solemn one to preserve, protect and defend it.[1]

For Lincoln to take an oath, swearing that it is registered in Heaven, if not genuinely sincere, would be sacrilegious and an affront to all believers in the Christian faith. By doing so, President Lincoln would have divested himself of honesty and self-respect.

4. Lincoln boldly and repeatedly asserted that only with the help of God could he successfully lead the country. Historians, sociologists, and psychologists debate how an unqualified backwoods country lawyer could unite the country and accomplish the impossible task of restoring the union. When beginning his inaugural journey from Springfield to Washington, Lincoln said, "Without the assistance of that Divine Being, who ever attended [George Washington], I cannot succeed. With that assistance I cannot fail."[2]

A true patriot, Lincoln was also spurred on by the vision of a reunited country that truly operated under the principle "All men are created equal." He viewed himself as an instrument in God's hand, equipped to preserve the government of the people, by the people, and for the people. In the end, it was his reliance on God and love of America that produced as early twentieth-century Indiana senator Albert Beveridge said, the "wizardry that has mystified historians of all lands."

PRESIDENT LINCOLN'S LEGACY TO YOUTH

My interest in Lincoln has intersected with my fifty-plus years of working with youth through the Kare Youth League in Arcadia, California. On my desk I keep a small statue that perhaps best represents how those two interests converge.

It is a small replica of a sculpture of Lincoln created by Bryant Baker, whose works adorn not only the Capitol in Washington, D.C., but Westminster Abbey in London. The actual "Young Lincoln" sculpture stands in a wilderness background in Delaware Park in Buffalo, New York.

The sculpture depicts the young Abe Lincoln. He has been cutting with his axe, but now he rests and has a book in his hand. He is holding his place with his fingers, lifting his eyes as he ponders the future. He has a serious look, for life is important to him.

Like any youth today, this young Abe has not the faintest idea of what life holds for him. Clearly, as a boy from the backwoods without education and normal cultural advantages, neither he nor anyone else would have expected him to become one of our greatest presidents.

So I turn to Lincoln when considering how to inspire the children with whom I work to discover their life's purpose. If I had to distill that wisdom down to nine key lessons, they would be:

1. The Bible is given by God to man, and a person serves his spiritual needs by reading it regularly.

2. The Creator places uniqueness and greatness in every child. In his Lecture on Discoveries and Inventions (chapter 10), Lincoln writes that God implants special gifts in persons.

We possess dignity because we are related to God. President Lincoln declared to a delegation of African Americans: "It is difficult to make a man miserable while he feels he is worthy of himself, and claims kindred to the great God who made him."[1]

3. We must worship God. We must confess our sins, offer thanksgiving to Him, pray for His guidance, and submit to His will.

4. There are issues of right and wrong, and we must learn to tell the difference. Lincoln used the term "eternal right," recognizing moral laws that are fundamental to all rules of conduct set by men (*CW* IV: 7–8).

5. God has given each of us the privilege of being an instrument in His hand, helping Him perform His will on earth. Someday each of us will make a report to our Maker.

6. We can only fulfill our place in the Creator's plan with the help of God. Abraham Lincoln often expressed a twofold statement: "Without Him, I cannot succeed; with Him, I cannot fail."

7. Freedom is the golden apple, but it exists only as it rests in a silver frame of law.

8. The birthright of being an American is a great privilege and a greater responsibility. Privilege and responsibility form the two sides of a single coin; we cannot have one without the other. Americans are privileged while we bear the sacred trust of responsibility in sharing democracy with all other people of the world.

9. Others have sacrificed and paid the "last full measure" that we might enjoy the liberties that we enjoy. We must ensure that "government of the people, by the people and for the people shall not perish from the earth."

BIBLE REFERENCES IN *THE COLLECTED WORKS OF ABRAHAM LINCOLN*

Oral sources record many Scriptures used by Abraham Lincoln. This study is limited to those accepted by *The Collected Works*. It is the price we pay for certainty of usage by Lincoln.

The following chart includes the Scripture reference used, along with the verse or phrase as it appears in the King James Version. That is followed by source information detailing where it is found in *The Collected Works*, the date it was used, and the chapter in this book where more of that Lincoln document can be found.

In contrast to his use of biblical quotations in his great addresses to support his powerful advocacy of democracy, the Lecture on Discoveries and Inventions was secular. For that reason, I have listed his Scripture references in that document separately. (The lecture demonstrates careful study and the notation of chapter and verse—something that Lincoln does not do elsewhere in his speeches or other writings.)

Scripture	KJV Quote	*CW*	Date	Chapter
Genesis				
1:26-27	"Let us make man in our image and after our likeness."	II: 546	Aug. 17, 1858	11
3:1-3	good and evil	II: 278	Oct. 16, 1864	11
3:17	cursed of the race	III: 462	Sept. 17, 1859	11
3:19	"In the sweat of thy face shalt thou eat bread."	I: 411	Dec. 1, 1847	6
		VIII: 333	March 4, 1865	21
4:10	"the blood of Abel . . . crieth unto me from the ground"	I: 439	Jan. 12, 1848	6
5:24	"And Enoch walked with God"	II: 141	Aug. 14, 1852	8
Exodus				
12:37 (or Numbers 1:46)	"The children of Israel . . . about four (six) hundred thousand"	II: 409	June 26, 1857	9
14:13 (also in 2 Chronicles 20:17)	"Stand still and see the salvation of the Lord"	I: 289	July 4, 1842	4
Deuteronomy				
32:39	"I wound, and I heal"	V: 118	Feb. 1, 1862	14
Joshua				
24:15	"Choose you"	III: 410	Sept. 16, 1859	11

Scripture	KJV Quote	*CW*	Date	Chapter
Job				
2:4	"All that a man hath will he give for his life."	VII: 254	March 18, 1864	18
6:2-3	"My grief . . . heavier than the sand of the sea"	I: 229	Jan. 23, 1841	4
Psalms				
19:9	"The judgments of the Lord are true and righteous altogether."	VIII: 333	March 4, 1865	20
33:12	"Blessed is the nation whose God is the Lord."	VI: 155	March 30, 1863	18
67:4	"govern the nations"	V: 478	Oct. 26, 1862	18
90:10	"fourscore"	VII: 23	Nov. 19, 1863	19
111:10	"The fear of the Lord is the beginning of wisdom." (See Job 28:28)	IV: 482	Aug. 12, 1861	14
137:5-6	"Let my right hand forget her cunning . . . my tongue cleave to the roof of my mouth"	IV: 239	Feb. 21, 1861	13
Proverbs				
6:6	"Go to the ant, thou sluggard; consider her ways, and be wise."	II: 437	April 6, 1858	10
9:10	"The fear of the Lord is the beginning of wisdom." (See Job 28:28 and Psalm 111:10)	IV: 482	Aug. 12, 1861	14
16:33	"Man proposes, and God disposes"	VII: 301	April 18, 1864	
25:11	"A word fitly spoken is like apples of gold in pictures of silver."	IV: 169	Jan. 1861	13
		IV: 161 (note)	Dec. 22, 1860	13
Ecclesiastes				
1:4	"One generation passeth away, and another generation cometh: but the earth abideth forever."	V: 527	Dec. 1, 1862	19
3:7	"a time to keep silence"	IV: 195	Feb. 11, 1861	13
9:4	"A living dog is better than a dead lion"	II: 467	June 16, 1858	11
Isaiah				
7:14 and 8:10	"God with us"	II: 385	Dec. 10, 1856	9
53:1 (see also John 12:38)	Arm of Jehovah	III: 410	Sept. 16, 1859	11
Ezekiel				
37:9	"Come from the four winds, O breath, and breathe upon these slain, that they may live."	I: 278	Feb. 22, 1842	3

Scripture	KJV Quote	*CW*	Date	Chapter
Matthew				
5:48	"Be ye therefore perfect, even as your Father which is in heaven is perfect."	II: 501	July 10, 1858	11
6:34	"Sufficient unto the day is the evil thereof."	II: 260	Oct. 16, 1854	8
7:1	Judge not, that ye be not judged.	VIII: 333	March 4, 1865	20
7:6	"turn again and rend you"	III: 95	Sept. 11, 1858	11
16:18	"the gates of hell shall not prevail"	I: 115	Jan. 27, 1838	3
		IV: 194	Feb. 11, 1861	13
Luke				
15:7	Parable of the lost sheep—"joy shall be in heaven over one sinner that repenteth"	II: 510–511	July 17, 1858	11
16:31	"If they hear not Moses and the prophets, neither will they be persuaded, though one rise from the dead."	IV: 130	Oct. 23, 1860	12
John				
1:11	"He came unto his own, and his own received him not" (used facetiously)	II: 282	Oct. 16, 1854	8
6:26	desire to have the "loaves and fishes"	III: 461	Sept. 17, 1859	11
6:70	The Saviour chose twelve, one a devil	1: 167	Dec. 26, 1839	3
12:6	Judas "had the bag"	I: 167	Dec. 26, 1839	3
13:27	"That thou doest, do quickly"	Second Supple-ment: I	June 1, 1849	6
15:5	"He that abideth in me, and I in him, the same bringeth forth much fruit: for without me ye can do nothing."	IV: 190	Feb. 11, 1861	13
Multiple Gospels				
Matthew 6:9-13 Luke 11:2-4	Lord's Prayer	VI: 501	Oct. 5, 1863	17
Matthew 6:24 Luke 16:13	"No servant can serve two masters . . . hold to the one, and despise the other. Ye cannot serve God and mammon."	II: 275	Oct. 16, 1854	8
Matthew 7:12 Luke 6:31	"Whatsoever ye would that men should do to you, do ye even so to them;"	I: 473	May 21, 1848	6

Scripture	KJV Quote	CW	Date	Chapter
Multiple Gospels *(Continued)*				
Matthew 7:16-18 Luke 6:43-44	"Ye shall know them by their fruits. . . . Neither can a corrupt tree bring forth good fruit."	I: 347	Oct. 3, 1845	9
Matthew 8:28-34 Mark 5:1-20 Luke 8:26-39	Story of Legion	I: 272	Feb. 22, 1842	3
Matthew 9:13 Mark 2:17 Luke 5:32	"I am not come to call the righteous, but sinners to repentance."	III: 550	Feb. 27, 1860	12
		III: 554	March 2, 1860	12
		IV: 8	March 5, 1860	12
Matthew 10:29-30 Luke 12:6-7	"sparrows . . . one of them shall not fall on the ground without your Father. But the very hairs of your head are all numbered."	II: 97	Jan. 12, 1851	7
Matthew 12:25 Mark 3:25 Luke 11:17	"Every kingdom divided against itself is brought to desolation; and every city or house divided against itself shall not stand."	I: 315 (first of many uses)	March 4, 1843	3
Matthew 12:34 Luke 6:45	"Out of the abundance of the heart the mouth speaketh."	II: 271	Oct. 16, 1854	8
Matthew 12:30 Luke 11:23	"He who is not for us is against us; he who gathereth not with us scattered."	III: 462	Sept. 17, 1859	11
Matthew 18:7 Luke 17:1	"Woe unto the world because of offences! For it must needs be that offences come; but woe to that man by whom the offence cometh."	VIII: 333	March 4, 1865	20
Matthew 23:12 Luke 14:11, 18:14	"He that humbleth himself shall be exalted."	II: 90	July 25, 1850	16
Acts				
13:46	"turn to the Gentiles" (a facetious usage)	II: 282	Oct. 16, 1854	8
Romans				
3:8	"Let us do evil, that good may come."	I: 347	Oct. 3, 1845	9
8:31	"If God be for us . . ."	II: 385	Dec. 10, 1856	9
1 Corinthians				
1:19-21	"Hath not God made foolish the wisdom of this world?"	VI: 39–40	Jan. 5, 1863	18
15:52	the "last trump"	I: 115	Jan. 27, 1838	3

Scripture	KJV Quote	*CW*	Date	Chapter
Philippians				
2:6-8	regarding the humiliation of Christ	I: 278	Feb. 22, 1842	3
2 Thessalonians				
3:10	"if any would not work, neither should he eat."	V: 423	Sept. 13, 1862	17
Hebrews				
4:16	ascend "unto the throne of grace"	IV: 482	Aug. 12, 1861	14
9:27	"It is appointed unto men once to die."	II: 150	Aug. 14, 1852	18
12:1	"We also are compassed about with so great a cloud of witnesses."	VI: 383	Aug. 12, 1863	16
1 Peter				
4:12	"fiery trial"	V: 478	Oct. 26, 1862	18

SCRIPTURES USED IN THE LECTURE ON DISCOVERIES AND INVENTIONS

This lecture, covered in chapter 10, is recorded in *The Collected Works* volume II, pages 437–442 (April 6, 1858) and volume III, pages 356–363 (February 11, 1859). Uncharacteristically, Lincoln gave many chapter and verse references in this address.

Scripture	Reference
Gen. 2:15	Man put in the Garden to "dress it, and to keep it"
Gen. 3:7, 21	fig leaves for clothing "coats of skin, and clothed them"
Gen. 3:17-23	The first heir of the "curse—was a tiller of the ground"
Gen. 4:22	"Tubalcain, an instructer of every artificer in brass and iron"
Gen. 6:14-8:19	"gopher wood for the ark for the flood" and "the ark . . . belonging rather to the miraculous than to human invention"
Gen. 9:23	*garment*, used by two sons to cover Noah
Gen. 12:10-20	Abraham's sojourn in Egypt
Gen. 14:23	*thread*, mentioned by Abraham
Gen. 22:3	Abraham saddled a donkey, indicating "that riding had been in use some time."
Gen. 24:61	After the search for a wife for Isaac, "Rebekah arose, and her damsels, and they rode upon the camels, and followed the man."
Gen. 41:43	*chariot*, oldest recorded allusion to the wheel on occasion of Joseph being made governor by Pharaoh
Gen. 42:26	Animals bore burdens. Joseph's brethren "laded their asses wih the corn."
Gen. 49:13	*ships*
Ex. 14:9, 23	*horses*
Ex. 14:25	*chariot-wheels*
Ex. 15:1	*horse*, "Sang Moses and the children of Israel this song unto the Lord 'the horse, and his rider hath he thrown into the sea'"
Ex. 28:42	*linen breeches*
Ex. 35:25-26	"All the women that were wise hearted did spin with their hands and all the women whose hearts stirred them up in wisdom, spun goat's hair."
Ex. 35:35	weaver
Num. 35:16	*instrument of iron*
Deut. 3:11	*bed-stead of iron*
Deut. 4:20	*the iron furnace*
Deut. 8:9	"a land whose stones are iron, and out of whose hills thou mayest dig brass."
Deut. 19:5	"the axe to cut down the tree"
Deut. 22:10	*plows*
Deut. 27:5	*iron tool*

Scripture	Reference
Job 7:6	*weaver's shuttle*
Prov. 6:6	*ants and honey-bees*, referred to by Solomon
Isa. 33:21, 23	*oars and sails*, not mentioned until Isaiah (Reference not given by Lincoln.)
Matt. 24:41; Luke 17:35	mills, "Two women shall be grinding at the mill"

In the second part of his Lecture on Discoveries and Inventions, Lincoln gave no Bible references and briefly mentions only a few details from Genesis.

Scripture	Reference
Gen. 2–3	the Adam and Eve story
Gen. 2:20	the naming of the animals
Gen. 2:21-23	the making of Eve from a bone in his side
Gen. 3:7	the fig-leaf apron
Rev. 21:1	"There was no more sea"

BIBLE SUBJECTS USED AS ILLUSTRATIONS IN *THE COLLECTED WORKS*

(NOT INCLUDING THE LECTURE ON DISCOVERIES AND INVENTIONS)

Subject	Scripture Ref	*CW*	Date	Chapter
Almost Chosen People	Ex. 19:6	IV: 235,6	Feb. 21, 1861	13
Babel, Tower of	Gen. 11:1-9	II: 141	Aug. 14, 1852	8
		V: 416	Sept. 12, 1862	16
Bible				
Bibles owned by Abraham Lincoln: (1) Gift from Lucy Speed (2) Father's family Bible with three pages of records filled in by Abraham Lincoln (3) Personal Bible with family record (4) Presented by "Loyal Colored People" of Baltimore		 I: 261 I: 94–95 I: 304 VII: 542	 1841 1851 Nov. 4, 1842 Sept. 7, 1864	 4 17
"so long as the Bible shall be read"		I: 115	Jan. 27, 1838 Lyceum Address	3
"best cure for the 'blues' could one but take it according to the truth"		I: 261	Sept. 27, 1841	4
"I am fully aware that there is a text in some Bibles, that is not mine"		II: 130	July 6, 1852	9
"warred . . . as Satan does upon the Bible."		III: 305	Oct. 15, 1858	11
"The Bible says somewhere that we are desperately selfish."		III: 310	Oct. 15, 1858	11
"The good old maxims of the Bible are applicable . . . to human affairs"		III: 462	Sept. 17, 1859	11
"the Bible denounced oppression (slavery) as one of the highest crimes"		V: 421	Sept. 13, 1862	17
"This Great Book . . . is the best gift God has given to man."		VII: 542	Sept. 7, 1864	17
"the sublime truth, announced in the Holy Scriptures and proven by all history"		VI: 155	Mar. 30, 1863	18
"To read in the Bible, as the word of God himself"		VII: 368	May 30, 1864	
No audible answer to slavery, but such as "admits of a squabble"		III: 204,5	Oct. 1, 1858	
Facetiously, The Bible theory of slavery		III:445	Sept. 17, 1859	

Subject	Scripture Ref	CW	Date	Chapter
Birthright	Gen. 25:29-34	VII: 166	Aug. 22, 1864	16
		VII: 512	Aug. 22, 1864	17
		VI: 40	Jan. 5, 1863	18
		III: 63	Aug. 27, 1858	
Crucifixion (Niagara roaring when "Christ suffered on the cross")		II: 10	Sept. 25, 1848	6
Disciples, Twelve		I: 167	Dec. 26, 1839	3
Egypt and Egyptians (references to)				
Pharaoh, holding slaves for 400 years and the Red Sea	Ex. 7–14	II: 132	July 6, 1852	9
Egyptian angel of death to firstborn	Ex. 12:29	I: 278	Feb. 22, 1842	3
Four (six) hundred thousand out from Egyptian bondage	Ex. 12:37; Num. 1:46	II: 409	June 26, 1857	9
Moses leading the Children of Israel from Egypt	Ex. 14:1-31	II: 10	Sept. 25, 1848	6
Pharaoh's country cursed, hosts drowned in Red Sea	Ex. 12-14	II: 132	July 6, 1852	9
Enoch "Enoch walked with God"; remarks in jest of Douglas	Gen. 5:24	II:141	Aug. 14, 1852	8
Eternal See Right makes might "the high matter of eternal consequences, between him and his Maker"		I: 382	July 31, 1846	5
Feeding of 5,000	Matt. 14:15-21; Mark 6:34-44, Luke 9:12-17; John 6:5-13	III: 461	Sept. 17, 1859	11
Forgiveness Christian principle of		VII: 169	Feb. 5, 1864	16
Gold eagle (money blinds)	Ex. 23:8	II: 409	June 26, 1857	9
Goliath	I Sam. 17	II: 379	Oct. 9, 1856	8
Haman	Esther 3–7	II: 321	Aug 24, 1855	2, 9
Heaven, afterlife "joyous meeting with many loved ones gone before"		II: 97	Jan. 12, 1851	7
"not the sort of religion upon which people can get to heaven"		VIII: 155	Dec. 6, 1864	20
Instrument				
Word often used by Lincoln to signify a person being used in the hands of God	Rom. 6:13			

Subject	**Scripture Ref**	***CW***	**Date**	**Chapter**
an accidental instrument		IV: 194	Feb. 11, 1861	13
in encouraging relationship between friend Joshua Speed and his future wife, Fanny		I: 289	July 4, 1842	2
in carrying out wishes of the people		IV: 207	Feb. 14, 1861	13
a humble instrument in the hands of the Almighty		IV: 236	Feb. 21, 1861	13
very humble instrument; illustrated by insignificant part he played in hoisting flag		IV: 245 IV: 382	Feb. 22, 1861 May 22, 1861	13
Legion, story of	Matt. 8:28-34, Mark 5:1-20, Luke 8:26-39	I: 272	Feb. 22, 1842	3
Lie Lincoln's definition		I: 384	Aug. 11, 1846	5
New Birth	John 3:4-7	VII: 17–23	Nov. 19, 1863	19
Paul's doctrine regarding work	2 Thess. 3:10	V: 423	Sept. 13, 1862	17
Peter denying Lord with an oath	Matt. 26:35, 72; Mark 14:29, 68; Luke 22:33, 57; John 13:37, 18:27	IV: 71	June 5, 1860	12
Pharisees (illustration of those who believe themselves better than others)		IV: 274	March 5, 1861	14
Prayer				
"am upheld and sustained by the good wishes and prayers of God's people"		VI: 39	Jan. 5, 1863	18
"God knows how I prayed that this field of ambition might not be opened."		III: 334	Oct. 30, 1858	11
Responsibility before God				
"You have no oath registered in Heaven . . . while I shall have the most solemn one"		IV: 271	March 4, 1861	14
"I am responsible . . . to the American people, to the Christian world, to history, and on my final account to God."	Matt. 12:36, 25:14-30; Luke 16:2; Rom. 14:12; 1 Pet. 4:5	VII: 302	April 18, 1864	20
"when brought to my final reckoning"		VII: 268	May 30, 1864	
Right makes Might		III: 550	Feb. 27, 1860	12
"eternal right makes might"		IV: 9	March 5, 1860	12
		III: 554	March 2, 1860	12

Subject	Scripture Ref	*CW*	Date	Chapter
Sabbath Observance		V: 497	Nov. 15, 1862	16
Selfishness		III: 310	Oct. 15, 1858	11

NAMES FOR DEITY USED IN *THE COLLECTED WORKS*

Name	# of Times Referenced	*CW* Reference	Date	Chapter
Almighty	66			
Almighty Architect	1	I: 178	Dec. 26, 1839	3
Almighty Being	1	IV: 190	Feb. 11, 1861	
Almighty God	13			
Almighty God the beneficient Creator and Ruler of the Universe	1	VIII: 55	Oct. 20, 1864	18
Almighty Power	1	VI: 245	June 2, 1863	
Almighty Ruler	3	IV: 270 VIII: 326	March 4, 1861; March 1, 1865	14, 20
Author of man	1	III: 479	Sept. 30, 1859	
Creator	11			
Divine Guidance	1	V: 186	April 10, 1862	18
Divine Providence	1	VII: 533	Sept. 3, 1864	18
Great Disposer	1	VIII: 56	Oct. 20, 1864	18
Father				
Beneficent Father	1	VI: 497	Oct. 3, 1863	18
Common Father	2	VI: 536	Oct. 24, 1863	18
Father in Heaven	5	II: 501 V: 186	July 10, 1858; April 10, 1862	11, 18
Father of all men	1	V: 128	Feb. 4, 1862	15
Father of Mercies	1	VII: 533	Sept. 3, 1864	18
Father of us all	1	VI: 152		
Heavenly Father	3	V: 478 VIII: 55 VIII: 117	Oct. 26, 1862; Oct. 20, 1864; Nov. 21, 1864	18, 18, 16
God				
Divine Providence	9			
God bless you	10			
God in Heaven	1	III: 488	Oct. 14, 1859	11
God of battles	1	II: 121	July 6, 1852	9
God of Nations	1	VI: 40	Jan. 5, 1863	18
God of our fathers	1	IV: 191	Feb. 11, 1861	13
God (use of name)	228	III: 410		
Jehovah	1	III: 410	Sept. 16, 1859	11

Name	# of Times Referenced	*CW* Reference	Date	Chapter
Living God	1	III: 333	March 4, 1865	20
Lord	15			
Maker	5	I: 382 II: 10 II: 89 II: 97 III: 358	July 31, 1846; Sept. 25, 1848; July 25, 1850; Jan. 12, 1851; Feb. 11, 1859	5, 6, 12, 7, 10
Maker of the universe	1	IV: 226	Feb. 18, 1861	13
Most High God	1	VI: 496	Oct. 3, 1863	18
Omnipotence	1	I: 278	Feb. 22, 1842	3
Omniscient mind and Almighty arm	1	IV: 191	Feb. 11, 1861	13
Providence	18			
Ruler				
Almighty and Merciful Ruler of the Universe	1	VII: 432	July 7, 1864	
Almighty Ruler of Nations	1	I: 270	March 4, 1861	14
Supreme Being	1	VII: 533	Sept. 3, 1864	18
Supreme Ruler of Nations	1	IV: 246	Feb. 26, 1861	13
Supreme Ruler of the Universe	1	III: 10 VII: 431	Aug. 21, 1858; July 7, 1864	
Savior/Saviour	6	I: 167 II: 442 II: 501 II: 511 III: 17 VII: 542	Dec. 26, 1839; April 6, 1858; July 10, 1858; July 17, 1858; Aug. 21, 1858; Sept. 7, 1864	11, 17, 13
Supreme Authority	1	VI: 155	March 30, 1863	18
Supreme Being	3	IV: 220	Feb. 16, 1861	13
Supreme Government of God	1	IV: 482	Aug. 12, 1861	14
Under God	3	IV: 243 VII: 23 VII: 234	Feb. 22, 1861; Nov. 19, 1863; March 9, 1864	13

ENDNOTES

Foreword

1. F. Lauriston Bullard, *Lincoln in Marble and Bronze* (New Brunswick, NJ: Rutgers University Press, 1952).
2. Albert Beveridge, *Abraham Lincoln 1809–1858*, vol. 1 (Cambridge: Riverside Press, 1928), 606–07.
3. Abraham Lincoln, *The Collected Works of Abraham Lincoln*, Roy P. Basler, ed., vol. VIII (New Brunswick, NJ: Rutgers University Press, 1953–1955), 332–333.

Chapter 2: New Salem

1. Joyce Appleby, *Inheriting the Revolution* (Cambridge, MA: Belknap Press, 2000), 89.

Chapter 3: Legislator

1. Benjamin P. Thomas, *Abraham Lincoln: A Biography* (New York: Random House, Inc./Alfred A. Knopf, 1952), 52.
2. Ibid., 78.
3. *The Collected Works*, vol. IV, 439.
4. *The Collected Works*, vol. VII, 17–23.
5. Thomas, *Abraham Lincoln*, 75.
6. Carl Sandburg, *Abraham Lincoln: The Prairie Years*, vol. 1 (New York: Harcourt, Brace and World, 1939), 235.

Chapter 4: Friends and Family

1. In *The Collected Works* the title for this letter is "To Thomas Lincoln and John D. Johnston." Lincoln was writing to his father and his brother, but in this excerpt only the message to his brother is included.

Chapter 5: A Questioning Faith

1. Quoted phrases from *U.S. News and World Report* (February 21, 2005), featuring a summary of *Herndon's Informants: Letters, Interviews, and Statements about Abraham Lincoln*, Douglas L. Wilson and Rodney O. Davis ed. (Chicago: University of Illinois Press, 1998).
2. Thomas, *Abraham Lincoln*, 37–38. Interesting details on Lincoln's honesty—and his financial situation—are included in Harry Pratt, *The Personal Finances of Abraham Lincoln* (n.p.: The Abraham Lincoln Association, 1943).
3. Ralph Waldo Emerson, "Greatness," in *Letters and Social Aims* 8.318 23.

Chapter 6: United States Congressman

1. Stephen B. Oates, *With Malice Toward None* (New York: Harper and Row, 1977), 70.
2. Thomas, *Abraham Lincoln*, 111–14, 119.
3. Thomas, *Abraham Lincoln*, 116.
4. Wayne C. Temple has written in great detail about Lincoln's involvement with the canal system in his book *Lincoln's Connections with the Illinois & Michigan Canal* (Springfield, IL: Illinois Bell, 1986).

5. Mark E. Neely, *The Abraham Lincoln Encyclopedia* (New York: McGraw-Hill Book Company, 1982), 161–62.
6. David Herbert Donald, *Lincoln* (London: Jonathan Cape, 1995), 141.

Chapter 7: Faith Rekindled

1. G. S. Boritt, *Lincoln and the Economics of the American Dream* (Memphis: Memphis State University Press, 1978), ix.
2. In checking the story regarding the book by Dr. Smith, I found the limited edition sold out quickly. The most fortunate incident in my own study of Lincoln was that one hundred and fifty years after Dr. Smith's book sold out, I came upon and purchased a very rare copy.
3. Wayne C. Temple, *Abraham Lincoln: From Skeptic to Prophet* (Mahomet, IL: Mayhaven Publishing, 1995), 37–43.
4. Ibid. Other books that contain details about Lincoln's relationship with Reverend Smith are William J. Wolf, *Lincoln's Religion* (Philadelphia: Pilgrim Press, 1970, originally published 1959 as *The Almost Chosen People*), 80–87; Elton Trueblood, *Abraham Lincoln: Theologian of American Anguish* (New York: Harper and Row Publishers, 1973), 20–25, 59–63; Stewart Winger, *Lincoln, Religion, and Romantic Cultural Politics* (DeKalb, IL: Northern Illinois University Press, 2003), 195–201.

Chapter 8: Aroused, Ignited

1. Oates, *With Malice Toward None* (New York: Harper and Row, 1977), 107.
2. Henry Whitney, *Life on the Circuit with Lincoln* (Boston: Estes and Lauriat, 1892), 88.
3. Thomas, *Abraham Lincoln*, 143.

Chapter 10: A Lecture on Inventions

1. Despite the titles given in *The Collected Works* for the two parts of Lincoln's Lecture on Discoveries and Inventions, these excerpts were actually part of one lecture covering two topics, according to Dr. Wayne Temple. For additional background on these lectures, see Wayne C. Temple, "Lincoln the Lecturer, Part I," *Lincoln Herald* 10[2], no. 3 (fall 1999), 146–163.

Chapter 11: The Lincoln-Douglas Debates

1. Donald, *Lincoln*, 209.
2. Ibid., 210.
3. Harold Holzer, *The Lincoln-Douglas Debates* (New York: Harper Collins, 1993), 6.
4. *The Collected Works*, vol. III, 38–76.
5. *The Collected Works*, vol. III, 102–44.
6. Holzer, *Lincoln-Douglas Debates*, 185.
7. A complete concordance of the King James Version does not have a listing either for the word *selfish* or *selfishness*. However, the concept is certainly expressed in many other terms. Both Titus 1:7 and 2 Peter 2:10 use the term *selfwilled*. In 2 Timothy 3:2, Paul uses the Greek word *phil-auto*, the parts of which mean "love-self."
8. *The Collected Works*, vol. III, footnote on 335.
9. Holzer, *Lincoln-Douglas Debates*, 373.
10. Thomas, *Abraham Lincoln*, 193.

Chapter 12: National Prominence

1. Thomas, *Abraham Lincoln*, 182.
2. Allan Nevins, *The Emergence of Lincoln*, vol. 2 (London: Charles Scribner's Sons, 1951), 183.
3. Nevins, *Emergence of Lincoln*, vol. 2, 184.
4. Ibid., 184, 187.
5. Harold Holzer, *Lincoln at Cooper Union: The Speech That Made Abraham Lincoln President* (New York: Simon and Schuster, n.d.), 128.
6. Ibid., 52.
7. *The Collected Works*, vol. IV, 1.

Chapter 13: The Inaugural Journey

1. *The Collected Works*, vol. IV, 160–61.
2. Alexander H. Stephens, *History of the United States* (San Francisco: J. Dewing and Co., 1883).
3. Thomas, *Abraham Lincoln*, 241.
4. John G. Nicolay and John Hay, *Abraham Lincoln: A History*, vol. 6 (New York: The Century Company, 1890), 339–40.

Chapter 14: President of a Divided House

1. Harry V. Jaffa, *A New Birth of Freedom* (New York: Rowman and Littlefield, 2000), 3.
2. William H. Rehnquist, *All the Laws but One: Civil Liberties in Wartime* (New York: Vintage Books, 1998), 3.
3. Thomas, *Abraham Lincoln*, 272–74.
4. Nathaniel Wright Stephenson, *Lincoln* (Brooklyn: Bobbs-Merrill Co., 1924), 257.

Chapter 15: The Divine Will

1. *The Collected Works*, vol. V, 128.
2. *The Collected Works*, vol. V, 404.
3. Francis Carpenter, *The Inner Life of Abraham Lincoln: Six Months at the White House* (Lincoln, NE: University of Nebraska Press, 1995), 30–31.
4. *The Collected Works*, vol. IV, 270–71.
5. Nicolay and Hay, *Abraham Lincoln*, vol. 6, 341–42.
6. Ronald C. White, *The Eloquent President: A Portrait of Lincoln Through His Words* (New York: Random House, 2006), 161.

Chapter 16: The Military

1. Kenneth P. Williams, *Lincoln Finds a General: A Military Study of the Civil War*, vol. 1 (New York: The Macmillan Company, 1949), ix.
2. Ibid., 10.
3. T. Harry Williams, *Lincoln and His Generals* (New York: Alfred A. Knopf, 1952), 215–229.
4. *The Collected Works*, vol. VII, 169–170.

Chapter 17: A Nation Unshackled

1. This is a theme covered in multiple Scripture passages, including Job 10:8-12; Psalm 100:3; 119:73; 139:13-16.

2. Donald, *Lincoln*, 454.
3. Nicolay and Hay, *Abraham Lincoln,* vol. 6, 158–59.
4. John Hope Franklin, *The Emancipation Proclamation* (New York: Doubleday and Company, 1963), 83.
5. Carpenter, *Inner Life*, 269–70.
6. Oates, *With Malice Toward None*, 339.
7. Carpenter, *Inner Life*, 196.
8. Ibid., 197.

Chapter 18: Appealing to the Almighty

1. Frank E. Edgington, *History of the New York Avenue Presbyterian Church* (Washington, DC: New York Avenue Presbyterian Church, 1961), 243.
2. Emanuel Hertz, *Abraham Lincoln: The Tribute of the Synagogue* (New York: Bloch Publishing Co., 1927), xix.
3. Eliza P. Gurney, *Memoir and Correspondence of Eliza P. Gurney* (Philadelphia: J. B. Lippincott and Co., 1884), 309–12.
4. *The Collected Works*, Vol. V, footnote on page 478.

Chapter 19: Securing America's Birthright

1. *Merriam-Webster's Dictionary*, 11th ed., s.v. "Dogma."
2. Walt Whitman, "When Lilacs Last in the Dooryard Bloom'd," stanza 15.
3. Louis A. Warren, *Lincoln's Gettysburg Declaration* (Fort Wayne, IN: Lincoln National Life Foundation, 1964), 112–13.
4. Ibid., 145–46.
5. J. G. Randall and Richard N. Current, *Lincoln the President*, vol. 2 (New York: Dodd, Mead and Company), 346–347, *Lincoln the President*, vol. 4, 303.

Chapter 20: An Enduring Legacy

1. Proudly, Lincoln noted that Illinois was the first state to ratify this amendment.
2. *The Collected Works*, vol. VIII, 356.
3. The phrase appears in three dramatic Old Testament stories: (1) David to Saul before he faced Goliath (1 Samuel 17:26-36); (2) King Hezekiah, regarding the reproach of the Babylonians to the Living God (2 Kings 19:4-6; repeated in Isaiah 37:4-17); and (3) Daniel in the lions' den (Daniel 6:20-26).
4. Trueblood, *Abraham Lincoln: Theologian of American Anguish*, 137–38.
5. Randall, *Lincoln the President*, 303.
6. Oates, *With Malice Toward None*, 423.

Conclusion: The Faith of Abraham Lincoln

1. *The Collected Works*, vol. IV, 271.
2. Ibid., 190.

President Lincoln's Legacy to Youth

1. *The Collected Works*, vol. V, 373.

BIBLIOGRAPHY

Appleby, Joyce. *Inheriting the Revolution.* Cambridge, MA: Belknap Press, 2000.

Barton, William E. *The Soul of Abraham Lincoln.* New York: George H. Doran Co., 1920.

———. *The Life of Abraham Lincoln.* 2 vols. Indianapolis: The Bobbs Merrill Company, 1925.

Basler, Roy P., ed. *The Collected Works of Abraham Lincoln.* 10 vols. New Brunswick, NJ: Rutgers University Press, 1953.

Benet, Stephen Vincent. *America.* New York: Farrar and Rinehart, 1944.

Beveridge, Albert J. *Abraham Lincoln, 1809–1858.* 2 vols. Cambridge, MA: Riverside Press, 1928.

Blackstone, William. *Commentaries on the Laws of England.* London: Strahan, 1809.

Boritt, G. S. *Lincoln and the Economics of the American Dream.* Memphis: Memphis State University Press, 1978.

Bullard, F. Lauriston. *Lincoln in Marble and Bronze.* New Brunswick, NJ: Rutgers University Press, 1952.

Burlingame, Michael. *The Inner World of Abraham Lincoln.* Chicago: University of Illinois Press, 1994.

Carpenter, F. B. *The Inner Life of Abraham Lincoln: Six Months at the White House.* Lincoln, NE: University of Nebraska Press, 1995.

Chapmen, Ervin. *Latest Light on Abraham Lincoln.* New York: Fleming H. Revell Company, 1917.

Charnwood, Lord. *Abraham Lincoln.* New York: Garden City Publishing Co., 1917.

Donald, David Herbert. *Lincoln.* London: Jonathan Cape, 1995.

———. *Lincoln at Home: Two Glimpses of Abraham Lincoln's Domestic Life.* White House Historical Association in cooperation with Thornwillow Press, 1999.

Edgington, Frank E. *History of the New York Avenue Presbyterian Church.* Washington, D.C.: New York Avenue Presbyterian Church, 1961.

Emerson, Ralph Waldo. *The Works of Ralph Waldo Emerson.* 12 vols. New York: Fireside Edition, 1885.

Fehrenbacher, Don E. *Prelude to Greatness.* Stanford: Stanford University Press, 1962.

Franklin, John Hope. *The Emancipation Proclamation.* New York: Doubleday and Company, 1963.

Goodwin, Doris Kearns. *Team of Rivals: The Political Genius of Abraham Lincoln.* New York: Simon and Schuster, 2006.

Guelzo, Allen C. *Abraham Lincoln: Redeemer President.* Grand Rapids: William B. Eerdmans Publishing Company, 1999.

Gurney, Eliza P. *Memoir and Correspondence of Eliza P. Gurney.* Philadelphia: J. B. Lippincott & Co., 1884.

Hamilton, Charles, and Lloyd Ostendorf. *Lincoln in Photographs: An Album of Every Known Pose.* Norman, OK: University of Oklahoma Press, 1963.

Herndon, William H., and Jesse W. Weik. *Herndon's Life of Lincoln.* New York: The World Publishing Company, 1942.

Hertz, Emanuel. *Abraham Lincoln: The Tribute of the Synagogue.* New York: Bloch Publishing Company, 1927.

Holland, J. G. *Abraham Lincoln.* Springfield, MA: Gurdon Bill, 1866.

Holzer, Harold. *Lincoln at Cooper Union: The Speech That Made Abraham Lincoln President.* New York: Simon and Schuster, 2004.

———. *The Lincoln-Douglas Debates.* New York: Harper Collins, 1993.

Jaffa, Harry V. *A New Birth of Freedom.* New York: Rowman and Littlefield Publishers, 2000.

Jones, Edgar DeWitt. *Lincoln and the Preachers.* New York: Harper and Brothers Publishers, 1948.

Kunhardt, Dorothy Meserve, and Philip B. Kunhardt Jr. *Twenty Days: A Narrative in Text and Pictures of the Assassination of Abraham Lincoln.* New York: Castle Books, 1965.

Luthin, Reinhard H. *The Real Abraham Lincoln.* Englewood Cliffs, NJ: Prentice-Hall, Inc., 1960.

Macartney, Clarence Edward. *Lincoln and the Bible.* New York: Abingdon-Cokesbury Press, 1949.

McClure, A. K. *Abraham Lincoln and Men of War Times.* Philadelphia: Times Publishing Company, 1872.

McPherson, James M. *Abraham Lincoln and the Second American Revolution.* New York: Oxford University Press, 1990.

———. *Battle Cry of Freedom: The Civil War Era.* New York: Oxford University Press, 1988.

Mellon, James. *The Face of Lincoln.* New York: Bonanza Books, 1979.

Miers, Earl Schenck, ed. *Lincoln Day by Day: A Chronology.* 3 vols. Washington, D.C.: Lincoln Sesquicentennial Commission, 1960.

Neely, Mark E. *The Abraham Lincoln Encyclopedia.* New York: McGraw-Hill Book Company, 1982.

———. *The Fate of Liberty: Abraham Lincoln and Civil Liberties.* New York: Oxford University Press, 1991.

———. *The Last Best Hope of Earth.* Cambridge, MA: Harvard University Press, 1993.

Nevins, Allan. *The Emergence of Lincoln.* 2 vols. Norwalk, CT: Easton Press, 1988.

Nicolay, John G. and John Hay. *Abraham Lincoln: A History.* 10 vols. New York: The Century Company, 1890.

Niebuhr, Reinhold. *The Children of Light and the Children of Darkness.* New York: Charles Scribner's Sons, 1944.

Oates, Stephen B. *With Malice Toward None.* New York: Harper and Row, 1977.

Pratt, Harry E. *Concerning Mr. Lincoln.* Springfield, IL: Abraham Lincoln Association, 1944.

———. *The Personal Finances of Abraham Lincoln.* Springfield, IL: Abraham Lincoln Association, 1943.

Quarles, Benjamin. *Lincoln and the Negro.* New York: Oxford University Press, 1962.

Randall, J. G., and Richard N. Current. *Lincoln the President.* 4 vols. New York: Dodd, Mead and Company, 1955.

Rankin, Henry B. *Personal Recollections of Abraham Lincoln.* New York: G. P. Putnam's Sons, 1889.

Rehnquist, William H. *All the Laws but One: Civil Liberties in Wartime.* New York: Vintage Books, 1998.

Rice, Allen Thorndike, ed. *Reminiscences of Abraham Lincoln by Distinguished Men of His Time.* New York: North American Review, 1888.

Sandburg, Carl. *Abraham Lincoln: The Prairie Years.* 2 vols. New York: Harcourt, Brace and World, Inc., 1939.

———. *Abraham Lincoln: The War Years.* 4 vols. New York: Harcourt, Brace and World, Inc., 1939.

Schwartz, Thomas F. *Abraham Lincoln Chronology.* Springfield, IL: Illinois Historic Preservation Agency, 2002.

Shaw, Albert. *Abraham Lincoln: His Path to the Presidency and The Year of His Election.* 2 vols. New York: Review of Reviews Corp., 1930.

Shaw, Archer H. *The Lincoln Encyclopedia.* New York: The Macmillan Company, 1950.

Smith, James. *The Christian's Defense.* 2 vols. Cincinnati: J. A. James, 1843.

Stephens, Alexander H. *History of the United States.* Philadelphia and Chicago: The National Publishing Company, 1882.

Stephenson, Nathaniel Wright. *Lincoln.* Brooklyn: Bobbs-Merrill Co., 1924.

Stoddard, William O. *Abraham Lincoln: The True Story of a Great Life.* New York: Fords, Howard and Hulbert, 1885.

Temple, Wayne C. *Abraham Lincoln: From Skeptic to Prophet.* Mahomet, IL: Mayhaven Publishing, 1995.

———. *Lincoln's Connections with the Illinois and Michigan Canal.* Springfield, IL: Illinois Bell, 1986.

———, and Sunderine Temple. *Abraham Lincoln and Illinois' Fifth Capitol.* Mahomet, IL: Mayhaven Publishing, 2006.

Thomas, Benjamin P. *Abraham Lincoln: A Biography.* New York: Alfred A. Knopf, 1952.

———. *Portrait for Posterity: Lincoln and His Biographers.* New Bruswick, NJ: Rutgers University Press, 1947.

Trueblood, Elton. *Abraham Lincoln: Theologian of American Anguish.* New York: Harper and Row Publishers, 1973.

Warren, Louis A. *Lincoln's Parentage and Childhood.* New York: The Century Company, 1926.

———. *Lincoln's Youth: Indiana Years.* Indianapolis: Indiana Historical Society. 1959.

White, Ronald C., Jr. *The Eloquent President: A Portrait of Lincoln Through His Words.* New York: Random House, 2005.

———. *Lincoln's Greatest Speech.* New York: Simon and Schuster, 2002.

Whitman, Walt. *Leaves of Grass.* New York: Bantam Books, 1983.

Whitney, Henry C. *Life on the Circuit with Lincoln.* Boston: Estes and Lauriat, 1892.

Williams, Frank J. *Judging Lincoln.* Chicago: University of Illinois Press, 2002.

Williams, Kenneth P. *Lincoln Finds a General: A Military Study of the Civil War.* New York: The Macmillan Company, 1949.

Wills, Garry. *Lincoln at Gettysburg.* New York: Simon and Schuster, 1992.

Wilson, Douglas L., and Rodney O. Davis, eds. *Herndon's Informants: Letters, Interviews, and Statements about Abraham Lincoln.* Chicago: University of Illinois Press, 1998.

Wilson, Rufus. *Lincoln in Caricature.* New York: Horizon Press, 1953.

Winger, Stewart. *Lincoln, Religion, and Romantic Cultural Politics.* DeKalb, IL: Northern Illinois University Press, 2003.

Wolf, William J. *Lincoln's Religion.* Philadelphia: Pilgrim Press, 1970; originally published as *The Almost Chosen People*, 1959.

Woodworth, Steven E., and Kenneth J. Winkle. *Atlas of the Civil War.* New York: Oxford University Press, 2004.

Zall, Paul M. *Lincoln on Lincoln.* Lexington, KY: University Press of Kentucky, 1999.

MONOGRAPHS AND PERIODICALS

Donald, David, ed. *Inside Lincoln's Cabinet: Civil War Diaries of Salmon P. Chase.*

Douglass, Frederick. *Narrative of the Life of Frederick Douglass.* Recorded Books, LLC.

Ewers, Justin. "The Real Lincoln," *U.S. News and World Report*, February 21, 2005.

Gurley, P. D. "Faith in God: Dr. Gurley's Sermon at the Funeral of Abraham Lincoln." Philadelphia: General Assembly of the Presbyterian Church in the U.S.A., 1940.

Lowell, James Russell. *Abraham Lincoln.* The Harvard Classics.

Morris, Hal. *Hayne-Webster Debate*, 1996.

Pope, Alexander. *An Essay on Man.*

Schwartz, Thomas F., ed. *Abraham Lincoln Chronology.* Springfield, IL: The Illinois Historic Preservation Agency, 2002.

Shenk, Joshua Wolf. "The True Lincoln." *Time*, July 4, 2005.

Welles, Gideon. *The Diary of Gideon Welles.*

INDEX

G

H

I

J

K

L

M